We Don't Know What We're Doing

We Don't Know What We're Doing

Adventures with the extraordinary
fans of an ordinary team

ADRIAN CHILES

sphere

SPHERE

First published in Great Britain in 2007 by Sphere

On the back cover: Baggie Bird, Danny, Mystic Emma, Bernie,
Andy Thompson, Dawn Astle and Matthew, the Super Singhs,
Alan Cleverley, Dave Watkin, Waltraut Ball née Grubbe,
Emily, Sauce, Rev Ken and Nathan.

A CIP catalogue record for this book
is available from the British Library.

ISBN 978-1-847-44013-6

Typeset in Palatino by M Rules
Printed and bound in Great Britain by
Clays Ltd, St Ives plc

Sphere
An imprint of
Little, Brown Book Group
Brettenham House
Lancaster Place
London WC2E 7EN

A Member of the Hachette Livre Group of Companies

www.littlebrown.co.uk

For Jane, Evie and Sian. And in memory of
Arthur John Chiles 1906–1987.

Prologue

Les James weaving his magic

I love West Bromwich Albion. If West Brom are doing well, I'm good company. I'm a nice colleague to work with, a good friend, a doting father, a loving husband. If, as is more often the case, we're doing badly, I am none of the above.

My whole attitude to life is shaped by the Albion. For a start, I'm inclined to pessimism. I am lucky enough to have a fantastic job as a broadcaster, but you'll never catch me saying anything positive about my career, because to do so would be to tempt fate. I live my whole life with the same feeling I have in my stomach when the Albion are winning 2–0 with half an hour left. In other words, it's all going terribly well, but it'll still quite possibly end in misery.

Not that I've ever let my career get in the way of the Albion. In the spring of 2000 we were seriously threatened with relegation to what was effectively the third division. On a Tuesday evening we played Tranmere Rovers. That day had been quite an exciting one at work. The job of succeeding Anne Robinson as presenter of *Watchdog* was up for grabs and apparently I was on a shortlist of two with Nicky Campbell. On the drive up to the Hawthorns I asked myself the following question: what did I want more, the *Watchdog* job or a win against Tranmere? I thought about this for nearly two hundred yards of the M40 before deciding that I definitely wouldn't swap anything for a win that night.

We beat Tranmere 2-0 and Nicky Campbell got the *Watchdog* job. But I was happy. Never once did I advise myself to be careful what I wished for in the future.

Why do I feel like this? Why am I so obsessed? My brother's upbringing has been the same as mine, so why doesn't he feel the same way? He's still an Albion fan, and he'll go when he can, but he doesn't let it blight his life. I wish I could be like him.

On the other hand, I've also met people who make me look like a real lightweight. People who've more or less not missed a West Brom game, anywhere, well, ever. There are nervous fans and calm fans. Fans who are sure we'll win; fans who are sure we'll lose. Some become obsessed late in life; others spend half their lives obsessed, then just stop. When I hear fans chanting at the referee thus: 'You don't know what you're doing', I often think we should all be chanting to ourselves that we don't know what we're doing because I really don't think we do.

It doesn't help that because I work on television I'm often recognised when I'm out and about. In the rare moments the Albion slip from my mind, somebody in the street, a pub, a restaurant or in a taxi will raise the subject. The apotheosis of this was in January 2005 when we were bottom of the Premiership and, in all likelihood, would be come the end of the season. It was a wet Tuesday afternoon and I was walking through Leicester

Square in the West End of London when a tramp approached me. He had this determined look about him which had me reaching in my pocket for some money to fob him off with. But, as he approached, something didn't feel quite right. Instead of having his palm outstretched, it reached up and rested on my shoulder. 'Adrian,' he said, his eyes full of compassion, 'I'm afraid the Baggies have had it this season.'

It was around this time that a literary agent called John Saddler suggested I write a book about being a football fan. I thought this an extremely bad idea for two reasons. Firstly, I'd got to the stage where, as well as boring my family, friends, listeners and viewers on the subject of West Brom, I was actually boring myself. Secondly, my team's form was as bleak as the weather. We were certain to go down because we had been bottom at Christmas and, as every football fan knew, no team had ever been bottom of the Premiership at Christmas and survived. Still, if we managed to get a result at home against Liverpool on Boxing Day then maybe, just maybe, we could start to prove history wrong. We lost 5-0.

We were simply hopeless. Since Bryan Robson had taken over as manager in mid-November we'd played eleven matches in the Premiership and won precisely none of them. The thought of documenting our inevitable, laughably incompetent demise didn't appeal.

'No,' I said, 'I just can't do it.'

And we left it at that. John rang me every other week to check I hadn't changed my mind and, as the Albion's form hadn't changed much, my mind remained unchanged, too. I wasn't going to write a book.

Bad move. Four months later on the morning of the last day of the season we were, just as we had been at Christmas, bottom. But, due to a heady mixture of luck and skill – and no small measure of incompetence on the part of the three other struggling teams – we were in a position where, improbably, we could avoid relegation. It was like this: if we beat Portsmouth at home and

Norwich didn't win at Fulham, Southampton didn't win against Manchester United and Crystal Palace didn't win at Charlton, then we'd stay up.

'Survival Sunday', 15 May 2005

There's something special about watching football in summery sunshine. It's either the start of the season when hopes are high, or, as now, it's the sharp end when hopes will finally, at last, be realised (or, more likely, dashed).

For once I'm not nervous. It's the hope that kills you in football and I lost mine several weeks ago. Because I have so little hope I'm really quite relaxed. What will be, will be. But I can't have given up completely because when a friend of mine says, with an air of certainty, that 'it's not going to happen, is it?' I feel a lump forming in my throat.

There's no football ground in the world that doesn't feel fantastic when it's full, and this one is full to bursting today. Portsmouth's fans have come in numbers, intoxicated by the thought that if they lose today they could send Southampton down. During a televised West Brom–Wolves derby I once heard a commentator describe the Hawthorns as 'one of those grounds'. I think it is, too, but I'm obviously biased. It's one of the smallest grounds in the Premiership, but when it's full to its relatively meagre 27,877 capacity it's some place to watch football.

When I was a kid I used to sit in the Rainbow Stand with my granddad, right on the halfway line. Opposite us was the old Halfords Lane Stand, lavishly redeveloped sometime in my teens with features including a new phenomenon called 'executive boxes'.

It's in this all-new Halfords Lane Stand where my season ticket is now. These days, though, it's the oldest part of the ground, the other three sides having been redeveloped since.

It feels like a proper grandstand when you're in it, but seen from anywhere else it's pitifully small. When it's full it's terribly cramped down beneath our seats, next to the burgers and beers and betting shops and toilets. This forces a certain physical intimacy upon us when we need it least – on days like this we're on hugging terms anyway.

Roy Mitchell normally sits in the Halfords Lane Stand but, to his enormous regret, he's not here. Like the rest of us, he thought we were relegated a long time ago, so he went ahead and booked a golfing holiday, not thinking for a moment that anything would be left to play for by now. I don't hold it against him because, to me, you demonstrate your love for the club by how much you care, not how many games you get to. And I know that however beautiful the weather is on the golf course he's at, and however well he's playing it, he'll be in bits for the next two hours. Having said that, if someone had offered to fly me out to play Augusta National today with Tiger Woods I would still be here.

Roy writes for television. I first got in touch with him because a character called Koumas appeared in the cast of *New Tricks* on BBC1. We had a player called Jason Koumas and I knew it couldn't be a coincidence because there were other characters in the show with the same names as West Brom players. I called the office of the controller of BBC1, who called the production company, who unenthusiastically agreed to leave a message for the writer, whose name I'd spotted on the credits. I thought, If he is an Albion fan, he'll call; if he isn't, he'll think I'm a nutcase and won't bother. Roy called almost straight away.

'Generally,' he explained, 'thinking up names is a very boring part of being a writer. I just thought it would be hilarious to name the entire cast after the '68 cup-winning side. So for one of the first episodes there were characters called Osborne, Fraser, Williams, Brown, Talbut, Kaye, Lovett, Collard, Hope and Clark. I couldn't get Astle in,' he said apologetically, 'because it would have been too obvious. And I often used Albion dates, like the date of that final, 18 May 1968, for some murder or some event important to the plot.

'As for the main characters, well, they're all named after the Halfords Lane Stand. James Bolam plays Jack Halford, Alun Armstrong is Brian Lane, and Dennis Waterman is Gerry Standing. Halford Lane Standing,' he says triumphantly. 'When I first took the script in, they said how interesting the names were and they asked me where I got them from. I told them Halford was just a good English name, Standing was for the character's nickname, Upstanding, and Lane was as in Memory Lane. Of course that was all rubbish; it was just for the Albion connections.'

At half-time all is going swimmingly everywhere but here. Charlton are beating Palace 1-0, Fulham are 2-0 up against Norwich and Southampton are 1-1 with Manchester United. The trouble is, for the Miracle to come to pass we have to win and to win we have to score, and we don't look like scoring.

My mate Andy Thompson, with whom I've travelled up today, has a spare seat next to him in the East Stand on the other side of the pitch, nearer the goal we'll be attacking in the second half. It's no longer called the Rainbow Stand but as it's geographically where my granddad and I sat, I convince myself it'll help the cause if I go round there. My granddad would have considered me a right daft sod for thinking this.

Andy's a tall, swarthy music business executive from Kent who's never been able to adequately explain why he supports us. 'It's not going to happen, is it?' he says when I join him. I just shrug.

Then our great big earthmover of a striker, Geoff Horsfield, comes off the bench and scores. We are jubilant, but it reminds me a bit of childbirth in that you think all your troubles will be over when the child is born; in fact they're just beginning. We were desperate for a goal but now it's happened we have to start worrying about what might go on elsewhere. My stomach lurches all over the place. My God, this really could happen. Norwich are being trounced and Man Utd are ahead at Southampton. Worryingly, though, Palace have equalised at Charlton. I felt all right five minutes ago. Now I'm in bits: the hope is suddenly really starting to kill me.

But hope evaporates as quickly as it came. I seem to be the only person in the East Stand wearing a radio, so it falls to me to break the news to everyone that Palace have a penalty at the Valley. Everyone looks at me pleadingly. 'He's missed one against Charlton this season,' I say, parrotting Ian Brown, Radio Five Live's commentator there. 'Scored', I say miserably, a moment later. Everyone looks away.

Here, we then score to no great acclaim. With Palace winning we are going down anyway. Five Live's commentators at the Valley are making very unpromising noises. 'There's only going to be one winner here,' says Steve Claridge. 'There's only going to be one winner there,' I say to no one in particular. Absurdly, I start to feel a bit better again. The hope's ebbing away.

Then a cheer sweeps around the ground. It starts in the Halfords Lane Stand, opposite us, and soon everyone is cheering. The players look at each other and at the crowd. Charlton, against the run of play, have equalised.

Except they haven't. I know they haven't because I'm listening to the live commentary. But, ludicrously, desperately willing it to be true, I join in the celebrations anyway, even though I'm listening to Ian Brown tell me no such thing has happened. Soon everyone calms down and a resigned silence falls again. We're going down.

But then, astonishingly, Charlton do actually score. I jump up pumping my fists, and the rest of the East Stand, though suspicious of another heartbreaking false alarm, seem to believe the man from the BBC with the earphones on. It's unlike any celebration I've ever seen or heard. It starts cautiously; builds quickly to something approaching hysteria, and then dissipates as we consider the quite awful possibility that, having come so close, one Palace goal now would save them and relegate us.

The next ten minutes are the longest of my life. I'm crouched in a kind of foetal position, my fingers pressing the headphones ever harder into my ears. I judge that if the worst happens and Palace score, I will simply never recover. With about five minutes to go, the tension becomes so unbearable I simply crack up: 'No!' I scream, 'I just can't fucking take any more of this!'

'What's happened?' demand about fifty people all at once, the whites of their eyes blazing in the afternoon sun.

'Nothing,' I shout back. 'I just can't take this, that's all.'

Hearts breaking with relief, they sink back into their seats – as much as you can sink into your seat when your buttocks are clenched so tightly your backside's harder than the plastic you're sitting on.

Our final whistle is blown but nobody celebrates: Charlton and Palace are still playing. The crowd sub-divides into pockets of people crowding round those with radios. Thirty agonising seconds later, that feel as if they go on for hours, the final whistle goes at Charlton. After being bottom at Christmas and winning only six miserable games all season, we've survived. Pandemonium. The players jump around hugging each other. Other players in suits emerge from the crowd to join them and the fans start streaming on to the pitch. Andy and I hang on to each other like we're twins just reunited having been separated at birth.

Everybody hugs everybody else. Most people are in tears. Men and women I've never met kiss me full on the lips. Like Pat Cash climbing up to the box from which his father watched him win Wimbledon, I run up to where our directors are sitting. Our chairman Jeremy Peace is looking on, a little bewildered. I know him very well but I've never bear-hugged him before. 'My God, you're sweaty,' he says. Andy, unbidden, hugs him, too.

I then make for Denise, Mrs Bryan Robson. I don't know Bryan so I can hardly kiss him, but I met his wife at Villa Park a month ago and she's going to get kissed and no mistake. Smack on the cheek. Then I set about kissing all, and I mean all, the directors' wives. Some of them seem happy to be kissed by me, others less sure.

Finally, the jackpot: Cyrille Regis, my all-time favourite player. I barely know him but I'm puckering up as soon as I clap eyes on him. And as his partner is by now the only man, woman or child in the soft seats who hasn't had me slavering all over them, she gets the full treatment as well.

I return to Andy who is standing there taking in the scene before us. The pitch invasion has been so comprehensive that there's no grass visible. The celebrations are just starting yet I suddenly feel shattered. I nudge Andy and say, 'Shall we go?' He nods. We both feel as if we've reached such a peak of absolute happiness that staying would serve no purpose: we simply couldn't squeeze any more pleasure out of it. 'Our work here is done,' I say as we walk out on to the deserted car park. Everyone else still seems to be in the ground. We get in his car and drive off. There's so much joy in this car that an image of Chitty Chitty Bang Bang flying away comes to mind. But we just about manage to keep all four wheels on the ground as we head back towards London. We both wonder if we'll ever stop smiling.

That's how it was for me. For others it's been the same but different.

In Raglan, a seaside village near Hamilton, New Zealand, it's the early hours of an autumn morning. Mark Reynolds is crying softly into his pillow; tears of joy that the Albion have stayed up, as well as sadness that he's not there to witness it. A nurse who moved from Birmingham for a better life, Mark remains a committed supporter. His wife is less fed up with his obsession now than she was when they lived in Birmingham. Tonight, having been woken by the sound of him crying, she finds herself crying, too.

In New York City the editor of the *Daily News* is in pieces. Martin Dunn was born and bred in the Black Country. At what he knows to be roughly final-whistle time, he gets a text from his brother: 'I don't believe it.' He can't tell whether this is good or bad news.

In Portugal on a golf course near Lisbon, overwhelmed by a script he could never have written himself, Roy Mitchell is sprinting wildly the wrong way down the eighteenth fairway, screaming.

In Cannes, at the film festival, David Gritten, a writer on film for the *Daily Telegraph,* is taking part in a round-table interview with the terribly important film director David Cronenberg. There's much placing of index fingers along the lips and murmurs of appreciation.

David's mobile vibrates in his pocket. Quite unable to resist the temptation to answer it, he ducks under the table, affording himself a magnificent view of several film buffs' legs. It's his son. 'Dad,' he says, 'we've got another season of Premiership misery to look forward to.' Dave lets out a huge roar of delight and shoots up, firmly banging his head on the underside of the table. Glasses tinkle, the bubbles rising in the Perrier deviate slightly from their upward trajectory. 'Sorry,' he mutters, and the congregation's attention shifts back to the famous director.

In Laos, Adam Cotton is in the jungle with a German moth collector. He's humming 'The Lord's My Shepherd' and other Albion anthems to himself. Back at his hotel, which has no internet or even a working phone, it's only the following morning when he learns from Thai television that his team has survived relegation.

Garry Mottram is in the ground. He won't be again for some time. He is drunk, but happy. For just this short while he has managed to forget that he's robbed six banks and building societies and will surely get caught.

Lee Hughes has been caught. One of our best strikers of recent years, he is serving six years for causing death by dangerous driving. In his cell in a prison the other side of Wolverhampton, he's with five other Albion fans listening to it all on the radio. Afterwards he celebrates with two chocolate milkshakes.

On the Isle of Man, Stacey Cregeen, a very quiet man of advancing years, astonishes his family by hugging the lady who lives next door and swinging her around. He has been supporting the Albion since 1946 without ever actually visiting the Hawthorns.

Somewhere in the West Midlands, Nicola Rhodes is at her mother's house. For a long time Nicola never missed a game, home or away. She can't afford to go any more, though. She is glued to Sky Sports and runs around the house with joy when we survive.

Dave Chapman, owner of the Albion pub in Shoreditch, east London, sits on a stool at the bar and surveys the scene: a hundred and fifty or more Albion fans jumping up and down, sobbing or just staring at the floor. East End-born and bred but fifty-one years an Albion fan, Dave's never seen scenes like it.

Dawn, daughter of our greatest ever player, Jeff Astle, looks up at the sky and knows, just knows, that her dad is delighted, too.

Wherever we are, whoever we are, we suspect it'll be a long time before the Albion make us this happy again.

At 2.30 the following morning my six-year-old daughter comes into our bedroom complaining of nightmares. I try to reassure her but I am suddenly seized with panic, a nightmare of my own. Surely I haven't dreamt one of the happiest days of my life? I check with my wife. 'No,' she says, even more wearily than usual, 'you're OK, it all happened.' My little girl goes off to sleep again. I lie there, willing myself to stay awake just so I can carry on going through it all over and over again, but soon I slip into a deep and dreamless sleep.

In the morning I wake up no less elated than I was the night before. I feel really, really happy. It's not quite as good a feeling as I had when my children were born, but, honestly, it's not far off. Why does it make me this happy? More importantly, why does it, most of the time, make me so miserable? And, most intriguingly of all, who are those people I was kissing and hugging and crying with? Some of them are friends, some I'm just on nodding terms with, but most are complete strangers. I have this massive bond with them, a really extraordinary intimacy, yet I know nothing about them. I want to find out who they are, what their stories are and why we feel the way we do about our football club. I'm going to write that book, after all.

One

One-legged Kev

Summer ends for me on the first of August because it's in August that the football season starts. I can never understand those fans who miss football during the close season. If you ache for the season to start then you can't be much of a fan. If you're truly passionate about your club, if it really does rule your life, you will have loved each precious football-free day of summer. And you'll mourn the coming of the new season and the trauma it's sure to bring.

In early August you'll already feel nostalgia at the sight of your kids playing on a beach, or of your garden blooming, or of the sun setting late and slowly. You'll mournfully admire a summer breeze whispering through the trees and realise that in the time it takes for all those leaves to fall and grow back again next spring, your life won't be quite your own. On top of all the other worries you have about your marriage, your children, your work, your health or whatever, you'll have to find huge reserves of emotional strength to deal with everything your team throws at you this season.

Men are supposed to think about sex every six seconds. I don't know if that's true, but I certainly think about West Brom more than I think about sex. During the season I think about them constantly. In fact I don't believe they're ever completely out of my mind. Whatever else I'm doing, from bathing the children to presenting live television programmes, there's a bit of my under-sized brain bothering about the blue and white.

Over the summer, though, I manage to forget about the Albion. My West Brom friends are dear to me but we have no real relationship in the summer months. We occasionally meet, but it never feels quite right. It's all out of context and confusing, almost embarrassing, like seeing one of your schoolteachers out shopping during half-term.

But now, driving up from South Wales where I am supposed to be on holiday with my family, I realise that I'm just dying to see everyone again. The nearer I get to the Hawthorns, the yearning replaces the guilt I felt earlier as I left my wife and kids alone on our family holiday. I hate this obsession as much as my wife hates me for being so obsessed. This thought stays with me on the M4 but dissipates on the M50 and has completely gone by the time I get on the M5, by which time I'm thanking God for football and for the Albion.

Saturday, 13 August 2005, Manchester City away

I cannot remember the last time we won the first game of the season. The day before last season's first game I happened to be flying back from Miami. As we taxied for take-off, a bloke sitting across the aisle clocked me and said, in a strong West Midlands accent, 'You going to Blackburn?'

'Yes,' I said grimly.

'And me,' he said, just as grimly.

This exchange couldn't have sounded any different if we were discussing the coincidence of us both going in for vasectomies the following day.

In the car park at the Hawthorns I join the supporters converging to board the coaches north. Under grey skies acquaintances are being renewed. Neither quiet nor boisterous, they remind me of nothing so much as schoolchildren on their first day back after the summer holidays. Everybody seems to be rolling their eyes at everyone else, wordlessly saying, 'Here we go again.'

Dave Holloway, who has been organising the fans' away travel for nearly a quarter of a century, is here as usual. He always wears the same XXL-sized sweatshirt, merchandise from a haulage firm somewhere in the Black Country. A model of weary efficiency, Dave takes calls, makes notes and points new recruits in the right direction.

A new coach firm, Johnson's, has won the contract to transport us this season. Apparently anxious to impress, their coaches are parked not in a straight line but in a geometrically precise staggered formation. The nose of each coach is exactly, artfully, five feet ahead of the one to its right. The effect, ludicrously, is somewhat impressive. The drivers, in identical uniforms obviously, stand in pairs or threes exchanging animated hand signals about routes and things.

I never used to go to away games as a kid and I have lived in London for a long time, so it's ages since I last travelled on a supporters' club coach. It was April 1986, the day we were relegated from the top division, away at QPR. I felt I just had to be there. A lad who worked in a foundry sat next to me, reluctantly. He kept looking back up the aisle, plaintively, to where his mates were sitting. Somebody was sick. On the way back our newly relegated team overtook us on the M1. We all looked at them but none of them looked at us.

There have only been three other occasions on which I've travelled by coach to an away game. And all three were with my granddad. Two were for cup semi-finals at Highbury in 1978 and 1982. We lost both and each time I cried at least part of the way home. In 1982 it was QPR who beat us. I was sitting next to a big biker bloke who must have been in his twenties. He cried himself dry and was just left with those painful, choked sobs that sound a bit like hiccups. My granddad stared straight ahead, pretending he wasn't that upset.

The time before that was the only away game I can remember going to as a kid, at Burnden Park, Bolton. We won 1-0, but walking back to the coach afterwards a bunch of youths sprinted past us and knocked my granddad off his feet. This seemed incredible to me. My granddad was indestructible, infallible. And yet here he was on the floor next to me, an old man, just lying there. It was then that I understood he wasn't immortal. But I couldn't grieve for long because in an instant, with a quiet grunt, he was on his feet again and holding my hand as we walked back to the coach. I was relieved: although his vulnerability had shocked me, he was still, essentially, made of girders.

A quarter of a century later I'm on coach number one, Dave Holloway's coach. It's first off the car park. Behind us, another dozen or more coaches fall into line. As we pull away from the Hawthorns, I feel suddenly, unashamedly, profoundly emotional. We are as one on these coaches. We're a small benevolent army. We are together, and being aboard one of this fleet fosters a special sense of belonging.

The lady sitting behind me hands out some fruit cake to the

man sitting across the aisle from her. 'I've missed you, Mary,' he says.

'I made it myself,' she says.

I look at them both ruefully, but no cake is offered to me. There's belonging, and there's belonging.

The man eating the cake is called Dave Taylor. I ask if he misses many games.

'No.'

'Well, when was the last one you missed?'

'Don't know. Must be twenty years at least.'

I am agog. I often feel that I operate at an absolute maximum of devotion to the Albion, but I'm a million miles from an attendance record like this. 'You haven't missed a game, home or away, for twenty years?'

'No,' he replies evenly.

Incredulously I look around for other passengers to share my admiration for this amazing feat. Blank faces stare back. It's soon apparent that hardly any of them have missed a single game in twenty years or more.

This is a whole new experience for me. I spend my life with people who look at me with amazement and pity in their eyes at my devotion to the Albion. So it's decidedly odd to be made to feel rather inadequate, not a proper fan. My fellow travellers aren't unpleasant about it. In fact there's kindness in their eyes. It is like it's my first visit to a stamp collecting club and I have whipped out my album, of which I'm very proud, and they've shown polite interest in it before producing huge volumes of their own that dwarf mine.

Alan Cleverley, head of the supporters' club, leaps to his feet.

'Tea break,' one of the regulars explains.

'White, no sugar, please,' I say, warming to the whole ritual.

'White, no sugar,' Alan says as he hands me a cup. It feels a bit like I suppose a first holy communion might feel. I think about how nicely a slice of Mary's cake would go with this. I almost say so out loud, but don't.

*

My seat at Man City is three rows from the front. To my left sits a little kid and next to him his dad.

'How old are you?' I ask.

He thinks. 'Eight,' he says.

'When did you come to your first match?'

He looks at his dad. 'When he was three,' his dad says.

'When I was three,' the little boy echoes.

The season starts. I suppose I ought to feel a surge of anticipation and hope but, for me at least, those days are long gone. And it seems that most of us here feel the same. It's a neutral feeling: neither happy nor sad. If, as one, we could vocalise our thoughts at this moment, we would wearily intone, 'OK, here we go again, bring it on. There'll be good bits and bad bits but together we'll get through it.'

The first chant of the season comes from Man City: 'Come on, City,' they shout together without noticeable enthusiasm.

'Fuck off, City,' our fans respond, reflexively, without any real malice.

Other rituals are observed. A corner kick is awarded in front of us. Somebody stands up, so the person behind them has to do so, too, and soon we're all struggling to our feet. As we do so knees crack and seats slap up with the sound of dominoes toppling. The corner comes to nothing. We sit back down again.

Neither side scores, although both come close. A couple of minutes before half-time, the bloke to my left stands up. 'Lucky piss,' he explains as he pushes past me.

At half-time I'm distracted by a girl of about fourteen with glasses on snogging a much taller and slightly older looking youth. They kiss incredibly passionately yet tenderly. It seems inappropriate somehow; we're not even winning, for heaven's sake. When I next look in their direction, the girl's talking to a younger girl who is obviously her sister and an older man who is clearly their dad. The lad who was doing the snogging is now just as engrossed in his programme.

In the second half, due to the usual combination of skill and ineptitude, both sides have chances to score but fluff them all. Our best opportunity comes when Kevin Campbell, Albion's experienced (in other words, old) striker, finds himself racing in our direction with only the goalkeeper and the goal standing between him and us. This time when we stand up we do so urgently, all at once, so the seats all snap up together. Time stands still in the instant before David James, City's goalkeeper, saves Campbell's shot with his legs. We all sit back down again.

The match finishes, to our fans' general satisfaction, nil-nil. Back on the bus we pronounce ourselves fairly happy. It's a point away from home and there's also a sense that it's a nice introduction to the season: a defeat would have been terribly disappointing and a win too much to ask. Either outcome would have plonked us straight on to the emotional rollercoaster we'll be on all season. It's been a nice way of easing ourselves in.

In the seat behind me, the man with Mary is eating some pasta out of a plastic box. I say that I haven't done enough preparation for this trip and next time I'll be certain to bring along something to eat. Many of them smile and I sit down. Mary taps me on the shoulder and says, 'Here's the last bit of my cake.' She does so in a tone of voice that suggests she knows this is what I've been after the whole time. The cake tastes good.

I'm back to the communion again: the tea on the way up was my wine and now I'm truly breaking bread with the faithful. I belong in a way I didn't when I boarded the coach.

Back in West Bromwich my car is parked the other side of the ground from where the coaches empty us out. I walk there with a neat, slightly built middle-aged woman who was sitting just across the aisle from me on the coach. She smiled at some of the things I said and sometimes nodded, but we've not really spoken. She read *Homes & Gardens* magazine and ate some low-fat crisps and some black grapes out of a small plastic bag.

Now, as we find ourselves walking in step, I ask her name – it's Yvonne – and if she misses many games.

'Not really,' she says, 'but I can't go to Chelsea because I'm working.'

'Where do you work?'

'In a law firm in Birmingham.' She pauses and there's a short silence before she says, 'Mind you, I've only missed four home games in forty years. Not bad for a female, is it?'

I can barely find words to express my admiration for her. 'People sometimes say I'm mad,' says Yvonne, 'but what do they get excited about? Shopping?'

It's funny she should say that because only last week I was reunited with a very old friend. He has two kids, a son of ten and a thirteen-year-old daughter. His son's really into football so I talked to him for ages about that. But I became conscious that I wasn't really connecting with his daughter. Eventually I asked her what she liked doing, what she was passionate about. 'Shopping,' she said, shrugging. Now, I ask you, what's a healthier obsession, shopping or football?

Saturday, 20 August 2005, Portsmouth at home

Most mornings I do this really stupid thing. I make myself and the kids some eggs. I put a bit of water in a pan on a high heat and I also put the kettle on. When the kettle's boiled, I pour the boiling water into the pan. But the barmy bit comes before that: as the water in the pan starts to bubble and the kettle comes to the boil, I say to myself that if the water in the pan boils before the water in the kettle then West Brom will avoid relegation.

I did this for all of last season. On the morning after we survived relegation I went downstairs, kissed the picture of Bryan Robson on the back of the *Daily Mirror* and put the water on. Anxiously, as usual, I watched to see who would win the race to boil, out of the kettle and the pan. And then – a beautiful moment this – I remembered we'd survived and it didn't matter any more. In fact I even started to suspect that the whole thing was a bit of a nonsense and it really was unlikely that two bits of water boiling could possibly have an impact on the performance of a football team in a different time and place.

Three months later I am putting the kettle and the pan on and, with a queasy feeling in the pit of my stomach, find myself willing the pan to beat the kettle. I feel real shame at this stupidity and, more than that, plain weary at the thought that this is how it's going to be for the next nine months. I know I'm in good company, though: even some of the most experienced and analytical of managers are susceptible to the same kind of childish superstitions. Gordon Strachan once related to me how 'there I was losing 5-0 at Old Trafford, standing in my technical area wearing my lucky shoes and lucky suit!'

Mascots are the clearest quasi-official manifestation of this ritual and superstition. I have always felt rather sorry for them myself. Everybody ignores them unless they get in a scrap with another mascot, in which case they may well get their picture somewhere in the *Daily Star*.

West Brom's nickname, for reasons which aren't entirely clear, is the Baggies. But their real nickname is the Throstles, apparently after a throstle – a thrush – kept in a cage in a pub near the original ground. Or something. So it is that a century on, grown men dress up as giant thrushes wearing Albion kits. There is one mascot called Baggie Bird and a slightly smaller one called Baby Baggie. They are thought to be related.

I never took much notice of either bird until our first-ever match in the Premiership, away at Manchester United. It was very moving to see our team, little old Albion, walk out at Old Trafford. Watching some of our players kicking a ball about with the likes of Beckham and Giggs was incongruous enough but, for some reason, it was the sight of Baggie Bird in that massive stadium which really got to me.

Last season I ran the London Marathon dressed as Baggie Bird. I did so to raise money for charity. I also thought it might do us some good in our battle against relegation – well, every little helps, after all.

But the main reason I did it was that I had always wondered how these people who run marathons in funny costumes actually train for the event. Does it cause car accidents if you run down a main road as the Pink Panther? So I did one training run around my local park. Very few people took any notice at all. Running back home, still in costume, a bloke begging outside a Tube station asked me, a giant thrush, if I could spare twenty pence.

Last week at Man City I saw Dave Challoner, the man inside Baggie Bird, who lent me his costume to run the marathon in. He looked a bit displeased.

'Got to go to a bloody wedding next week,' he grumbled.

This was an opportunity too good to miss: given my marathon run as Baggie Bird undoubtedly helped save the club from relegation last year, surely my presence as mascot for the first home game of the season could only propel us to further success? 'Do you fancy it?' asked Dave.

'Oh, go on then,' I replied.

This is why I now find myself in what looks like a boiler room, next to the dressing room, fighting my way into the costume again. I can still smell myself from the marathon four months ago. This time tights are involved. Richard, who is Baby Baggie, helps me on with them and works on sorting out the complicated arrangement of elastic that stops the head from falling off.

Richard's a small, bald, rather tough-looking chap. He is very rigorous and strangely macho in the way he dons the costume. He gets out a couple of pairs of brand new goalkeeping gloves and hands one of them to me. 'It's good to cover your hands up,' he advises. 'It hides them so the kids can't see them.' I wonder how many of the kids in the ground actually think that Baggie Bird is real.

Unaccountably, since no one will know it's me, I'm really very nervous. The players are out on the pitch warming up and we have to go out to join them. My problem is that I can't see where I'm going because the costume's summer clean-up has left the upper beak a bit flaccid and it's obstructing the view out of the mouth.

So we make our way out of the boiler room towards the tunnel. Baby Baggie leads the way with Baggie Bird somewhat geriatrically holding on to him. Baby Baggie tells me to be sure to wave as we emerge from the tunnel. Obediently I shyly raise one of my wings while Baby Baggie skips on to the pitch clapping his wings above his head, precisely in the manner of a popular player acknowledging the spontaneous acclaim of the crowd as he emerges for the first time. As far as I can tell, nobody is clapping either of us. I tilt my head back for a glimpse at the crowd through my beak and am disappointed and relieved in equal measure that nobody's paying us any attention at all.

We make our way around the track signing autographs. I explain to a bewildered little girl that I'm having some difficulty holding the pen because it's my first time. Richard taps me with a wing: 'Don't talk,' he says rather sharply, 'it spoils it for the kids.'

We then go on to the pitch for a kick around. Richard has a little pantomime routine involving falling over, miskicking the ball and so on. I'm quite hopeless at this so he abandons the idea.

I wave up to where my wife's sitting. Later she tells me she feels nothing but shame and embarrassment.

Nigel Pearson, our assistant manager, is helping the players warm up. I shout to him that it's me inside the costume.

'Is there anything you won't do to get on this pitch?' he demands.

I shake my big bird's head, but not too vigorously in case it comes off.

The players go back inside to prepare for kick-off and, as it's so hot, we follow them in for a breather. With our birds' heads off, we wait at the mouth of the tunnel for the players and officials to arrive. Richard gives me my instructions: 'Right, we run out before the players. I'll curve off to the left, you go to the right. You've got to encourage the crowd to make as much noise as possible.'

'This is the best bit,' he says. 'It's fantastic,' he grins. I feel a bit sorry for him as he's obviously able to suspend disbelief well enough to be convinced, if only for a moment, that the rapture is for him, or at least his giant thrush.

The players crowd up behind us. I have still got my head off. Mike Riley, the referee, recognises me, smiles and says, quite nonchalantly, 'Oh, hello, Adrian.'

I try to avoid making eye contact with any of the players, I just feel too ridiculous. So I put my head on. The sound of the crowd outside is drowned out by the sound of my own breathing. 'Go,' shouts Richard. And there I am running a beautiful parabola towards the Smethwick End, waving my wings. For just a moment I know what Richard is getting at. The applause is all for me. I just know it. How else will I ever get the chance to run out with the players at the Albion? This is the only way it can happen, so I might as well make the most of it. I flap my wings at our fans, encouraging them to make more noise, but they're going ballistic anyway.

Before the toss of the coin we line up for a photo. The Portsmouth captain is Dejan Stefanovic, a Serb. Because my mum's from Croatia, I can speak Serbo-Croat, in which language Baggie Bird now says to him, 'Hello, Dejan. Best of luck.' He looks at me, a little alarmed. I suspect he thinks he might be losing his marbles. He seems to conclude that he can't have heard what he's just heard as he doesn't reply.

The match starts and we return to the boiler room to put away our thrushes for another week. Almost immediately a cheer goes up. A member of the coaching staff walking up the corridor says, quite unemotionally, 'We've scored.'

'Good start,' says Richard, peeling off his tights. Soon we score again and, although Portsmouth pull one back, we win. All thanks to me, I'm sure.

Wednesday, 24 August 2005, away at Chelsea

There are some places where luck – unless it's delivered in lorry-loads – can't help you, and one of them is Stamford Bridge. I hate going to Chelsea. It involves conceding lots of goals and scoring none and, get this, you have to pay one of the world's richest men forty-odd quid to watch it all happen. For me, there's the additional memory of a domestic accident two years ago, which has left Stamford Bridge and pain forever entwined psychologically.

If we're playing on a Saturday, Friday night is always tricky in my house. Given that I'll be buggering off for most of the following day, there is a clear and present danger that things could get very frosty, very quickly if I'm not at the top of my game. On this particular Friday night, with Stamford Bridge looming the following afternoon, I was pulling out all the stops. By the time my wife got back from work, our two-year-old daughter was bathed, fragrant and sucking contentedly at her pre-night-night milk. In the kitchen, preparations for our dinner of fresh fish and chips were advanced. The potatoes were chipped, the batter was beaten, the salad was tossed, the oil in the fryer was reaching optimum temperature. Jane said she'd nip up for a shower before we put Evie to bed.

Evie watched me adoringly as I got the cod fillets out of the freezer. They were stuck together. Feeling rather heroic before her admiring gaze, I reached for my very sharpest paring knife and inserted it into the gap between the two stuck-fast fish fillets I was holding in my left hand. I pushed hard on the knife.

Entirely predictably, in retrospect, the fillets sprang apart and the knife made its way through the palm of my left hand just where it meets the middle finger. My hand went numb; a fountain of blood gushed out of it; my knees buckled and I slumped to the floor. As I slipped in and out of consciousness, death seemed a genuine possibility. I noted with interest how the blood seemed to be pumping out of my hand. It was also clear to me that I didn't want to die this way. But what really panicked me was the thought that I might not be able to get to Chelsea the following day.

'I'm Mladen,' said the doctor in casualty a couple of hours later.

This was good news. With a name like Mladen, he had to come

from the former Yugoslavia, so I'd be able to talk to him in his own language.

'I'm from Sarajevo,' he said.

I asked him which football team he supported. This is like asking a Glaswegian the same question in that the answer tells you a whole lot more than which football team he follows. 'Red Star Belgrade,' said Mladen. This meant he was a Serb. Needlessly seeking confirmation of this, I asked him who he'd be supporting when Dinamo Zagreb, the leading Croatian side, played Fulham in a few weeks' time. All he said was, 'I'm not keen on Croatians.'

Terrific.

He said I needed to go to a special hand clinic. Seeking to appeal to his love of football rather than his non-existent love of Croats, I explained that I was desperate to get to Chelsea the following day. 'I'll see what I can do,' he said as he closed the door.

Ten minutes later he was back and smiling, a little cruelly it seemed to me. 'I've got you an appointment with the specialist tomorrow,' he said. 'That's the good news. But I think you'll probably have a couple of spare tickets to the match.' I suppose I could at this point have offered him my tickets but I wasn't ready to throw the towel in just yet. I knew the hospital in question was just down the road from Stamford Bridge.

Hope springing eternal, I arrived early for a noon appointment. At 12.30 p.m. the surgeon called me in. 'Was this beefburgers or frozen fish?' he asked. Clearly I wasn't the first clown whose hand he'd had to sew back together.

'You've severed the artery and nerve and you'll probably never get the feeling back in your middle finger, but I can operate to give you the best chance of getting some feeling back.' I listened to this not without interest or regret, but my main concern was still being in the ground at kick-off. Over the surgeon's shoulder, the clock said it was 12.35 p.m.

'When can you do the operation?' I asked tremulously.

'This afternoon,' he said. Oh, brilliant, I thought. I assumed this would be a quick consultation and he'd have me back some other time to do the operation. Just my luck: you read all the time about everyone having to wait six months to go under the knife and here I was being fast-tracked into the operating theatre with the Albion warming up ten minutes down the road.

'There'll be a short wait,' he said.

'How long?' I demanded, rather rudely.

'Why? Is there a rush?' he asked, not a little brusquely.

'I was hoping to get to see West Brom at Chelsea this afternoon, that's all,' I stammered meekly.

'I'll see what I can do,' he said in a tone of voice which suggested not so much that he wouldn't do his best for me, but that he wouldn't cry himself to sleep if he didn't quite pull it off.

At 2 p.m. I went into theatre.

'These injections will hurt,' he promised.

He was right.

'You've got a quite a high pain threshold,' he remarked.

Nonsense, of course; it was just that I was too focused on the big hand on the clock to worry about any pain in my hand. Two-fifteen now. Surgery commenced. He had those funny specs on which look like little binoculars. Two-thirty came and went. I was resigned. I told myself that if I made kick off at three, having still been undergoing microsurgery at 2.35 p.m., that would be a miracle. At 2.38 p.m. he said, 'Right, that's done.' The nurse asked if I'd like a lie-down to get myself together. 'No, thanks,' I said. At 2.59 p.m. precisely, after an extraordinary twenty-four hours spent slicing open my hand, losing consciousness, being whisked to casualty and going in and out of theatre, I was in my seat, ready for the Albion to respond in kind to my efforts and deliver the sort of heroic performance that would make all my pain and suffering worthwhile.

We lost 2-0.

Three seasons on, I'm not handling any frozen fish, but I admire the impressive little scar on my hand on this its third anniversary. It seems to me that tonight's game is going to provide me with about as much enjoyment as I had running a sharp knife right through my palm. So, as I have a practically free afternoon, I decide to try a more liquid anaesthetic to help me through the evening. I've noticed many times that away fans drink very deeply: tonight, I aim to see if being extremely drunk makes getting a proper stuffing any easier to bear.

This process begins in central London over lunch with one of my bosses, the head of football at BBC Sport, an uncompromising Ulsterman called Niall Sloane. I tell him about my feelings for the Albion at length but it's not long before his eyes start glazing over. It's three o'clock by the time we finish. I go for a couple of pints in an empty pub round the corner and then walk across Hyde Park in the pissing rain to another pub in Kensington where one-legged Kev is to meet me. He's known as one-legged Kev because he only has one leg. He's an amputee, you see.

He is there with a neighbour of his in Worcester who supports Chelsea. Kev asks me how my plan to get drunk is going. I tell him I am so wet and cold that I'm becoming sober again. 'I'll get you a drink,' he says, hobbling to the bar.

Kev Candon first went to the Albion when he was eight. 'My cousin, he kept going on about what it was like going to a football match. Then I went and I was hooked straight away. Dad didn't like football but Mum liked it 'cos she'd been to the Albion when she was a young girl, in the late forties early fifties. Then I came along. When I started going regularly my mum started going, too. Went together, me and me mum. It was brilliant, brilliant. Wasn't ashamed or anything like that, big lad like me being out with my mum.

'Dad didn't mind me and Mum going 'cos he was working on Midland Red, on buses. He was a proper Paddy. He come with me to see Albion–Villa one Boxing Day when Jim Cumbes was in goal and let the ball into his own net. My dad didn't see any of the match. He was in the bar.' Kev laughs.

'Mum stopped going just after the 1970 League Cup final 'cos of the violence. The coach got bricked at Coventry. And that was enough for Mum. She wouldn't have stopped me going, though. I'd have left home. I was obsessed. Oh God, I was unbelievable with it, man, unbelievable. It was life. There was nothing else. Nothing else for me, just football and West Bromwich Albion.'

I feel faintly sorry for Kev when he says this, but my wife would argue, quite persuasively, that I'm no better. At the sharp end of one particularly nervy season, torn between pity and contempt, Jane sat me down and said, quite seriously, 'The reality is that you are in the grip of an obsession. And I dread to think what kind of awful thing has got to happen to you to put the Albion in perspective.'

This quite stopped me in my tracks and for several minutes I ceased worrying about whether the Albion would get promoted. And for the next few days I did wonder if I would become less obsessed with the Albion should, God forbid, something really dreadful happen to me.

I mentioned what Jane said to one-legged Kev once and he nodded, but then thought for a moment, and shook his head instead. 'No, that's crap. I had my leg cut off. Lots of really bad things have happened to me and I'm as obsessed with the Albion as you are.'

Kev's troubles began fifteen years ago: 'I had two operations on my back. First one was for a prolapsed disc. Then they had to go back in to clean me out because they never cleaned me out from the first operation. That was '91, then me leg and foot just went deformed, because of that back operation that went wrong. I still say it went wrong, but I never got any compensation. Different doctors have told me different things. My leg was withering away for a long time, four or five years maybe.'

All that time, as they tried to save his leg with three more operations, Kev was in unbearable pain. 'I was lying flat on my back in a block of flats in Nechells. Mum's place. Most games I couldn't go to but St John Ambulance took me. They drove me in and carried me on a stretcher high up into the stand. They put me down and I'd lie on my side to watch.

'For the play-off final, I went down to Wembley with St John Ambulance. Cost me a bloody fortune. There again, I was on the stretcher. They put me right by the royal box, flat on my back. People called me an idle bastard and everything. One bloke even said, the match ain't that boring, mate.

'I was on my back for five or six years. Couldn't walk. Well, I could walk, but I was very badly crippled in one leg so I couldn't get very far. The majority of the time I just had to lie down on my back because of the pain. It was absolutely unbearable.'

Kev had his leg amputated in 1996: 'My dad's birthday and the day England beat Holland 4-1 in Euro 96. I never saw the goals until six months afterwards. It was such a relief to have it amputated. I wasn't in so much pain and I could get down the Baggies again.'

In moments of excitement, Kev often becomes detached from his leg. 'Against Wolves once at our place, we scored and I jumped up and my leg hit somebody's wheelchair. The thing just hit the button on me leg and it just dropped off. It was a million to one chance. Everybody was pointing at me saying, his leg's fell off.'

Another time he lost it I was with him at Walsall on the first day of the season. We were losing 1-0. Kev, a St John's man and I sat in the Bescot Stadium's first-aid room contemplating Kev's stump. 'This is great,' announced Kev. 'We're losing, my leg's come off and he', he said, nodding at the first-aid man, 'hasn't got any talc.'

So while the Albion's season got off to its customary dismal start we sat in the first-aid room puzzling over what we could use instead of talcum powder to help ease the artificial limb back on. 'Got an idea,' said the St John's man, getting to his feet. Five minutes later he came back with some flour. 'This should do the trick,' he said. It did do the job, thankfully. Less happily, though, we lost 2-1.

'But I've always felt better off than most in the disabled section,' Kev continues. 'There's people with MS, paralysed from the waist down. Mine was minor compared with them. I'm in and out of a wheelchair. There's a lot worse off than me.' He pauses. 'There have been some shit times, though. When I was on me back for all those years in Mum's flat, she was suffering from cancer. She was an Albion fan to the end. She didn't go, but she'd get upset if we lost.'

When my wife asks what it would take for me to be cured of my obsession, I think of Kev, flat on his back for six years, living with his dying mother in Nechells, his love for the Albion never deserting him.

By the time Kev, his Worcester Chelsea mate and I get to Stamford Bridge, I have drunk a large gin and tonic, more than a bottle of wine and six pints of strong lager. It's all a bit dream-like. Kev goes off to sit with his mate amid the Chelsea fans. I tell him to mind his back. He says he won't be able not to cheer if we score. I don't worry much about that eventuality coming to pass.

Suddenly overcome with hunger, I buy a steak pie and through huge mouthfuls of it tell anybody who wants to listen that we're going to get stuffed. The team sheet suggests that the manager's giving up on this game in the hope of beating Birmingham on Saturday. There's much tutting about this, but some drunkenly expressed approval, too.

Then I have another beer, which I neck quickly as the kick-off's approaching and the law forbids drinking in sight of the pitch. On this occasion the law is not an ass, as I urgently need to stop drinking and sit down. In search of my seat, I stagger up a short flight of stairs and am blinded by the floodlights and the beauty of the pitch. However drunk I am, however pessimistic I am about a game, however disillusioned I am with anything and everything, the sight of a football pitch under floodlights always stops me in my tracks.

I gaze admiringly on, swaying slightly. And then I take my

seat. Remarkably I spot a Chelsea fan I know, a good friend, waving at me about thirty yards away. I make an obscene gesture at him and marvel at the constitution of those who use alcohol as a means of pepping themselves up for a fight. At this very moment I couldn't fight my way out of a paper bag. In an actual brawl the only hope I'd have would be to vomit on someone.

One joy of games like this is the women. There's a specific breed of woman who show up at our evening games in London. They are in their twenties or thirties and they come because they're going out with Albion fans of the same age. These men dress in the unmistakable uniform of West Midlands boys who have come down to the big city and done well for themselves. They are in suits and overcoats standing next to women in warm, practical but incongruously chic clobber. They are all really nice looking.

I just love the bewildered look on these beauties' faces when the first chant spouts angrily out from our fans all around them. They stare at the chanters, then at their men, then back out at the pitch, astonished at the side of their man they're seeing now for the first time. Does he really hang out with these people? they wonder. To a woman they are nonplussed. I always love watching and I stare at them now, drunkenly slack-jawed in amusement and admiration.

I am soon shaken out of my reverie by Chelsea scoring. They go on to get three more. Two of those I miss, though, as I have to keep staggering off to re-empty my bladder. We don't come anywhere near scoring at all.

Feeling shattered and queasy, I busy myself in the second half blinking a lot to try to keep my contact lenses from misting up as I start to dehydrate. I crave water but the queue is too long because a lot of Albion fans have given up on the game to concentrate on drinking instead. This is football as an excuse for a piss-up. I don't quite get it. If it's a piss-up you want, just go to the pub. The forty quid we've spent on the match ticket would be enough for twenty pints of strong European lager in the West Midlands.

On the way out of the ground someone nudges me and says, 'We were robbed.' I smile weakly. Getting drunk hasn't dulled the pain of heavy defeat at all. My throat's dry. I feel rubbish.

Two

'I'm not sure Steve Watson's the kind of player we should be signing if we want to establish ourselves'

Three matches in and the team has a win, a defeat and a draw to its name. We are doing better on the pitch than I am in my quest to find out why football fans are like we are. Still, as a manager might say, the season's a marathon not a sprint, and before our next fixture there is an opportunity to make progress: the annual general meeting of the supporters' club. It takes place on a Thursday evening at the Hawthorns. Like all football grounds when there's not a match on, the place resembles a deserted cathedral, with only a few functionaries and the most ardent of devotees in attendance.

We are in one of the hospitality suites in the East Stand. Maybe a hundred people gather to hear John Homer, the president, say membership is falling but a new branch has opened in Scotland.

In discussing the performance of the team, he uses the word mediocrity, which he pronounces 'mee-dee-OH-kritty'.

I get talking to Mike Thomas, whose collection of Baggies memorabilia is generally thought to be unmatched. He goes to most reserve and youth team games.

'What about the first team?' I ask.

'I've missed three in twenty-nine years,' he says. 'One when I had a heart attack, then when I had the angiogram after that heart attack and the third time was when I thought I was having another heart attack.'

There are those who would regard Mike as a nutter but I feel only admiration for this level of commitment. I ask him why it is that some people need to go to every game. I say that I love the Albion and you can really love them without going to every single match. In fact I believe that you can miss plenty of games and still be a genuine fan. Mike disagrees: 'The only reasons not to go to every game are time and finance,' he says severely.

A middle-aged bloke approaches me and shyly pulls a photograph out of his pocket. It's of some box hedging fashioned to read 'West Brom'. I tell him how impressed I am and ask how long it took to grow. 'Twenty years,' he says, pulling out another picture – this one twenty years old – of the hedge as a load of little baby hedges spelling out West Brom. His love for and pride in the hedge and the Albion are all rolled into the big smile on his face.

I end up chairing a discussion about why everyone feels the way they do about the Albion and, disappointingly, it turns out that nobody can really articulate why. They all keep talking about how passionate they are, but not why they are so passionate. I see a packet of crisps lying on the bar and wonder if asking someone to explain why they like football is as pointless as asking why they like crisps. They just do. And asking why they like the Albion instead of Wolves is like asking why they prefer cheese and onion to prawn cocktail. They just do.

'Perhaps,' I suggest, 'we do it for the love of each other, not for the club itself.'

Silence falls as, rather embarrassed in some cases, the congregation ponders this thought. Finally, with the air of a man sharing a definitive answer to the question, a bloke punches his chest really quite hard and says, 'It's in here, it's in the heart.'

Sandy Wolfson, a psychologist at Northumbria University with a special interest in the behaviour of football fans, has overseen research in which hundreds of football fans were asked why they came to support a team. Of those asked, 35 per cent said it was because of where they lived, but 36 per cent put it down to who their family supported. Sandy, I have to report, urges me to take some of this with a pinch of salt because hardly a single respondent cited the success of the team as the reason they started supporting them. 'Who are all those Man Utd fans, then?' she cries.

We're all agreed that family plays a big part. And it's not just our living relatives who exert this influence. As I drive away from the meeting, I'm reminded of some women I met at Manchester City: Pat, Jean and Jean's daughter Michelle. I was standing in the four-deep crush for refreshments. 'We can't see over the top,' said Jean to me pleadingly. 'Can you see if there's any red wine?' It had never occurred to me that you could buy wine in grounds, and there was no red wine, but there was white and I bought them a small, warm bottle each.

Jean told me she hardly ever missed a game and said something I couldn't quite hear about her husband's gravestone. Soon a rather doleful looking thirtysomething woman joined us, clad head to foot in Albion-branded gear. Even her white trainers had the club crest on. Her mother said, by way of introduction, 'This one's mad for it.'

'Tell them about Sunderland,' instructed her mother. Obediently, Michelle told me how she worked nights at Sainsbury's and how, when we last played at the Stadium of Light, she stayed up for forty-eight hours straight through. I asked how she got into being an Albion fan. 'Since my daddy died,' she said.

'Your daddy?' I asked, wondering what on earth she was going to say next.

'When he died we came and spread his ashes on the pitch, on the centre circle. And as we were walking off my mum says, "Well, do you want your dad's season ticket?" I've been going ever since.'

I wondered if it would be appropriate for me to say how desperate I am for my daughters to be as fanatical as me, and Michelle, but how I'm not sure I'd be prepared to actually die to make it happen. I decided to say it and all three of them laughed but exchanged glances once or twice as they did so.

Jean married Michelle's father in 1957. 'It was Gordon who got me into the Albion,' she explained. 'I was from Rowley and he was from Oldbury. I wasn't into the Albion at all, but if you can't beat them join them.'

Gordon Wilkes died in 1993. Martin, Michelle's brother, used to go with their dad every week but just couldn't bring himself to keep it up after he died. 'When we scattered his dad's ashes on the Albion ground, he couldn't go,' said Jean, 'and he's been up twice since then I think. He just said "I can't. My dad's there and I can't." Now when I go up I feel as though I can talk to Gordon but Martin couldn't. He used to idolise his dad. They used to go on the away coaches together. When his dad died he stopped going. He stopped and Michelle started.'

For Jean and Michelle, being at the Hawthorns is an opportunity to commune with their much missed husband and father. Jean said, 'Sometimes I say, Gordon, oh pick up the goalpost and don't let them get in, and I'm talking to him, you know. It's just like he's there.'

Michelle agreed. 'My dad's ashes are on the ground so I feel like I am going to see him, 'cos I can't go to the cemetery 'cos his stone's there but he isn't. When I go to the Albion, I really feel he's there.'

Pat Luke, Jean's friend, looked on. She is what my dad would describe as a handsome woman. She's sixty-six, well-spoken and really loves the Albion. Her experience is evidence that the family bond which ties us to our teams is often not as straightforward as parents or grandparents taking their kids along until they are infected.

Derek, Pat's husband, is not the least bit interested in football, and neither are her two children. But Pat follows the Albion everywhere. When I got the chance to speak to Derek, I asked him how far he was into their forty-five-year marriage when he realised he had hitched his wagon to a fanatic. 'Well, I suppose after the first twelve months,' he said thoughtfully. 'It didn't really surface straight away. I knew she was interested in football but she never went to a match until our son started coming home from school at about twelve, thirteen supporting a different team each day. She said, "No, you've got to support the Albion", because her brother used to take her. So I decided it was about time I tried to get my son into football.'

Derek, dutiful father, duly bought two season tickets, for him and his son, and proceeded to the Hawthorns. They went for a season and a half before they both realised that neither of them was enjoying it very much. 'Every time they kicked off I used to think, Oh my God, another hour and a half to go. And halfway into the second season I suddenly realised he wasn't going to get interested. He was no more interested than I was. I said to Pat: I can't keep this up, I've just got no interest in it whatsoever.' His tone even now was tinged with shame and helpless desperation. 'So we gave up. We just stopped going. And Pat said, well I'll have the season ticket, but my son still didn't want to go, so she took it on and we let the other one go, and she's been going more or less ever since. I think it's about eighteen years now since she took over our tickets. I can't understand why anyone is interested in football at all, but she obviously got the bug.'

I admire Derek's honesty and I'm more convinced than ever that supporting a team is, at least in part, a kind of genetic thing, like some say alcoholism is.

I asked him how he copes when she comes home miserable.

'Well,' he said, with quiet feeling, 'I often wish we'd got a cat and she could kick the cat instead.'

I feel rather sorry for Derek in this respect, but even sorrier for Pat because she has never had anyone in the family to share her joy on the rare occasions the Albion haven't let her down. Again this had Derek the football widower sounding rather sheepish. 'I say, oh good, and that's about the end of it, and I'm afraid she got the same reception from my son and daughter when they were both at home. It was just, oh, all right, then. Which must be quite sad really, but, you know, I just can't raise the thought, or the feelings for it.'

He paused and then said, as if he was making a plea for my clemency, 'On our fortieth wedding anniversary I went to the player of the year night with her.'

So poor Derek, quite unable to raise any enthusiasm for football generally or the Albion specifically, loyally attended a player of the year function – an event for aficionados if ever there was one. I pictured him sitting there, quite bewildered, all for the love of Pat. I could have hugged him. I hope she did.

'Derek's very good about it,' said Pat, rather proudly. 'It was our forty-fifth wedding anniversary last week. We've learnt how to get along with each other. I've got my interests, he's got his. The way we look at it, one of us is going to be left on their own.' These are the words of a typical Albion fan – spoken with love but with a hard edge of clear-eyed pragmatism.

Saturday, 27 August 2005, Birmingham at home

This match kicks off at midday on the advice of the police, who take the view that the less acohol is consumed, the better. At 9.30 a.m. I wander up to the Sportsman, a Pakistani-run pub in West Bromwich. It's heaving. Setting aside, for a moment, my quest to find out why we feel the way we do about our football club, I survey the mass of bodies and wonder if for many people football isn't just an excuse for a piss-up.

I fall into conversation with John Mitchell from Evesham. He runs a food transport company. 'Basically,' he says, 'I drive mushrooms around.'

I ask if he was at the last home game, against Portsmouth. 'Yes,' he says. 'Horsfield in the second and fifty-ninth minute. They pulled one back in the sixty-third.'

It turns out that John always remembers in exactly which minute goals are scored. I ask him how. And why.

'Don't know,' he shrugs. 'Can't help meself.'

The mushrooms he transports, by the way, are ordinary ones, not the narcotic variety.

A blamelessly happy half hour ensues in which I name a game and he tells me when all the goals went in. Somehow we get on to the subject of a League Cup tie against Bradford. 'We'd lost the home leg 3-1 and I was getting a load of stick from work – why you wasting your time going up there for that? that kind of thing – 'cos we were two goals behind and had no chance. But I went and after ten minutes it was 1-0 and after thirty-eight it was 2-0, 3-3 on aggregate. Then they got one back on forty-three, 2-1. And on forty-four they scored again: 2-2. On forty-five we made it 3-2, then on forty-six they made it 3-3! We scored on fifty-five and sixty to make it 5-3. Six-all on aggregate, so we had extra time then. Chris Whyte cleared it off the line in the 120th minute. In the next round we went to Newcastle and won 1-0. Chris Whyte on thirty-three. Or it might have been thirty-two.'

Impressed beyond measure, I go and buy him a drink. A middle-aged bloke at the bar smiles at me.

'Hello, mate,' I say. 'How's things?'

He stops smiling and says, 'Oh, not so good. Just had an operation on me sinus. Had a drip in my arm. Agony it was.'

I tell him how sorry I am to hear he's not been well and how glad I am that he's on the mend. 'Well,' he says, 'that's the problem. I don't feel well at all. I don't think I'm on the mend. I don't think the operation worked.' This stuns us both into silence. He stares into his pint and I go back to John.

Before we leave, John points at a bloke in his late thirties, slim built and unshaven with a baseball cap on. 'He', says John, 'is a proper hooligan.' I think about trying to get a quick word with him, but think better of it. How much better to busy yourself remembering goal-times than kicking anyone's head in.

In this match – as John Mitchell, mushroom transporter, will surely remember it – Heskey puts Birmingham ahead on ten. Horsfield equalises on twelve, but Jarosik on twenty-six and Heskey on thirty-three make it 3-1 before half-time. Horsfield pulls one back on sixty-four. On eighty-seven minutes, thoroughly pissed off, I leave the ground, get in my car and drive back home to London.

The following day I am at work presenting *Match of the Day 2*. It is a fantastic job, to be sure, but not quite so fantastic if we've lost. The trouble today is, the whole dynamic of the season has changed. After a vaguely competent start, we were thinking that the risk-free mid-table mediocrity we have dreamt of might even be within our grasp. But a home defeat at the hands of Birmingham has reminded us it's not going to be like that at all. It's going to be another long struggle. I find myself looking eight months into the future at our last five fixtures of the season, wondering if we'll survive. A dull ache of quiet panic runs through me as a long winter of unbearable tension hoves clearly into view. And, as a presenter of a programme about Premiership football, I'm going to have to report on it all.

Before I go to the studio I get something to eat in the canteen. I'm strangely cheered by a learned article about bird flu in the *Sunday Telegraph*. Apparently half of us could die. The prospect of such a calamity lifts my spirits. It puts the Albion's troubles into perspective, for sure, but it's also possible that if so many people perish, all football would be cancelled so we couldn't get relegated.

The titles of *Match of the Day 2* feature arty shots of each Premiership ground. From out of each stadium whooshes the club crest. When the Albion's is shown it's like a dagger to my heart. Will it be there next season? I swallow hard and try to raise a warm smile. 'Good evening, welcome to *Match of the Day 2* . . .'

Saturday, 10 September 2005, Wigan at home

Ahead of this one I have eschewed the baser pleasures of beer and goal-times in a packed pub for the marginally more sophisticated surroundings of one of the club's restaurants. In the Halfords Lane Stand, it is a touching relic of the early days of football hospitality. It's quite cramped and, though they've tried their best with it, the carpets and wallpaper put you in mind of your nan's house; even more so in winter when the smell of embrocation wafts up through the floor from the dressing rooms below.

Still in search of some answers as to what draws us here, I have got together some of my more learned Albion friends. In places like the Sportsman, surrounded by predominantly working-class blokes, you can construct an appallingly patronising as well as specious argument along the lines of: well, what else have they got in their lives? But my companions today give the lie to that in so much as though they would mostly claim to have genuine working-class origins, they have all done well for themselves in demanding walks of life.

Dave Gritten, film writer for the *Daily Telegraph*, looks up from the menu and says, 'I never thought I'd see the word "drizzle" on a menu here.' There are prawns, too. Somebody wonders if they've been fished out of a nearby canal.

Another film journalist is here, Garth Pearce. Like Dave, he was working in Cannes last year on the day we beat Portsmouth to survive relegation. While those of us at the ground inched our way through an agonising second half, he was in a suite at the Carlton hotel waiting for Sharon Stone to show up for an interview. She was fifty minutes late but, to be fair to the woman, couldn't have been aware she'd chosen one of the most important fifty minutes in West Bromwich Albion's history. Garth, not wanting to be distracted during the interview, had switched his phone off but as she still hadn't arrived he switched it back on. A voicemail from his daughter was waiting for him: 'Dad. Boing boing. You've made it. The other three all lost.' Garth punched the air and shouted, 'Oh YES!' at the precise moment Ms Stone entered the room. Apparently assuming he was merely pleased to see her, she smiled graciously.

Garth's brother-in-law is here, too. Quinton Quayle, British Ambassador to Romania. With a name like Quinton Quayle, I'm not sure what else he could have been but a high-ranking diplomat. (At his residence in Bucharest he once led me into a little room just off the main entertaining area. All over the walls were newspaper cuttings, pennants, posters and photographs about and of West Brom. 'Here's my little shrine,' he said proudly.)

And there's Dave Chance, who looks a bit like the actor Warren Clarke. So he looks nothing like an air hostess, which is what he was before he retired. He was cabin service director on Concorde, no less. But, more impressively for us, he worked on many of the charter flights in the seventies when West Brom were playing in Europe. Many a time we've listened at his feet to tales of flying Ron Atkinson and the team to Belgrade and Valencia in those fabulous days of yore when we never won anything but did compete in the UEFA Cup.

We get talking about the first time we went to see the Albion. For each of us, as for most fans, the experience is seared in the memory. Dave Chance takes us back to Easter Monday, 1948, against Birmingham City. 'It was 1-1. Billy Elliot took a corner for us and it finished up in the back of the net. Seemed to go straight in. Gil Merrick was in goal. He was England keeper at the time. I saw him years later, thirty-five years after the event, and I told him he let in the first goal I ever saw the Albion score. And do you know what he said? He said, "Easter Monday, 1948, at the Hawthorns. I had it in my hands and to this day I still don't know how it ended up in the net."'

43

'Pompey in 1955, here,' says Dave Gritten firmly. 'Beat them 4-1.'

His Excellency the ambassador says his first game was Man City in 1967.

Garth says his dad – good parenting this, in my book – warmed him up with some reserve matches then took him to see us beat Luton 4-2 in 1958.

Then it's my turn. Oddly enough my first game was against Luton, too, in 1974. We drew 1-1. It wasn't my dad who took me, though, it was my granddad. He was responsible for administering the first lethal doses that led to my addiction.

Every other Saturday at 12.15 p.m. precisely, my granddad would pick me up from my parents' house. From the age of eight to fifteen this was the ritual: I would get into his blue Volvo and head to the Hawthorns. On the way we'd stop at a chip shop in Oldbury. He would go in and buy me chicken and chips with curry sauce poured all over the top of it.

We would be on the car park at the Hawthorns for about one o'clock, at which point he'd go off to the Throstle Club and drink beer with his friends. I would open up the chicken and chips and curry sauce with not much less relish than I used to open my presents on Christmas Day. Even now the taste and smell and texture of soggy chips, fried chicken and chip shop curry sauce can have my eyes filling up with tears of nostalgia and love for my granddad and the Albion.

I sat there for at least two hours before every home game for seven years. I would do my homework and listen to all the pre-match stuff on BRMB or what was then Radio Birmingham. Sometimes I'd sit in my granddad's seat and pretend I was driving his car. And I used to love looking out of the car window as kick-off got closer. There'd be hardly anyone there when we arrived but then the windscreen would fill with people and cars and I would become more excited by the minute at the prospect of the match.

Occasionally there was the added thrill of TV cameras. The satellite trucks would park up nearby. I was nervous about the game at the best of times, but this made it worse: if we lost, we'd be seen losing on the telly. If we won, though, I'd be able to watch it all over again. I said quiet prayers, sometimes gripping the steering wheel so tightly that it made my hands ache.

I idolised my granddad so I never asked why it was that I had to sit in the car for so long before every game. And neither did I really object to leaving every match ten minutes before it ended. I would say a quarter of all the goals scored at the Hawthorns in that time happened while we were driving back down the M5. Why did we have to leave early? 'To avoid the traffic,' he would say. I accepted this totally, and it was years after he died before I dared to wonder what exactly he had to be home for. All he ever did on a Saturday night was sit with my nan, and often my brother and me, watching the telly.

I have never felt any rancour towards him for instilling in me a love for the Albion. Although I'm quite sure he would feel disappointment as well as pride if he could see me now – allowing my life to be blighted by the club he introduced me to.

Incidentally, the other taste of this time, apart from chicken, chips and curry sauce, is that of a Fox's Glacier Mint. There was a bloke sitting next to us who would hand them out every time we scored. The taste of those things still makes me happy.

Years later, after my granddad had died, I happened to be sitting near our old seats. To my surprise the man with the mints was still there. I introduced myself and was pleased that he remembered me. But then he said, 'What happened to that old bloke you used to come with?'

That old bloke? I thought, that's my granddad you're talking about.

But all I said was, 'Oh, he died.' Then I walked away and I didn't go anywhere near those seats again. And as that stand's since been replaced, I never will.

I sit here now looking across the pitch. I have had a bit too much cheap red wine with my meal and I find myself calculating that because the new East Stand is set a little further back than the Rainbow was, the exact spot where my granddad and I sat is actually in mid-air. I imagine him there, levitating, looking on.

In those days if we scored first, as long as it wasn't too early, it would make me happy. But now I'm much tenser. We score first and are coasting yet I still leave my fingerprints in my seat. I can't bear the tension of being 1-0 ahead because there is just so much to lose. I find holding on to a lead so nerve-racking that I'm almost relieved when Wigan equalise. Without a lead to defend, I feel more relaxed. And, pessimist though I am, on this occasion I feel sure we will take the lead again. But we don't. Every time I try on optimism for size, it lets me down.

There are many things in football that break your heart but there is nothing worse than a home defeat thanks to an injury time goal from the visitors, such as the one Wigan score in the ninety-second minute. Misery. If only my granddad was still taking me to the matches, I would have been long gone. As it is, after fifteen minutes stuck in solid traffic, I channel all my anger and misery into driving fiercely in whatever direction other cars don't seem to be going. I end up somewhere near Spaghetti Junction, stuck fast again. Perhaps my granddad had the right idea, after all.

It wasn't just me my granddad took to the football; he took my brother Nevil, too. I often wonder why Nev didn't fall for the Albion like I did. Stranded in traffic, I have nothing better to do than ring and ask him: 'When Granddad started taking you as well as me, why didn't you enjoy it?'

'I did.'

'You didn't.'

'I did. I remember, it was a night game. I loved it. I didn't stick at it because basically I played more than you and we trained on Saturdays. I preferred playing to watching. Watching just irritated me because I wanted to be playing.'

'So how would you describe your attitude now?'

'Interested.'

Interested. Pah. 'Not passionate, then?'

'No. Well, I am when I watch it. It does my head in and I start becoming like you. If I go up there or watch it on the telly, I start getting involved and feel the disease growing. Then I ease off a bit.'

He has got a point here. I feel it very deeply, but he finds the experience of watching us almost unbearably painful and frustrating, much worse than me, oddly. Perhaps you can actually be too passionate to go. Maybe there are some who aren't interested and others who have it in them to become too interested but see that, so guard against it happening. Still, I'm not going to give him that let-out, obviously.

'I'm a fair-weather fan. I'm no use to them at all,' he admits before I can start getting at him. 'Basically the only time I go is when you give me a free ticket. I don't think they'd thank me just for being there.

'And I suppose the other thing is that I was abroad a lot and when I was back here I went out with evil women who would have chopped my cock off if they suspected I'd been enjoying myself at all.'

Fair point, although if he had gone at that time – in the nineties – I doubt he would have got much enjoyment out of it at all, so his girlfriends' junior hacksaws would probably have stayed in the toolbox.

Saturday, 17 September 2005, Sunderland away

My marriage just now won't take another whole Saturday out following the Albion so I don't go. One of the many perks of my job on *Match of the Day*, though, is that if I can't make it to a match I can always watch the game at the office because live pictures of all of them are available.

Today Andy Thompson is with me, headphones on, squinting at the little monitor on my desk. Another friend, Anthony Kernan, a Chelsea fan, has come in to watch their game at Charlton. Seven minutes have elapsed when Sunderland score. Andy kicks the metal filing cabinet under my desk. It makes a startlingly loud noise and someone working a couple of desks away looks round. We are playing desperately poorly. Anthony, watching Chelsea at another monitor just a few feet away, seems a distant figure, operating in another world entirely.

At half-time I pop down to the *Match of the Day* production office where Gary Lineker, Alan Hansen and various other luminaries are watching all the matches on lots of different screens. I tell them morosely how badly I think we are playing. They look at me with a mixture of pity and contempt, and wonder that I am the least bit surprised.

In the second half we're even worse but in the ninety-fourth and last minute Zoltan Gera, our Hungarian international, scores. Andy and I both leap up, the headphones tearing from our heads as we do so. Suddenly the world is a better place. Anthony smiles benignly, drawing pleasure from our joy as a rich man might from seeing a beggar wolf down a sandwich he has just been given.

'Still think we're doomed,' says Andy as he drops me off at home. 'We were shit.'

Tuesday, 20 September 2005, Bradford at home in the Carling Cup

Being born locally with an Albion-mad granddad, my initiation into supporterhood was pretty typical. The same can't be said of Gurdial Singh and her children. I have arranged to go to tonight's game with her daughters.

The Singh's home is near Solihull. It's part of a tasteful new development of executive houses that are all very nice and all look the same apart from the Singhs', which is distinguished by the Albion paraphernalia in most of its windows. Outside there are two cars, their windows also full of West Brom stuff. Next to the front door there's a plaque: 'West Brom Fans Live Here'.

We chat in a sort of mini-living room next to the kitchen. Jadeen and Jeevan are idly watching *Sky Sports News*. 'Show Adrian the Sky Plus page,' says Gurdial to her younger daughter. Jeevan reaches for the control and the screen is filled with page after page of saved West Brom footage.

Gurdial came to West Bromwich from the Punjab when she was one. 'I take my kids and show them the wall I sat on when the Albion came past after they won the cup in 1968. I was seven at the time and didn't really know what was going on. All we knew was that West Brom had won the cup. Didn't know what cup or who they'd beaten or anything.

'On Saturdays when I heard the crowds coming past I'd go and stand in the window and pretend to be cleaning the sill just so I could look at them. I wondered what it would be like to be part of that, to be part of a crowd on your way to support a team – the unity of it and the anticipation of going there and watching. They were right noisy then, and there were a lot more of them. You'd see regulars going past. You'd set your watch by them as they came past the house.

'Whenever I went shopping with my mum to Birmingham, the bus would go past the ground, and I'd always make sure we sat on the top deck because there used to be a gap through which you could get a glimpse of the pitch, of the green. I didn't really know what went on there but I just found it fascinating.

'It wasn't until secondary school when I started to understand, when I met people who were fans, or had boyfriends who were fans, or were girls who actually went to matches. But I could never go. I suppose you could say I was forbidden, but it was so unthinkable it wouldn't even have crossed my mind to ask the question. A female Asian going to a football match just would not happen. My brother started to get into football but, like a lot of Asians at that time, he was a glory hunter and supported Leeds United. We used to watch on TV. It was on late at night and my mum never stayed up that late, so my brother and I could watch it. It was like something we shouldn't be doing.'

Gurdial got married in 1983, aged twenty-one. It was an arranged marriage. 'He's from Newcastle and luckily a football fan, but we lived away. As soon as we got married we moved to Kuwait and then Bahrain. He's an oil engineer, in Algeria at the moment.'

In 1990, they came back to the UK. It was in 1993, when the girls were seven and five and their brother was on his way, that Gurdial finally found herself at the Hawthorns. 'We were living in Solihull and football still didn't matter really. We had an interest and watched the big games on TV but I was more concerned with bringing up the kids. Then one Saturday, I think Newcastle were playing Coventry or something, and I said to my husband, why don't you go. And he's like, OK. And then, for me, it was suddenly like an awakening. It was so weird. I suddenly thought, Hang on a minute, what's stopping me going to the Albion?

'The first game I went I was eight months pregnant with Jo, and had my two girls with me and my husband. I was there, finally, in that ground. And I couldn't believe it. Could not believe it. I stood there staring at the pitch.'

Gurdial goes quiet, quite emotional at the memory. 'I did feel a little bit uncomfortable being pregnant and we were the only Asians there. But it was just . . . just . . . after all those years. And it didn't let me down.'

We talk about taking her children. 'It was a real effort sometimes getting the kids to go. They didn't want to. But whenever they were asked they always wanted to go.' It sounds to me as though they were told to go more than they were asked. I ask Gurdial if to some extent her kids obeyed her by going to the Albion just as she obeyed her parents by not going. I'm not sure she's thought of it like that before.

'I suppose that's true. I mean, if they really didn't want to go, they didn't have to but, then again, I didn't give them much choice. The alternative was probably just to go and sit at my mum's. Thinking back, it was so cold sometimes they were turning blue.'

I ask if she gets anxious when she sees the kids upset about the Albion. Does she ever wonder why she put them through it? Gurdial shakes her head. 'They suffer with me; we suffer as a family. We do this as a family thing.'

In the ground I sit with Jeevan and her older sister Jadeen in the Birmingham Road End, right behind the goal. Jeevan looks up at the stand to the left where they used to sit and says, 'We were so bored at first, and cold. We never really used to watch the game, we just looked around and played games and things.'

Now, though, they, and their younger brother Joshan, are hooked. I quickly become very attached to these two young women. It's not just that they're young and attractive and intelligent, it's that they really are Albion mad and they say things like, 'I'm not sure Steve Watson's the kind of player we should be signing if we want to establish ourselves' and 'I don't know why we don't play Kanu in the hole every week.'

Jadeen says she is going back to Leeds tomorrow to university but then will come back down on Friday for Saturday's match against Charlton. 'My friends think I'm mad. The girls don't get it, 'cos I'm a bit of a girly girl as well. I like pink things, I like shopping, so I've got that side. Do you remember the Blackburn game last season and if we won we had a chance but we drew? I was desperate and saying to my friends, We're relegated, we're relegated, and they said, are you actually relegated? and I said, well, no. And they just didn't understand,' says Jeevan helplessly.

Tonight, though, the challenge is to get past Bradford. Say that word to a West Brom fan and watch them gaze into the middle distance, lost in thought. In 2002 Bradford was the penultimate match of a season in which we, improbably, thrillingly, overtook Wolves, our archest of rivals. We had to win at Bradford.

It is a long, beautiful story but the essence of it is that in the dying minutes of the game, just as we were resigning ourselves to a heartbreaking and calamitous draw, the Albion were awarded a penalty. A Slovakian called Igor Balis scored. I was standing next to a short, middle-aged man with tattoos and a shaven head. He started crying when the penalty was awarded and continued to do so once it had been scored. He wept for the remainder of the game and long after the final whistle. He might still be there now. Just as Humphrey Bogart said to old what's-her-name in *Casablanca*, 'We'll always have Paris', so we can always say to each other that, no matter how bad things get, 'We'll always have Bradford.' No one can take that away from us.

There are lots of kids in the ground tonight because prices have been reduced. If the aim is to enthuse and indoctrinate them, then the team, for once, does its bit by scoring a couple of goals. Behind us sits a bloke called Alex, probably in his late twenties. With him is his nephew, Aaron, who looks about four. Both have very closely cropped hair. The little boy is agog with the whole experience. He fires questions at his uncle. 'Who's playing best?' he demands, 'Albion or Bradford?'

The answer, as it happens, is Albion. We go 2-0 up but just before half-time Bradford pull one back, a significant event for another fan close by, Elena Sergi. She's twenty, a law and history student at Keele University, and has a season ticket with her dad. She has not seen us concede a goal in ten years. This is because any time the ball comes anywhere near our penalty area she buries her face in her dad's coat. But tonight, disaster strikes: 'I went to get a hot chocolate and as I came out in sight of the pitch I just saw the ball go into the net. I was holding hot drinks so I couldn't cover my eyes. I just stood there holding these hot chocolates.'

At half-time little Aaron earnestly leafs through the programme with a frown on his face: 'Where', he demands of his uncle, 'does it say in here that we're winning 2-1?'

We score twice more in the second half to win 4-1. In the morning I call Gurdial Singh and congratulate her on a quite magnificent parenting job. I find myself telling her about an accountant I recently met at a conference. He was from Cannock. 'I feel a bit guilty when I meet a West Brom fan,' he said, 'because

I used to go, but I stopped. I was one of a long line of Albion fans, but my son turned into a Man Utd fan.'

And this is the bit that really made my jaw drop: 'And I wasn't going to try to stop him being a Man Utd fan. I didn't want him to be a Albion fan. I didn't want him to grow up with a loser's mentality.'

Gurdial is as aghast to hear this now as I was to hear it at the time. 'No,' she says quietly but firmly, 'no. It makes them stronger.'

Three

Newsagent, anti-aircraft gunner, strict timekeeper: Vic Stirrup

Whatever family pressures have been brought to bear on you, the question of why you are a fan is a different one to how much of a fan you are. How do you measure loyalty?

The simplest measure is how many games you get to. Obviously that is relevant, but my measure is this: it comes down to how much you know and how much you care. I've got a friend who supports Birmingham City. One Saturday he came down to London to stay with me. We talked a bit about the Albion who, not unusually, had lost that day. Then I asked him who the Blues had played.

'Oh, don't know,' he said.

To me, my friend is not a fan. He can't be. If you're a proper fan, your fixture list will be hard-wired in your head. You'll know who your next three games are against at least, and you'll certainly know if, and who, you are playing that day. And if you're not at the game, whatever you are doing, wherever you are in the world, you will be totally in bits until you find out what the result is.

Before any theory can be considered proven, it has to be tested to the extreme and Allan Ahlberg's the man who subjects my theory to the sternest test. Allan is a fan who cannot remember the last time he went to the Hawthorns.

He's a hugely successful writer of children's books. I had him down as a Jewish American, so was astonished to see on a TV documentary that he's from Oldbury in the Black Country. I knew, just somehow knew, that he was an Albion fan. I called the producer of the programme, who gave me a number for his publisher but warned me that he was notoriously difficult to get hold of. I left a message and forgot about it, until about an hour later when I got a note to call him. It was a Bath number. 'Up the Baggies,' he said when he answered.

We have arranged to meet at Paddington Station. Even as we shake hands, Alan is talking about Ronnie Allen and Ray Barlow and the team that almost won the double in 1954. There's a sparkle in his eyes as he talks about those days, yet even then he didn't go to many games. 'I used to play football on Saturday morning and in the afternoon I played for another club and Sunday mornings as well. I used to come home on Saturday afternoon all covered in mud and have a bath. I'd always try and buy the *Sports Argus* and I'd listen to *Sports Report* on the radio.'

'So you never went much,' I ask, 'but it was still in your guts?'

'Oh, yes,' he says with feeling, 'Oh, definitely.' He pauses. 'It's not been an even thing, it's ebbed and flowed but for some reason it's accumulated in the last seven or eight years. I don't know why. As you get older, as men get older, they become more emotional. I think that might be it. But I've become a comic figure in my larger family. They find it curious.

'On Survival Sunday I was in the garden, my wife was there. I had the radio on and I kept going inside to check Ceefax. The whole thing was incredible with those four matches, like poker, the four hands being laid out. When we were safe, I was rushing up and down the garden going mad. The neighbours wondered what was up.'

He shakes his head at the memory. I tell him this is bad news indeed for me, because I've always hoped it would wear off when I get older.

'Perhaps it'll work the other way with you,' he says, 'or perhaps you're already old.'

I tell him I often feel old, watching the Albion.

'It's absurd,' he continues, 'but it's become a stronger feeling. When they lose, I don't buy a Sunday paper at all, but when we win,' he says with real relish, 'I get the papers and walk down to this café in Bath. I spread the paper out and have some breakfast and read all about it.'

'Paradise,' I say.

'Paradise,' he agrees.

Another supporter who never shows up to support the team is Steve Lloyd. It's his wife, Sandra, I meet first. She has been recommended to me as a fan whose love for the club knows no bounds. When I called her, she was in a pub in Sunderland. Above the din she told me which pub in West Bromwich she'd meet me in before our next home game. I asked how I would recognise her. 'Oh, you'll know me,' she said, 'I've got this haggard look about me.'

I see her before she sees me. She is not the least bit haggard – an elegantly dressed woman, even if everything she's wearing does seem to come from the club shop: WBA jumper, neck scarf, brooch, ring, pendant and, I have to assume, knickers. It would be premature for me to ask if she's wearing West Brom knickers, although she looks the kind of woman who wouldn't be that offended if I did put the question to her.

I buy some drinks. It is a classy little pub in its own real-ale sort of way. There is a beer called Dirty Bitch. 'Get yourself a Dirty Bitch,' Sandra says, laughing in a bawdy, cackly tone.

She's with Rob, her son, and her daughter Kate, a student at Aberystwyth University. And a bloke called Brian is here, too, one of her brother's friends. I ask how she got into football. She shrugs and says, 'Well, I was born in 1955 while my dad was at the match so I suppose it was always going to happen. I had three brothers and I went to the football with them. That's what you did. Why I got hooked I have no idea. I was seven or eight. I don't know. I just took to it more than my brothers.'

I ask if her loyalty's every wavered. 'Yes, the Ron Saunders days. Eighty-five to eighty-six. They were the pits. I never stopped going, though, I just found it hard. I haven't got a fantastic record, but I didn't miss one last season or the season before and I think the season before that we just missed Crystal Palace midweek.'

These are the kind of people I mix with now – those for whom missing two games in two seasons constitutes something other than a fantastic attendance record.

'At the 1968 cup final there was an old bloke there who told me to make the most of it 'cos it'd never happen again in my lifetime. Miserable old sod, I thought, but wasn't he right? In the Hillsborough 1969 semi-final against Leicester when Allan Clarke scored, I cried all the way home.'

Her love for the Albion isn't unconditional. 'I get annoyed at away games now, especially. At the end I'm really pissed off if the players don't come over and clap. We're not asking a lot, are we, having come all that way? Just a clap. It's not much to ask.'

I ask Kate if the Albion affects her life as much as her mother's. 'Yeah, it does.'

'How?'

'Well, I have to travel back from Aberystwyth every week, don't I?'

This isn't quite what I was driving at. 'But do you get emotionally as wound up about it as your mum?'

'No,' she says, 'I think I've mellowed with age.'

I look at her mum, and at myself, and wonder why the age-mellowing process hasn't kicked in with either of us yet. I tell Kate I'm getting worse all the time, that I remember when I was fourteen feeling the pain of losing and looking forward to getting older when, having grown out of it, I surely wouldn't feel as bad.

'It never worked out like that, Kate,' I say sadly.

Kate smiles kindly.

Shortly afterwards, in the Gents, Brian says to me, 'You know what you said about taking it worse as you get older. Well, I do, too.' He shakes his head and his appendage at the same time, zips up, and says again, 'I do, too.'

Sandra tells me about Steve. 'When I first met my husband it would have been about 1972. We went everywhere, home and away, with the Albion. Then Kate was born. I don't think he went to many games after Kate was born. And then when Regis left he stopped completely, because he loved Cyrille Regis. He never went again. Must be twenty-five years. Even now if I've got a spare ticket 'cos Kate can't go, he won't go. He loves them. He wants them to win. He wants them to do well, but he won't go.'

I find this fascinating: a real fan who stopped going because his favourite player left. 'I just stopped,' confirms Steve simply when I get to meet him, 'and we played rubbish football for a number of years.' And that's a perfectly understandable attitude even though I feel the opposite: the worse they're playing, the more inclined I am to go. I think this is because subconsciously I believe they need me more when they're bad, like a sick relative. If they're doing well, they'll be fine without me.

What I don't get in Steve's case is why he can't go to the odd game; why stop completely? He opens his mouth to reply but in the end he just says, 'Er, er, I really can't answer that.' He pauses again. 'Once you get out of the habit of going on a Saturday afternoon, that's it. It's, er . . . ' he trails off again.

There were other circumstances, though: he had a business to run and he had babies to hold while Sandra was travelling the length and breadth of the country. I ask if this ever offended his macho sensibilities. 'No,' he says firmly, 'I can honestly say it never concerned me. I never thought about it once.'

I ask him if he can understand her passion, can he share it with her? 'Oh, yes. And with my son and daughter.'

I recall Sandra and Kate telling me how they burst into the bedroom at four in the morning the day after we beat Crystal Palace to win our first promotion to the Premiership. They jumped up and down on the bed chanting, 'We are Premiership.' This sounds to me pretty much like the perfect marriage. I try to imagine my wife and daughters jumping up and down on my bed chanting about the Albion, but the mental picture just won't come to mind.

I ask Steve where he was on Survival Sunday. Wasn't he tempted to go that day? 'God, no. No, no, I couldn't stand it. Jesus, it was bad enough watching on the telly, let alone being there.'

I'm almost exasperated with him now: 'So, you still want us to win; you care enough to be hardly able to watch; you fully understand your family's passion, and even share that passion, but you haven't been at all for twenty-five years? Steve,' I say, 'I plain don't understand.'

Again, he has no answer for me. He just says, 'Well, I'm not saying I'll never go again . . . '

I honestly don't think Steve really thought much about this until I started bothering him. Having reflected upon it, though, I sense he shares some of my bafflement. But neither Sandra nor I can see him coming back into the fold any time soon.

Another fan who doesn't go any more is Nicola Rhodes. But her reason is straightforward: she can't afford it. Watching football has become eye-wateringly expensive, and I know plenty of fans who beggar themselves to go, but Nicola, a school secretary, is the first person I've spoken to who has actually been priced out.

'I was at secondary school when I started,' she explains over the telephone. 'I was about fourteen, I think. I didn't hardly miss a match for years. I used to send notes in to school about going to the dentist, all that kind of thing, to go to midweek matches. I went regularly for about ten years. We were in the old third division. I went to all the bottom league clubs. I got a boyfriend, and he started coming with me. And then we bought a house and then there was a baby on the way. And you can't afford to do everything, can you?'

'So was it the time or the cost that stopped you?' I ask.

'A bit of both, but mainly the cost.'

'Would you go back if you could afford to?'

'Oh, God, yeah, I do miss it. My boyfriend – I'm with someone else now – he goes to Liverpool week in week out. I see him going to football and I'm stuck here at home or I go shopping. I'd rather be at the football.'

'So,' I ask, 'could you not afford to go to the odd game?'

'Well, I could, I suppose,' she says, faltering, 'but I just couldn't do it like that – I'd either have to go all the time or not at all.'

'It's like giving up smoking, then,' I suggest.

'Yes,' says Nicola, as though the analogy's not occurred to her before, 'exactly.'

I ask if she keeps in touch with how we're doing. Is she always aware that we're playing? 'Oh, yeah. I watch mainly on Sky Sports News, I watch the results coming in. And I'm always ringing the fans I know on the coaches who still go. I speak to them, like, regular and they keep me updated. And I'm always looking at the internet and things.'

Although she won't admit to seeing it in these terms, the real tragedy for Nicky is that she picked precisely the wrong years to be watching the Albion. In the 1990s, with Nicky always in attendance, we were hopeless. We got relegated to the old third division. But, just as she stopped going in 2000, the rot stopped with the arrival of Gary Megson as manager. We survived relegation, nearly got promoted, got relegated, got promoted again and then, thrillingly, under Bryan Robson, survived relegation on the last day of the season.

Poor Nicky missed all that. Survival Sunday was especially painful: 'I couldn't stop thinking about it. I spent the morning shopping. My mum was at her sister's and I arranged to meet her there for the afternoon and basically I sat in front of their telly. I was running in and out of the kitchen, going mad. I couldn't believe it.'

This is more than I can bear, the thought of her missing that great day. 'So,' I say again, still incredulous, 'you missed hardly a game for a decade or more and now you haven't been for five years.'

'Yes,' she says simply. 'Well, I went to last Boxing Day, against Liverpool, with my boyfriend.'

That's the one we lost 5-0.

We are slipping into bathos here and I can't take much more so, without sounding like a host on commercial radio, I ask Nicky if she'd go to a match if she got a free ticket.

'Of course,' she says.

Because of *Match of the Day* commitments, my regular seats will be going spare at a match next month. 'Well, I've got two you can have for Newcastle.'

'Ooooh,' she says, just like they do on radio at moments like this.

I feel a bit callous really. Callous for exposing Nicky to her addiction again and callous because I've forgotten to be grateful for the fact that I can afford to go every week and make myself bloody miserable there without worrying about the money.

Then there is the case of Francis Cregeen. Francis, or Stacey as he's known, is the father of a colleague of mine, Melissa. She has always told me her dad's a massive Albion fan but rarely comes to matches because he lives on the Isle of Man. When I heard he was coming over for the weekend to see Mel in Maidenhead, I organised for him to come to the match. I also asked my friend Garth to give him a lift. When Garth called Mel to arrange this, he asked when her dad had last been to the Hawthorns. She didn't know and shouted the question to Stacey.

'Never,' he said.

'Never?' said Melissa to her dad.

'No, never,' he repeated.

'Never,' she said to Garth.

Saturday, 24 September 2005, Charlton at home

This is Stacey's first visit to the Hawthorns in fifty-nine years of supporting the club. He's very smartly dressed, although nothing seems quite the right size and nothing really matches anything else. Sartorially, he reminds me a bit of myself.

We're in the East Stand, where most of the corporate entertainment goes on. There is memorabilia all over the walls. It's beautifully done. There are shirts, boots, trophies, rosettes, tickets from the century before last and magnificent photographs of great moments in the club's history. Stacey's never been here before but this past is his to share as much as anyone else's. 'Great players,' he says under his breath, looking at a picture of the 1954 cup-winning team that he could hardly ever have seen play, even on television.

Stacey Cregeen, like his father before him, is from the Isle of Man. Which begs the obvious question: why Albion? He smiles as if a little ashamed and says, 'I really can't remember why. I don't know, Adrian, I couldn't tell you that. I've been an Albion supporter since the football started after the war. They've given me nightmares ever since. Strange, isn't it?

'I just used to follow them on radio. The sport programme on

Radio 2. Before that it was the Light Programme. Eamon Andrews used to do it.

'Most fellas round by me have got their favourite teams. My wife tolerates me, just about. She and Melissa are both Liverpool fans. I listen to the matches on Five Live. I'm normally in the garage or doing something in the garden, or whatever. I've got an Albion friend of mine down the road here who lives a hundred yards away. He never goes either. He's red-hot Albion. I don't know why he's an Albion fan. I don't think he knows. He must be mental like me.'

As we walk to the area reserved for directors' guests, I keep losing Stacey as he lingers over one exhibit or another in the glass cases; a newspaper cutting or a signed shirt. At our table he drinks tea, I drink beer. Every two minutes he gets up anxiously, asking if he can buy me or anybody else a drink. Somewhat incongruously Jim Davidson sits at the next table, apparently a guest of the Charlton directors.

Stacey is a little hard of hearing. I shout to everyone I introduce him to that he's been a fan since the Second World War but this is his first time at the ground. Nobody quite knows what to say. Carl, a son of one of our directors, congratulates him on finally making it. Stacey smiles.

We take to our executive seats in the directors' box just as the players run on to the pitch. 'It's perfect,' he says softly to himself, 'just perfect.' He sits bolt upright and very far forward on the edge of his seat, and claps as the players take their bows. His clapping sounds to me somehow separate, distinct from everyone else's.

This is one of those occasions when I am desperate for us to score, not for my sake, or even the team's, just for Stacey. It takes me back to a time I brought a woman called Liz, who I was trying to woo. We were losing 1-0 but she seemed to be quite enjoying it. I wanted her to fall in love with the Albion as much as I wanted her to fall in love with me. In fact I supposed the one would lead to the other. We pressed and pressed that day (the Albion, not me and Liz)

63

and I could see she was beginning to get into it. She wanted us to score and this made me more infatuated. Finally we did score, and she and I went mad together. It was a beautiful moment. Then it was ruled offside. 'Why?' she said. 'Why's it no goal?'

We lost 1-0. I don't think I ever saw her again after that day. She never fell in love with me. And, as far as I know, she never fell in love with the Albion.

I was engaged to someone before I got married to Jane. The one game I remember taking my fiancée to was one of the most vital in our recent history. We had to win at Portsmouth on the last day of the season to avoid relegation to what was then known as Division Two. Fratton Park was like a mental asylum that day. She didn't get it. How could she? No newcomer could have begun to start getting it that day. It was just too big an experience – like trying to play St Andrews in a gale on the day you take up golf.

We won 1-0. After the final whistle my fiancée took a picture of me and my mate Duncan. We looked so in love, so happy, me and Duncan. We are still close friends. The engagement was broken off within months.

With my wife, I should point out, it was rather different. The first game I took Jane to was away at Norwich. We were 2-0 up but ended up drawing 2-2. As an analogy for a relatively successful marriage that seems about right. I knew I was going to marry her the day we played QPR in London. I couldn't go but she went on her own and stood behind the goal with all the Albion fans. And we won 2-0.

Since then she's gone from finding my devotion to the Albion rather charming to finding it ludicrous, corrosive, selfish, immature and many other adjectives, none of them complimentary. In a rare moment of conciliation, she suggested that 'in promotion and relegation' ought to be inserted in the marriage vows along with 'for richer, for poorer' and 'in sickness and in health'.

Back with Stacey, it is soon clear I'm hoping in vain for a happy outcome today. On the pitch, things go very badly for us.

We concede a penalty. As the referee points to the spot, I feel Stacey's whole body tense up for a moment. 'Oh, no,' he groans, as they score. And when Charlton make it 2-0, I feel him sort of convulse. 'Oh, no,' he groans again.

They're murdering us. Our fans boo our team, but Stacey, utterly focused on the game, still offers encouragement. 'C'mon,' he pleads under his breath during a rare attack, 'let's have a ball.' Let's have a ball. The expression is archaic, somehow. It's Stacey's own. But we don't get a ball. A straightforward cross is fluffed.

Another chance goes begging for us, and for them. We are all over the place. Poor Stace is leaning forward in the football fans' foetal position, his head in his hands. Nearly sixty years an Albion fan and this is what they do to him when he finally gets to see them in the flesh on their home ground.

During half-time we sit quietly in the directors' guests area. He sips tea. I pray he'll have something, anything, to celebrate. Just one goal would do, even if we concede another ten. For once my prayers are answered. We come out for the second half playing much better and soon score. He is on his feet cheering and clapping, again, it seems to me, slightly out of sync. I gingerly hug him by clasping both of his shoulders. 'At least we've got hope now,' he says.

I trot out the old line: 'It's the hope that kills you, Stace.'

He laughs. And we go on to lose.

Afterwards he won't stop thanking me for the experience. He begs me to take some money from him for the ticket, but I won't. I'm normally desolate after a defeat, especially at home, yet I am humbled by the experience of watching with Stacey. The result doesn't matter because it meant so much to him just to be in the ground.

I'm surer than ever that his devotion is just as valid as that of someone who has not missed a game in thirty years. Does Stacey care any less than me? Does Allan Ahlberg? Steve Lloyd? Well, the answer is, yes, but not much less.

As Stacey and I part company I tell him again how amazing it is to have an affinity for something you never actually see.

'Strange, isn't it?' he says.

I suppose football is a bit like religion in that you can believe in God without going to church. That's not a view, on football at least, that Vic Stirrup would share. Having watched the Charlton match with a supporter who's never been to the Hawthorns before, I'm going to my next game with a war veteran whose attendance record stands comparison with that of anyone in the world.

Saturday, 1 October 2005, Blackburn away

I am late to pick up Vic Stirrup from his home in Smethwick. He wants me to collect him at 10.30 a.m. It's 10.35 and I'm not quite there yet. We have to be at the Hawthorns for eleven to catch the coach to Ewood Park. I don't want to be late because Vic has only missed five matches, home or away, since serving as an anti-aircraft machine-gunner in the Second World War. I really don't want to be responsible for him missing his sixth.

He is waiting for me in the bay window of his semi-detached house, tapping his watch in that way old people have of pretending to be pretending to be annoyed. The door opens to reveal Vic and two generations of his family forming a guard of honour in the doorway. There are two grandsons in their early teens, Vic's daughter and her husband. In front of them, there's Mrs Stirrup, Brenda. And in front of them all, Vic. He taps his watch again. I apologise profusely and everyone laughs.

He grabs his stick and walks towards the car. Martin, a long-time Albion friend travelling with us, offers him the back seat. Vic says he prefers the front. I offer a helping hand but he refuses. He puts his stick in the footwell and levers himself in. On the way to the ground, assuming that at eighty-six he's hard of hearing, I find myself shouting at him as we chat, as does Martin, who raises his voice from the back seat. Then, in a lull in the conversation, Martin asks me quietly how much the coach costs.

'Fourteen quid,' says the not-the-least-bit-deaf Vic.

*

We're travelling on HATS coaches – the Hawthorns Away Travel Service. Long before I knew what an acronym was, I remember much admiring it as a kid reading their announcements in the programme. For political reasons I'm not entirely sure about, HATS has not been the club's official away travel service for some time. Today it's only running one coach. Dave Gutteridge, head of HATS, as it were, is keen to explain. Even before we've left West Bromwich, he comes to my seat and tells me about a meeting he had with a previous chairman who said there was a chance to make some money with the travel membership scheme. 'I got up and walked out,' says Dave, turning abruptly and walking back to his seat at the front.

Les James is on board, too – Old Les, as Vic calls him, even though he's seven years his junior. Les is a fabulous-looking old bloke, like someone from central casting. Leathery skin, flat cap, pointed chin, brilliant smile and a soft but firm handshake. He looks around at me from five seats ahead and gives me a thumbs-up.

Also with us today is Elena Sergi, who has never – at least until the Bradford match ten days ago – seen the Albion concede a goal. She is here with her dad, George. They're quiet people who smile a lot. I expected to find Elena a bag of nerves, but she couldn't be more relaxed.

'I'm fine now. I'm fine afterwards, too. It's just during the game I can't bear it. I don't know why, I just can't watch the games. I love going but I get so nervous. I think it's because my dad always used to say that since I was born we'd always been terrible, we'd gone downhill. Thanks a lot, Dad.'

Her dad is Greek Cypriot. He originally went to Wolves but decided he preferred the Albion, if only for practical reasons: 'Most Greek Cypriots are based around the Tipton area, so Albion was the only ground we could really get to.'

He laughs when I congratulate him on bringing up his daughter so well, but I also wonder if he feels guilty at all for getting her into it when she obviously finds it so stressful. 'Yes,' smiles George, 'but what can I do? She's hooked.'

Vic has a scrapbook of photos of him following the Albion all over Europe. Vic in Amsterdam; Vic in a group photo in Bruges; Vic and a little boy in Bucharest; Vic smiling in Belgrade. On every other page there is a typewritten itinerary for that particular trip, handed out by the organisers: David Dryer Sports Travel Ltd. I ask how much money this all cost him. 'Ooh dear dear dear,' he says, shaking his head.

There are pictures of Vic with his dad, who looks just like him. There is a great one of them standing next to the bus on which they travelled to the 1954 cup final. His dad is always very well dressed with a three-piece suit and pocket watch. And there are pictures of Vic with a little boy, one of his sons. On one the little boy has pinned to his scarf the badges of all the teams whose grounds he has visited. There are lots of them.

'He stopped going,' says Vic.

'Why?'

'Don't know.'

There are a number of newspaper cuttings in which, perversely, his loyalty seems to become more impressive the further back you go. There is one from 1986 which tells us that 'Vic Stirrup, aged sixty-six, has only missed two games since the war.' But then another one from 1979, in which he's pictured with our goalkeeper Tony Godden, tells us he hasn't missed a single solitary match since the war. He tells me that Tony Godden is one of his top five all-time favourite players. I wonder if this is based as much on his willingness to pose for a picture with Vic as his goalkeeping skills.

Other scrapbooks Vic has brought with him are devoted to the 1968/69 and 1969/70 seasons. There is no mention of any home games; it's all about the away trips. And there are no match reports, because this scrapbook, bizarrely, is concerned only with logistics. At the top of each page is the result and sometimes, but not always, the scorers. Below, glued or sellotaped in, is the match ticket, often torn in half, and the coach ticket. On some pages the coach or match ticket is missing, in which case he has written, 'Not available.' An entry for Arsenal explains the absence of a coach ticket thus: 'Went by train – no coaches.' He has also written the departure and arrival times of the coach.

Hence:

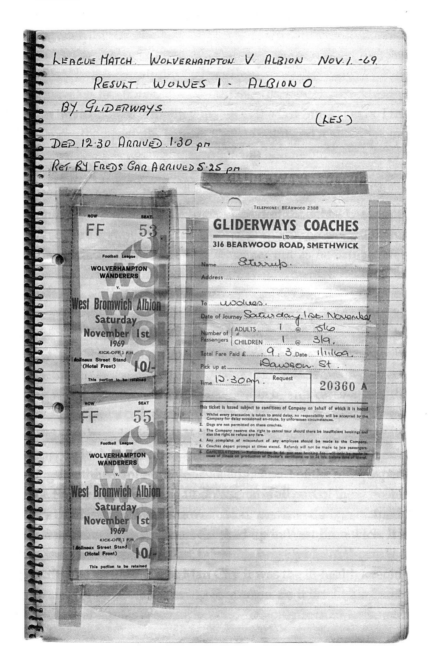

Most extraordinarily, he has entered the name of the coach driver for each trip. It is usually 'Fred', or 'Les', but sometimes it's 'Colin Smith'.

I tut indulgently. I remember keeping a scrapbook myself, although it was, like most schoolboys' football scrapbooks, mainly match reports and photos of players rather than coach tickets. Kids, I think, the daft things they do. I smile at Vic and we raise our eyebrows to mourn the passing of the innocent pleasures of our youth. But then it strikes me that he was into his fifties when he was sticking coach tickets into this book.

Later I tell my wife about the scrapbook and how it made me wonder if Vic is possibly a little bit mad. 'Mad? Do you really think so, Ade? How wise of you. Of course he's bloody mad!' she explodes. 'He's only missed five games since the Second World War. We knew he was mad in the first place.'

Troubled by the thought of a fifty-year-old war veteran putting coach tickets into a scrapbook, I work up the courage to ask Vic if this isn't somewhat disordered behaviour for a grown man. He flails around trying to explain himself but comes up with nothing. 'No, I just don't know why,' he says helplessly. 'I only done it for two years anyway,' he offers in mitigation, before adding: 'But I still got all the tickets from the other matches. I've got a tin full of my away tickets.'

Vic makes to hand me another photo, this one of him in uniform, but he hesitates, as though there is something in it he hasn't spotted before. He is quiet for a while before he says, 'The worst trip was to Malta. Thirty-four ships in convoy. Seven arrived. I was on the Malta run three or four times and that was a terrible run that was. You was attacked twelve hours a day.'

I ask Vic Stirrup, anti-aircraft gunner, rather childishly, if he ever shot down any planes. 'Don't really know,' he says. 'Each ship used to have an area into which you'd fire continuously whether there was a plane there or not. So the whole area was more or less covered. You didn't look for an aircraft to fire at. Otherwise you'd have four or five ships all firing at the same

70

plane and then you'd have another plane coming from some-where else.'

Fascinated, I absorb this presumably elementary lesson in mil-itary strategy as we pass Stafford, Stoke and Holmes Chapel on our way north. It seems rather unsatisfactory to me that you spend the whole war firing into the sky and never find out whether you shot anything down. I suppose it's like following a football club all your life and not knowing at the end of it whether your support really made much of a difference.

I say to Vic that I suppose all that metal is still down there at the bottom of the sea. 'I suppose it is,' he says, looking out of the window. I imagine Vic's bullets, all lying there.

As the coaches park up at Ewood Park I ask Vic if he wants to go for a drink. 'Don't drink, don't smoke,' he says triumphantly, 'and never had a car. You asked how I can afford it. Well, that's how I can afford it.'

As we walk to the ground, I ask if he's got butterflies. 'No,' he says.

'Nervous?'

'No. I used to get excited, but not any more. I do stand up and clap when we score. If we score.'

We struggle up several flights of stairs to our seats. Vic has enough breath to tell us that this climb's not as bad as the one you have to do at Newcastle.

Next to the pie counter we find nervous Elena and her dad. The smiles have all gone; she's unrecognisable from the relaxed, chatty woman on the bus. Wringing her hands, she says, 'It's started ear-lier than usual today, which is usually a bad sign. We normally lose if I feel this bad.' Her dad says, 'She's always like this, Adrian, she's not making it up for you.'

We take our seats, Elena to my left, Vic to my right. Only now does he put his glasses on, reminding me that, two weeks and a day short of his eighty-seventh birthday, he doesn't normally wear them.

71

Once we've kicked off, Elena's body gets more rigid next to mine. Facially she becomes madly mobile: smiling, wincing, flinching, grimacing. I ask if she has a hood to pull over her head but, before she can answer, her dad smiles and taps his shoulder. As soon as the ball looks like it might be entering our penalty area, she hides her face in the arm of her dad's coat. As soon as the danger passes her dad taps her knee and she looks up again.

Vic, by way of contrast, is impassive.

Six seats to my left, on the row in front, sit five teenagers who I judge to have hooligan tendencies. The nearest one to us has a nose that is either congenitally unusually shaped or has been broken. Otherwise he is quite a good-looking lad. He swears a lot. And he's wearing a black T-shirt on which, in large white letters, is printed the legend, 'Who the fuck are D & G?' Vic doesn't seem to be aware of him. And he doesn't seem to be aware of Vic.

Every now and then these boys jump to their feet and turn round to face the crowd behind them. With their little faces twisted in passion and pain and their arms outstretched, they exhort the rest of us to join them in song: 'Fucking come on!' one of them squeaks at everyone. 'The West Brom! The West Brom!' they chant. Largely ignored, they soon give up, snarling their disgust at the apathy of those around them, and at the world in general.

I have them marked down as grotty little cretins, but then one recognises me and gets them all to sing my name. 'One Adrian Chiles, there's only one Adrian Chiles.' In my notebook I cross out 'cretins' and write 'rascals' instead.

Vic mutters occasionally about the game but passes no audible comment.

'Stand up if you hate the Wolves!' demand the rascals. Everyone ignores them. 'Fucking come on!' they command in vain.

We nearly score, Blackburn nearly score. But nobody does score. As the half-time whistle goes, Vic promptly removes his specs, pops them into his pocket and delivers his verdict: 'They

72

done well.' I ask him if he wants anything to drink but he says he can't because then he would have to go to the toilet.

The second half begins promisingly. Before long we're awarded a corner, right in front of us. Vic nudges me, grins and rubs his hands together. 'Here it is!' he says happily. For a moment he looks fourteen years old. This remains the only time I have ever seen him betray any sense of excitement.

We never score from corners, but I trust his instinct, he has been watching us take corners for eighty years now, after all. The ball comes across and I feel the ancient body next to mine momentarily lose fifty years. Yet there is no goal. The moment passes. There is more than half an hour left but this turns out to be our last corner, indeed our last appearance in their penalty area.

As the game progresses Elena's tolerance for tension seems to diminish still further and her head is burrowing into her dad's shoulder as soon as the ball enters our half of the pitch. I tell her she wouldn't make much of a goalkeeper. She laughs into her dad's coat.

I ask how she knows what's going on if she can't see. She says it's the crowd noise that gives it away and, daftly, that, 'A good way of knowing what's going on is to look at other fans.'

'But isn't an even better way of knowing what's going on to actually look at the game?'

She has no answer. I tell her she might as well leave her head buried in her dad's coat as the ball doesn't seem to be spending much time far away from our penalty area. Ten minutes from the end, Blackburn score. And then they score again. Vic is unmoved. The final whistle goes and there are a few boos from our fans. Vic pockets his specs, plants his stick on the ground and rises to his feet.

Back on the coach, everyone is opening their packed lunches. I moan that I haven't bought anything and cheese sandwiches are held out towards me from all directions. Snatches of dissatisfaction, voiced through mouthfuls of sandwich, echo flatly around the coach. 'He's got to go.' 'They were bound to score with all those corners.' 'Give him a chance – he'll get it right.'

Elena is perfectly relaxed and happy all over again. She doesn't join in the grumbling and moaning. All her angst is focused into the ninety minutes, which is in many ways preferable to carrying it around with you all week like I do. She is so over the disappointment that she is even looking forward to watching *Match of the Day* tonight. I'm plain baffled that the woman who refused to watch the ball come anywhere near our goal is going to watch it on the television tonight. 'I like analysing how they scored,' she says.

'How? Why?' I demand.

'I don't know,' she laughs. 'Even at the game, if there's a big screen I'll try to watch it if they show the replay.'

I never ever watch us lose on *Match of the Day*, and I present the flaming programme on Sunday nights. When I was a kid I had a friend called David 'Bobby' Charlton, a Birmingham fan, who would watch *MOTD* or *Star Soccer* on ITV even if the Blues had lost. This seemed to me the height of maturity as I couldn't bring myself to watch even if we'd drawn (unless we'd come from behind). If we had been ahead and the opposition had equalised, I wouldn't watch.

I'm not proud to say that after a defeat on a Saturday I have often gone into work to present *MOTD2* on the Sunday completely ignorant of all the football results. Having left the ground at the final whistle, I will have put some music on in the car, refused to speak to anyone and kept away from all news sources that evening and the following morning. One time I got in to work on Sunday lunchtime and Mark Demuth, my editor, said, 'Of yesterday's games, we'll pull Liverpool out for a longer look at it, for obvious reasons.'

'Yes,' I said, 'obviously.' The last I'd heard of Liverpool, or indeed any game the day before, was the half-time scores. I made my excuses and took some sports pages to a quiet corner to find out what exactly had happened in the games I was shortly to broadcast about.

Back on the coach, Old Les says something to me about a carpet he has got in the back of his car that he wants to show me. I assume I have misheard him but I smile and say I'd love to see it.

We are on the slowest coach. The rest of the convoy are out of sight by the time we get on the M6 and when we arrive back at the Hawthorns the car park is nearly empty. As we drive off, I remember I've forgotten to go and see whatever it was that Les wanted to show me.

In the dark on the way back to Vic's house, he says, mainly to himself, 'Got to be off to the ice hockey tomorrow afternoon.' He is also a season ticket holder at Coventry Blaze ice hockey team. 'Face-off at six o'clock,' he says.

At home Brenda emerges from the front room to greet us. 'One minute it was nil-nil,' she says, 'then next time I switched it on it was two-nil.'

Vic and I grunt.

I ask if she's got his tea on. She snorts. 'He's been out all day. He can get his own tea.'

Our first chance to make amends for the defeat at Blackburn is an unpromising home match against Arsenal next Saturday. Before that, though, on Monday night, the reserves are at home to Wigan. Attendance at reserve games seems to me to be rather like Catholics attending mass on weekdays as well as on Sundays and holy days of obligation. There can be few greater demonstrations of devotion.

I've arranged to meet the Hayden family at tonight's match. They are all Albion mad. 'The Albion's our life, really,' Amanda Hayden once told me. Her dad Roy's not missed a league game for thirty-eight years this week. His wife Barbara has missed only half a dozen home games in that time. Their son Steve is equally passionate, but he won't be there tonight. He hadn't missed a game in twelve years until he missed the first of this season because he'd just gone into hospital, which is where he has been ever since.

As usual, the Haydens spent part of their summer holiday on tour with the Albion. This year that meant a trip to Spain and Portugal. It was at Benfica that Barbara thinks Steve caught a cold. 'It was quite windy,' she says. 'Steve had a cough. He said he thought he just had a cold, or hay fever, or something. He made an appointment but cancelled it. But then he got a bit breathless walking up a hill and he said, I'm fed up with this. So I told him to go and book another appointment – other folks go for nothing, don't they? The doctor took a blood test and by that night he was in hospital. He had leukaemia. It was the Thursday before the start of the season. And all he could think about was getting to Man City on the Saturday. But there was no way he could go.'

It is with some trepidation that, on the way up from London to the Hawthorns, I turn left on to the M5 instead of right, to go and visit Steve in Worcester Royal Infirmary. I have never met him before and all I really know about him is that his life's in danger. I am not sure what I'm going to say to him. I'm armed with a *Match of the Day* book signed by Gary Lineker, whose youngest son had leukaemia when he was a baby. His little boy made a full recovery and I judge the book to be a good omen for Steve.

Before being allowed on to the haematology ward, I have to clean my hands with some alcohol solution dispensed from a contraption on the wall. I'm led to the door to Steve's room, where I am asked to rub my hands with more of the stuff before being fitted with a pink plastic apron. It's made clear that germs really can kill round here.

Steve has his own room, not, I take it, because this is any kind of luxury establishment, but because of the risk of infection. His sister Amanda is with him. Having been through chemotherapy, Steve is bald bar a few fluffy wisps of hair. He jumps to his feet in delight when I open the door. The gap between his two front teeth is widened by the huge breadth of his smile. Given the risk of infection, I'm not sure we should shake hands but he says it's fine.

He thanks me for the book with a sincerity I find really quite hard to deal with, and he settles back into his armchair. He's wearing an Albion T-shirt, Albion tracksuit trousers and blue Albion slippers with the letters W, B and A woven into the instep. On the bed there is a box with the pieces in it to build a plastic model Ferrari. On the walls are hundreds of cards, a small team poster and a big picture of Curtis Davies, our close-season signing from Luton. I can't imagine Steve's seen him play yet.

I ask him what he was really more worried about when he came in on that Thursday to be told that he had cancer. Surely it was his health rather than the possibility of not being able to get to Man City?

'Man City,' he says firmly.

'Honestly?'

'Yeah. That was the big thing. That was all my mind was set on, getting to the football. But your red cell count should be between twelve and fourteen. Mine was 3.5. They said most people like that would just pass out, or lay in bed. But I just thought I want to go to the game.'

Steve, having had a blood transfusion and been diagnosed with leukaemia, couldn't possibly have gone to the game. 'It really cut his legs off,' his mum told me. The Albion are as important to me as they are to Steve but if my life was in danger I assume I would be more pre-occupied with survival.

'No, no. Definitely not,' says Steve. 'It's a passion. You just forget about everything else for the football basically. It's a release.'

He is very ill and obviously in some discomfort but he only looks really pained when he tells me he has no radio and has to rely on *Sky Sports News*. 'It's just not knowing what's going on during the game. My sister and dad phone me from the ground at half-time and full-time.'

Even for the first game of the season, within hours of the diagnosis, half the family went to Man City. 'Mum come down to watch it on the telly with us,' says Steve. 'Just had results coming through and regular phone calls off my sister and dad.'

Amanda tells me that neither she nor her dad really considered not going to Man City even given the calamity that had just befallen the family. 'You must be joking,' she grins. Steve tells me there is no way his dad would have missed the game. 'I wouldn't have let him,' he says firmly.

I ask whether, lying awake at night, he worries about his health or the Albion's parlous league position. 'Bit of both actually. Basically, with my levels in my blood you've just got to give it time. And there's not much I can do about my health.' I say that I hate to break it to him but there isn't a lot he can do about the Albion either. 'No,' he says, 'I suppose you're right. I hadn't thought of it like that.'

I ask Amanda how she felt when all this first happened. 'It was horrible. I was in London and drove straight up. When you're told things . . .' her voice trails off. 'It really hits you when they say things like, if this hadn't been discovered X, Y & Z would have happened.' X, Y and Z is what Amanda says to avoid saying words linked to death. 'It really puts life in perspective – there's a lot more than work, there's a lot more than anything else going on in the world.'

'Does it put the Albion in perspective, then?'

She falters and laughs and doesn't answer the question directly. 'Well, our house is just all Albion. We don't talk about anything else apart from football, do we? It is quite demoralising.'

I'm not quite sure whether she is talking about the Albion or Steve's health now. It turns out to be both: 'That's all he's known and he's missing it a hell of a lot. He's just got to really look forward to the day that he is back there.'

I tell her she seems to talk less about the illness in its own right than in its relation to the Albion. She doesn't talk about him getting better as much as she does about him being well enough to go to a game again.

'Yes, but that is our life,' she explains patiently. 'In our house everything relates to the Albion. Even when we book our holidays it will either be between the end of the season and the beginning of the pre-season or we'll go away with the players on the pre-season.'

I ask Steve an unbelievably crass question: 'What's worse, being told you've got leukaemia or hearing that Wigan have scored in the last minute?' Significantly, possibly, Steve thinks before answering and says, 'I'm just determined to beat it. At the moment I'm just sat here waiting for my counts to come up and looking at the fixtures and which game I can possibly go to when I get out. And sort of planning through the season to see when I can get back there. That's like the inspiration for the end of this – to get back to the football.

'I went to the Charlton game but had to go in an executive box because of infection, which wasn't quite the same, but it was great to see them. It was just great to be there, to see familiar faces and familiar surroundings. I'm hoping I might be out for the Newcastle game at the end of October. Hoping that might be the one.'

I drive away from the hospital quite light-headed with the enormity of what Steve and his family are going through. Ordinarily, at moments like this, I'd be inclined to dismiss the Albion as totally unimportant but that hardly seems appropriate here as Steve clearly remains as fanatical as ever.

He'd certainly like nothing better than to be at the reserve game tonight. As I walk up Halfords Lane I find the peace and quiet of the scene strangely soothing.

Just outside the players' entrance, I'm recognised by a forty-something man with a gentle kind of northern accent. We shake hands. His name is Pete Moran. Surely, not a Wigan Athletic reserves fan?

'Stoke,' he says, as if by way of explanation.

'So what are you doing here?'

'Just fancied watching a game and I saw this was on.'

'Do you get to many?'

'I did two on Saturday, two non-league games. There were no others because of the international. This is my fifty-third of the season.'

'Fifty-three?' I echo in wonder. It's the tenth of October.

'Sad, aren't I?' he smiles, challenging me to agree or disagree.

I disagree. 'I never think it's sad to have a passion. But fifty-three?' My voice trails off.

'My record for one season is 263. Sad, aren't I?' he says again.

There's a purity about reserve games. There are no fair-weather fans here, it's just for the truly committed. Tonight they, we, are 386 in number. Alan Cleverley and John Homer, leaders of the supporters' club, are here, neatly dressed, wearing club ties. They're meeting and greeting at the glass doors of the executive entrance. This is their night and the club seems happy to let them believe that they really are in charge. These two stalwarts are afforded the privilege of sitting not in their usual places but on the cushioned seats of the executive club. They remind me of us train-users who pay the extra ten pounds to travel in the first-class carriage at weekends.

Vic Stirrup is here of course, sitting next to John Evans, the club secretary, and Roger Rimmer, the former club doctor. Behind Vic are a row of coaches, with the first-team manager, Bryan Robson, looking balefully on.

Elsewhere, my presence has been noted, somewhat reproachfully, by the regulars. Oh yes, they seem to say, you've finally decided to show up at a reserve game, have you? It's like I have distant relatives who I rarely see and now I've shown up unannounced at some family party. Where've you been all this time? The atmosphere is serious, rather cliquey. I'm sure everyone is here to enjoy themselves but there is an aficionado's earnestness about the place.

Barbara Hayden taps me on the shoulder. 'Steve's putting on a brave face,' she says, her eyes suddenly glistening a little. 'I know he does lie awake at night worrying.' And of Roy, she says: 'He puts on a brave face, too. He was really hurting for the first game of the season. He was in tears when he got on the bus.' To which any rational observer would simply say, so why did he go, then? But she has only sympathy for her husband as she recalls his heartbreak, travelling up to Man City without Steve.

Barbara also relives the moment the consultant broke the news that the first round of chemotherapy hadn't worked. 'His levels were still too high and he said that Steve still couldn't go to a game. Steve looked at me and said, "It hasn't worked, has it?" She pauses. 'They said he could have a break from the chemo but he definitely couldn't go to the football. That really hurt him. In the end he went anyway though.'

The players run out. Incongruously, as they do so, the speakers pump out the same music as for the first team. The band's name is totally inappropriate, too: Faithless. It echoes around the all but empty ground.

There are fans who don't miss a first team game and there are fans who don't miss reserve games either. Improbably there exists an even more hardcore minority: those who turn up to watch training. These aren't children hanging around for autographs, but adults who can't resist the chance to nose around. Five grown men standing on the bank, hands in pockets, looking on.

It is a chilly autumn Thursday when I come across them, but it could be any day between July and May. One of them is Tim Higgs, who's in his fifties. He runs a small silver business. 'I come occasionally, that's all I want to say. Otherwise my wife might hear it. I usually come up towards the end of the week if I can manage it just for half an hour, to see what's going on.'

He says Gary Megson, our previous manager, wasn't too welcoming: 'In the end he seemed to hate us but Robbo, Bobby Robson, is absolutely brilliant with us.'

'Bryan Robson,' says another bloke, Mick, tiredly, as if Tim's always getting his names muddled up.

'Oh, I get mixed up, it's me age,' says Tim.

Mick works for an estate agent. 'I just pop down in my dinner hour to see what's going on.'

Paul Doherty is self-employed as a painter. 'I come down about once a week to get a bit of inside information. I just slip out when I can.'

Dave Rolfe is a bit younger than the others. He's a good-looking lad who I've seen about for years. He has always had a pony
tail and works in IT. He used to play a bit, on Everton's books.
'I've been coming for years. It's more of a social thing, isn't it? You
get to moan about things. Why did we play like that? Why's he
picking him?'

'But surely,' I say, 'you could do that on the phone, couldn't
you?'

'Could do, but this is just like a little social club, ai' it? These are
the people who'd love to be doing their job, wouldn't we? No
doubt about it.'

Darren Clarke supplies cutting tools to the aerospace industry.
'I'll pop in Thursdays or Fridays to see what the team looks like.
It's about finding out something that other fans generally don't
know. Just having a preview of the team and stuff like that. And
finding out how the atmosphere seems to be, 'cos that's changed
quite a lot under Robson compared to what it was like before.
We've all become quite good friends now as well. If there's not
much going on, we'll pop down here for a chat and run over
what's gone on really.'

'Whatever the weather?'

'Whatever the weather. Snow, whatever. We go for it.'

Tim says they have seen some worrying sights in their time:
'That first session when Megson took over they were playing
against nobody, literally nobody, doing moves and so on. We were
here half an hour and we didn't see them score! Nobody scored
against, literally, nobody; fresh air. We were looking at each other
and saying we're doomed.'

This, surely, must represent some kind of nadir in the life of a
football fan: you go to the training ground and stand in the freezing cold to watch your team fail to score against no players at all,
against 'fresh air', as Tim puts it. His tone is still incredulous and
despairing at the memory.

I ask if the players ever acknowledge them, if they show any
recognition of the devotion which coming to watch training

represents. 'Some of them do,' says Dave, 'and you know the ones what am good lads, don't you? I think they'm quite a good bunch.'

'Nigel Pearson came to speak to us the other day,' adds Tim. 'He explained why they weren't playing Inamoto, which was fair play. Mind you, we still didn't think he was right, did we?'

'No,' they all agree.

These people are football mad, obviously. But there is a method to their madness. Ninety per cent of a footballer's work is done at the training ground, so if you really are passionately interested in your team this is the place to come. The vast majority of us, who just – just! – go to the matches, are essentially operating on incomplete information when we criticise the team. As Tim puts it, 'There's only about a dozen who come down here and twenty-odd thousand who go up the Albion and they don't see what we see.'

When we 'normal' fans see a poor player picked week in week out, the cliché we use, in despair, is often 'they must be good in training'. I ask if this sometimes really does apply. Tim says, 'Sometimes we can see why he's picked players, from what he's seen down here.'

'On the other hand,' says Dave, 'sometimes we're as mystified as everyone else because they've been crap in training, too.'

Four

Val Ball née Grubbe and her daughter Sue

Saturday, 15 October 2005, Arsenal at home

There are 26,604 fans in the ground today and I can't imagine one of them has a more captivating life story than the woman I'm sitting next to. Her name is Val Ball and I'm between her and her daughter Sue who is a very fine-looking woman indeed. It is probably for this reason that I've noticed her over the years. We've had the odd chat about the column I write in the programme. Sue has a proper Black Country accent as evidenced by the fact that she says 'her' instead of 'she'. She, or her, as Sue would say, is usually here with Val (short for Waltraut). Val's accent is a surprisingly easy mix of German and Black Country.

She was born Waltraut Grubbe in Lauenburg, Germany, in

1925. Danzig was the next big town, 'but if you went down there you had to have a special pass to go through the Polish Corridor,' she says. 'Towards the end of the war we had to leave school to do war work – in a factory, farm or hospital or anything like that. I went into nursing in a civilian hospital. But as the war was coming towards us, the hospital was taken over by soldiers and so the nursing staff were, too. And all of a sudden we had notice given that in just a few minutes we had to go, had to get out 'cos they were really coming fast towards us.'

'Who was coming fast?' I ask, just wanting to hear her say the words. 'The Russians were coming,' she says, unconsciously obedient. I catch Sue's eye as Val pauses for a second before continuing. 'I didn't know what to do, you know, and I thought I better stay with my mother and my grandmother. And she says, no no, you go with the soldiers, you go with the hospital and you'll be all right.

'So I went. We went towards Danzig, where we made a field hospital. The wounded kept coming; the soldiers who were fighting in the war. And they, the Russians, got closer and closer to us. It was absolutely shocking. We had no way of getting out. The only way was by sea. My mother and my grandmother and my aunt, they went on their own. The bombing was so bad they all had to go in a church and stay there. And all of a sudden someone shouted, whoever can run, run – there's a boat going and you'll be able to be shipped out. And so my mother ran. My grandmother, through the bombing, just collapsed and died. My mother put a blanket over her and ran for her life. She was shipped to Dresden. Didn't know what happened to my grandma, whether she was buried or anything.'

As I listen to this story spill out of her, I am dumbfounded. There are even moments when I forget the Albion's perilous league position.

'We had some relations in Danzig and a driver said, we'll take you down there, but when we got there, there was no one. I didn't know where anybody was. Then we were in one of the schools and they were doing amputations and things. They said the Russians were going to take over everything, and it all – papers, everything – had to be burned. And then they said, what are we going to do with the women? We're not going to let the Russians have our women.

'Then I cut my wrist,' she says, pulling up her sleeve. 'I had to because they didn't want us to be taken, and if we didn't do something like that our soldiers were going to shoot us. But all of a sudden there was this screaming and they said, come on, come on, we can make it, we can make it. And we were running again.'

'When the Albion are relegated,' I say, as carefully as I can, 'and you hear people say they want to slit their wrists, well, you know what it's like to slit your wrists . . . '

'Yes. It's terrible. It's terrible. I don't know how the soldiers saved us in the end. I still have dreams about being chased.'

Val got on a cargo boat that was bound for Denmark, but ended up in Hamburg. Later, looking up Lauenburg on the internet, I'm spellbound to come across the following text that places Val in a historical context and, chillingly, shows just how lucky she was:

Soviet submarines torpedo countless passenger ships and tens of thousands drown in the icy Baltic Sea. All who do not escape by sea attempt to leave in wagon caravans or by railway. Pomerania is now overrun by the Red Army. Between the sixth and tenth of March the eastern Pomeranian towns of Bütow and Lauenburg are occupied. Entire streets go up in flames. Many citizens decide to end their own lives out of fear of the Soviet cruelties they have heard about from refugees. .

Once Hamburg fell Val found herself a job with a British major and he set her up as a nanny in Scarborough. This didn't suit Val: 'They had a little boy and they wanted a German nurse 'cos they were doing a lot of entertaining and different things but the baby was young and teething, so I said, bugger it, I'm going home. But there were no jobs going, so the British said, you've been in England, would you like to go back again? That's how I came to West Bromwich to the District General Hospital. I was a nurse there.'

This couldn't have been a barrel of laughs – a German nurse working in an English hospital straight after the war. 'It was all right. I had a rough time at first. One of the patients felt sorry for me. They had a pub in Wednesbury, the Leather and Bottle, and I went on my days off down there. They showed me what to do and I started pulling pints and helping out.

'Then my husband's mother came in and noticed me. So she went home and told her sons, they've got a German barmaid there, you know. Oh, you should see her, she's all right.'

Sue adds: 'My dad was one of five brothers, so they were all clamouring to get up there first.'

'They came down to look at this German barmaid,' says Val, 'and that's how I met him.'

I asked when she first heard the words West Bromwich Albion.

'As soon as I met him!' Val shouts. 'It was West Bromwich Albion this, West Bromwich Albion that. His father's house was called the Hawthorns because one of his sons was playing for the Albion before the war, so it was very much Albion through and through. Over the years he told me everything about it whether I wanted to hear it or not.'

They got married two years later.

'In 1954 they won the cup and brought it around the ward and I held it. And I was going home saying, you don't know what I've been doing, I've been holding the cup! And my father-in-law said, she's only been in the country a few years and she's already got a cup! We've been here years and we don't get a chance like that. That's how it all started and from then it's been all Albion.

'We used to go to the supporters' club, the Throstle Club. He went and I could go as well to do all sorts of different things. There was entertainment and that. Not having a family of my own here apart from, you know, the children and the in-laws, the

Albion was an extended family. Going to the Throstle Club made me feel like part of a big family.'

Val's husband Cyril died in 1993 from cancer. 'He should have been there when we were promoted because he never got the chance to see them in the Premiership and what a joy it was. The year he died we got promotion to the first division. The players came round here on the open bus and we all went to see them.'

Gurdial Singh also went to this parade, heavily pregnant with her third child. In fact she gave birth to Joshan that evening. I'm intrigued to think of Joshan there so close to Cyril. A fanatical West Brom fan not quite born and another one shortly to die.

Just before we kick off, I ask Val how she thinks we're going to get on. Can we win?

'I don't think so.' Pause. Thinks. 'I would like a draw. I know they've got players out but I'd like a draw.' She says this as though beating Arsenal is so unlikely it might even be an inferior outcome to drawing.

Call me sentimental, but it warms the cockles of my heart to be discussing the possibilities of a West Brom game with an eighty-year-old woman from the German-Polish border with an accent born in Nazi Germany but polished into pretty pure Wednesbury.

'I hope you're not going to get all lairy and use bad language,' I say. Val nods in the direction of our most vocal fans thirty yards away in the Smethwick End. 'I pick up a lot of slang from that lot,' she says. 'I don't understand it properly so I keep saying to Sue, what do they say? What do they sing?'

Sue has to tone down the language when she's telling her mum, but once Val's got the general idea she runs with it. Sue says: 'We were queuing up at M&S and I said, I better get some sweets for the match. The young chap serving behind the counter asked us what match we were going to. When I said we were Albion fans he said he was a Villa fan and all of a sudden my mom started singing, *stand up if you hate Villa!* I couldn't believe her said it.'

'I couldn't believe I said it,' says Val.

'And then,' Sue continues, 'the lad was so shocked he swiped the card the wrong way or something. Anyway, it wouldn't work and this time her started chanting, *you don't know what you're doing!*'

'I can't believe I came out with it,' says Val.

'Now they're best of friends, her and this chap,' says Sue. 'He was going to come to her birthday party, but he was on holiday.'

The match starts. When Arsenal come close to scoring, Val says, quite softly, 'Ooh no.' On the odd occasion we nearly score, she just says, 'Oooh.' After six minutes, in which we have started brightly, I look at her and she purses her lips and nods approvingly. 'So far so good,' she says carefully.

Then Arsenal score a soft goal from a corner. Nil-one. 'Not even twenty minutes gone,' groans Val. It seems to all of us that Arsenal will go on to score several more goals without reply. The young chap sitting in front of Sue begins to get very animated indeed. He has tanned skin and bleached hair but as his anger rises his face turns from brown to red, the colour even showing through his short bottle-blond hair. His occasionally falsetto shrieking is background noise for a while.

Sue pulls a bag of sweets out of her handbag. 'These normally help,' she says, a little desperately. I have a chocolate eclair and Val goes for a humbug. Our football doesn't improve much. 'I wish I'd put my dad's lucky socks on,' says Sue.

Unaccountably, we start getting better. Our left back has a shot from a long way out. It just misses the post, eliciting a slightly higher-pitched 'Oooh' from Frau Ball. Another chance elicits an even higher-pitched 'Oooh.' Sue says: 'He's pushed Greening out wide, hasn't he? That's why we're doing better.' I hadn't noticed; I never notice things like that. But Sue is right.

And, joy, we equalise. We're right behind Kanu when he whacks it into the Arsenal goal. Sue and I jump up. Frau Ball stays in her seat but claps happily. She looks up at me and says,

'Draw.' Sue shouts that the sweets worked. The crowd starts singing 'The Lord's My Shepherd', at which point Sue takes a monogrammed handkerchief out of her handbag. This she passes to her mum who, with some ceremony, dabs her eyes with it. She then passes it back across me to Sue, who also dabs her eyes with it, before putting it back in her handbag.

As Arsenal restart the game I ask what that was all about. 'It's my dad's hanky. We always do that when the 'The Lord's My Shepherd' comes on.'

At half-time I present Vic Stirrup with his Barclays Premiership Supporter of the Year trophy. Malcolm Boyden, the announcer, calls him on to the pitch. There is a disinterested smattering of applause but, as Malcolm describes Vic's achievements, the acclaim grows with gasps and groans that wouldn't shame a quiz show audience: ' . . . a season ticket holder since 1925, he's missed only five games since the Second World War . . .' By now he has a standing ovation right round the ground. He beams. I kiss him on the top of his head.

Vic has succeeded where the club he's so doggedly supported has failed for so long: he's got some silverware in his trophy cabinet. As he struggles to carry the heavy trophy a member of staff asks if he wants to leave it with them and have it sent on. 'No,' says Vic firmly, 'I should like to have it at home with me tonight.'

As I help Vic back to his seat he tells me that Les has got something to show me. I suspect this is whatever Les had in the boot of his car when we got back from Blackburn. I am right. Les comes towards me, grinning, with a huge plastic bag he has somehow dragged into the ground. Inside there is a rug he's been making all summer. It features the club crest and bears the legend: WBAFC The Great Escape 2004 2005.

Ever since my nan died I have been short of friends who are in their eighties. Not any more. Vic, Les and Val, combined age somewhere north of 240, are now among my favourite people in the world.

The second half starts and, as the Albion's momentum builds, Frau Ball becomes more animated. When Arsenal fluff a free-kick we believe to have been incorrectly awarded, she claps and cheers sarcastically. She nudges me and says: 'I think this is the best I've seen Albion play for a long time.' And exactly halfway through the second half she suddenly dares to think of ditching her hope for a draw: 'Wouldn't it be great if we could beat Arsenal?' she says dreamily, as if it has just occurred to her that this is not an impossibility. At this point I genuinely wonder what part of my body I wouldn't now give for a West Brom winner, just for Waltraut Ball née Grubbe.

Sue gets the sweets out again. I choose an eclair as it worked in the first half, but Frau Ball doesn't go for a humbug. I confuse her by suggesting she should have a humbug again because it'll be good luck, but she looks at me as if I might be mad. Then – a moment I will still not have forgotten when I'm Val's age – we score. It is an absolutely unbelievable goal from a not especially well-loved recent signing, Darren Carter. This time there is no sitting down and applauding for Frau Ball. She's on her feet going wild. The three of us hug, clinging on to each other for dear life. 'The Lord's My Shepherd' is sung again. Once more, Sue pulls her dad's hanky from her handbag. Her mum dabs her eyes with it; Sue dabs her eyes with it. My eyes are filling up and could do with a wipe, too.

The Albion cling on. Dennis Bergkamp and Neil Clement have a bit of a scuffle right in front of us. Everyone stands up to shout things and be annoyed. I stay seated to keep Frau Ball company but she springs up to join everyone but me for a look at the aggro. There are fifteen minutes to go. The thought of throwing this lead away is too horrible to contemplate. I want the final whistle to go so I can hug the Balls all over again. For once, we cling on. We've won, joy.

'Fanfuckingtastic.' I get Sandra's text the moment the final whistle goes. She must have written it before the ref blew. I will talk to her about that.

Sunday, 23 October 2005, Bolton away

Sunday matches are a good and bad thing for me. Good because if we are playing Sunday we can't be playing Saturday, which means the temperature doesn't drop in my house on Friday evening and Saturday morning. It means Jane doesn't have to harbour homicidal feelings towards me every time she sees other fathers with their kids happily playing in the park. It means I won't have to beg my friends who are fathers to keep out of Jane's sight if they are in the park. It means my bewildered children won't have to watch me pace around in the morning, distracted, then disappear before returning, shattered and usually totally pissed off, six or seven hours later.

For these reasons Saturdays without West Brom games are beautiful things, but Sunday matches are hell. I can't go to them because I have to be at work presenting *Match of the Day 2*. It could be worse – I can still watch as the pictures are fed into TV Centre – but the problem is that when we lose I have to broadcast the whole sorry business.

This makes life very difficult for my colleagues. The first season I presented the show I worked with Gordon Strachan with whom I soon became quite friendly, but he tired very quickly of spending time with me on days like these. On one occasion, watching us lose against Middlesbrough, I was moaning and groaning and muttering to myself and cursing everything. 'Will somebody please shut this bloke up!' he suddenly exploded. 'It's like sitting next to the Grim Reaper. Honestly, I come in here every Sunday all happy and cheerful and you suck the bloody life out of me.'

By the end of that season, though, I think I infected him with a bit of what I've got. There was a vital home match against Everton on a Sunday. We scored with about twenty minutes to go. Graeme Le Saux was watching with us. It was an odd situation – he was with Southampton at the time, for whom a West Brom win would have been bad news as they were also fighting relegation. When the goal went in Graeme asked, 'How long left?'

Gordon looked at me. 'Fucking for ever,' he said with feeling. I said nothing. I had momentarily lost the power of speech.

We won that one, which made presenting the *606* radio phone-in on Five Live straight afterwards much easier. There have been occasions when those phone-ins have been absolute misery, such as a couple of months earlier when we played at Fulham in a 4 p.m. Sunday kick-off.

At 5.45 p.m., with about a quarter of an hour left, it was nil-nil and we'd had the better of the match. It's at this time that I have to leave the *Match of the Day* office and go to the radio studio for the phone-in. Heart thumping, I sprint-walked to the other side of the building. I was so nervous by the time I got there I was almost faint with worry. It was still nil-nil. I was quite beside myself with relief that we hadn't conceded a goal but also, fatally, stupidly, I had the nerve to be disappointed that we hadn't scored.

The way the studio is set up you can see television pictures but the commentary is from the radio and it is a couple of seconds ahead of the pictures; you hear what's happened fractionally before you see it. So it was that with no time at all left in the match Fulham had a corner. As I watched their player prepare to take it, I heard the Five Live commentator scream that it was in the net. For a precious moment I clung on to the hope that there was some mistake – like a man falling from a mountain might grab hold of a little branch sticking out of the cliff-face even though he must know it will come away in his hand.

There had been no mistake. The ball came over, Fulham scored and I was that man falling to his death with the twig in his hand. It had just gone six o'clock. I heard the commentator say, 'Adrian Chiles is waiting for your calls – if Adrian Chiles is still with us, of course.'

A couple of minutes later I was on air. I ended my introduction by saying, 'Please call me quick, before I do something stupid.' At home as my (obviously bad) luck would have it, Jane was listening while she bathed the kids. Evie, our eldest, looked up at her in alarm. 'Mummy, what's Daddy going to do?'

When the phone-in finished Jane took part in a personal phone-in with me on my mobile – a rather one-sided affair involving her bollocking me and me listening, stammering the occasional apology.

But back to today against Bolton. They played in Turkey on Thursday night so will be very tired and they have some key players out. We, on the other hand, have a full team out and beat Arsenal last week. So many reasons to be hopeful always convince me that only a defeat is possible.

Not so Frank Skinner: the most optimistic fan I have ever met. I've only watched one game with him before, an unforgettable draw at Villa six months ago. We played badly and were losing. I was disconsolate for the last half an hour but three minutes into injury time Frank was still reassuring me that we could get a goal. Unbelievably, with all but the last kick of the game, we scored. Since which time, I have held him to be invested with mystical powers.

Suspecting he wouldn't be making the trip to Bolton either, I have invited him in to share the privilege of watching a live game not being shown on Sky. We are in an area away from the rest of the production team. I just can't bear to be sitting with non-Albion fans at times like this. It's just the two of us. I am sure we'll lose. Frank is sure we'll win.

After twenty minutes we get a penalty. We both leap up and, though we hardly know each other, sort of grab one another. We sit back down. We score the penalty. We both leap up and sort of grab each other again in exactly the same way. The referee orders the penalty to be retaken. We sit back down. The retaken penalty is missed. 'Shit,' we both say.

No goals are scored until ten minutes before the end. At this point I am praying that we hold on for a draw. Frank will have none of this, though, insisting that would be a disappointment. Bolton score. Silence. 'I still think we'll get something out of this,' says Frank finally, 'but I'm beginning to think I might have to settle for a draw.' Then Bolton score again in injury time.

Afterwards, morosely, we shake hands and he goes off on his way already formulating reasons to be positive about this defeat which he will probably text to me later.

On *606* a caller from Bolton appears on the screen, along with a line from the producer on what he wants to talk about. This reads: 'West Brom are heading for relegation.' I steel myself to keep my language clean. I am ready for him. If he says how rubbish we are, I'll make various points about how Bolton are spending a fortune on wages and how we are concentrating on the future, developing our academy, while they are spending pots of money on ageing foreign mercenaries. But all he says is 'Be afraid, Adrian. Be very afraid.' This catches me out. I come out in goose-flesh all over. I'm momentarily rendered speechless and the best piece of invective I can come out with is, 'Yes, you're probably right.'

Tuesday, 25 October 2005, Fulham away in the Carling Cup

If Sunday fixtures have their plus and minus points for me, evening kick-offs are broadly positive because they are not so dis-ruptive of family life. Ones in London are especially good as they're closer to home. I can think of no greater pleasure than to meet a load of friends in a pub at about four in the afternoon for an evening game.

Sandra 'I've got this haggard look about me' Lloyd is waiting for me there. I'm keen to meet the hardcore of ever-present, appar-ently ever-pissed away fans she travels with, particularly two blokes she's given me advance warning of, Pete and Nathan: 'I warn you, just so you know, one of them will be pissed and the other one will be, well, he's just got a lot of problems.'

It's going to be an interesting evening. I am bringing a couple of friends from work: two non-football fans from whom I want outsiders' views of proceedings. Rob Finighan is a television producer who likes his rugby and isn't averse to football but is never quite sure what we fans are on. Adam Shaw is my co-presenter on BBC2's *Working Lunch*. He has a very tepid interest in football and has hardly ever been to a game.

When we arrive at the pub Sandra and her team are well settled in, talking to a couple of men. One looks like he is in his early fifties. He reminds me of the Paul Whitehouse character, Ron Manager. He looks very happy to me, sitting here with a pint in his hand and a smile on his face. The other is very tall, quite bulky, unshaven and clad head to foot in denim. He is good-looking in a Stourbridge kind of way. I wonder who is the pissed one and who is the one with loads of problems.

Pete used to be a fireman. The big guy, Nathan, tells me he works for himself as a courier, driving a van. 'It's not a bad job and I'm self-employed, which is the main thing. When I was employed I sometimes couldn't get to away games.' It's Nathan who Sandra thinks has all the problems, and Nathan agrees. 'My problem, Adrian,' he says earnestly, 'is that women just use me for sex and I'm getting sick of it.'

Keen as I am to explore this so-called problem, I begin by asking about how he got into the Albion. 'My family were born and bred in Smethwick. You can trace it back generations. Me dad died when I was eight. He was a big Albion fan. I think that since the loss of my dad I needed something to belong to. And I think because he was a big Albion fan I felt obliged to follow me dad in a way. My uncle started taking me up there, actually my cousin. My mum's mum's brother's son. Second cousin.

'My mum used to tie in family visits with dropping me off at my uncle's house so I could get to the Albion. Up until 1992/93 it was just home games but since then I've only missed five or six away games in thirteen years.'

Nathan is a young man but talks about his life as if it has already passed him by, as if he is a failure, an underachiever, and it's always going to be like that. 'I'm thirty next year and I'm feeling as if I'm being left behind, so I would dearly love to find my way into a career. I regret a lot of things in life. In education I had the ability and intelligence to be successful but never had the attitude, always a bit carefree. Other priorities. Since my dad died I just always lived for the moment. If I knew then what I know now, I'd probably have taken a different path.'

One of Nathan's problems is that he has limited his options in the jobs market because he won't countenance doing anything that might involve missing the Albion. 'I worked in a leisure centre. I was offered a job there and I thought it'd suit me. It was an opportunity, but it was all shift work. And then we had this night game at home against Watford. As soon as I realised my shift clashed, I said, look, I can't work because I've got to go to the football. I know I shouldn't have been so hasty, but I left there and then.

'And I had this job as a driver for a paint firm in Birmingham. The first season in the Premiership we played Arsenal away right at the start of the season. They wouldn't give me the afternoon off so I dropped the van off that morning and said, there it is, see you later. And that was that.'

Wherever I sit at away games, it's impossible to miss Nathan. He is invariably near the back, on his feet, clapping and chanting. Winning or losing, he seems to be leading the noise. And he has always got a massive smile on his face.

'I've been kicked out the ground a few times both home and away. Nothing too serious – once for threatening behaviour, a couple of times for persistent standing, refusing to sit down.'

Later I check this out with one of the coppers responsible for the Albion. 'Yeah,' he says, 'I do know Nathan but he's no trouble, he's just daft.'

For no other reason than Nathan's mentioned the subject, we turn from the Albion to his sex life. He says his problem is that all the women who go for him are ten or twenty years older than he is. 'They just use me for my body,' he says morosely. 'We'll have sex a few times over a couple of weeks, then they just move on. Women round by me want to be driven about in decent cars,

Mercedes and stuff. All I've got is a long wheelbase Transit. I'd love to settle down with someone.'

His latest encounter, while typical, was slightly more exotic than usual. 'I got chatting to this woman in the pub. She's nice looking, fortysomething. And it's going quite well. Then she holds up her hand and says, have you noticed something? She had a ring on, so I said, oh OK, I'm sorry, I didn't meant to come on so strong. But she says, no, it's fine, my husband don't mind me shagging anyone else as long as I tell him about it. And then she says that he likes to join in sometimes and we could have a three-some. So I shagged her that night and now she wants to get him involved!'

I quickly mark Nathan down as a compulsive bullshitter but, right on cue, he gets a text from the woman: 'Gary's mentioned u few times 2day, says ur a good looking guy and if i meet u out and we get chatting i can do what i like as long as i tell him!' I tell Nathan that in all my years following the Albion I have never associated it with erotica. I ask if it ever gets in the way of going to the game. He thinks seriously about this for a moment before saying, rather thoughtfully, 'Well, it's always a balance, I suppose, but I can't remember missing a game 'cos I was shagging.'

When he goes to the toilet I ask Sandra if he is for real. She rolls her eyes and nods. I tell her I can't help feeling rather envious. 'You wouldn't if you saw some of the ones he takes home with him, I promise you.'

The turnstile operator at Fulham says to everyone, 'Enjoy the game.' This stops me in my tracks – I'm sure at first that he's taking the mickey. 'What's football coming to?' I hear someone ask. Neither Rob nor Adam can see what the fuss is about; it seems perfectly normal to them for a paying customer to be wished an enjoyable evening. They just don't understand football.

We score almost immediately. Everybody leaps about happily: everybody, that is, except Adam and Rob. They seem pleased enough but, like all non-fans, don't really know how to celebrate properly. They don't jump about and go crazy. They just smile and clap, which is a perfectly sensible response when something good happens. But, I wonder, when in their lives will they ever leap about beside themselves with joy, punching the air? Adam is really into theatre, which is great. But no one, no matter how good the production was, ever put their arms into the air and leapt about with joy in a theatre. Olivier could have just done the seminal Hamlet with Dame Judi Dench as Ophelia and, come the curtain call, still no one would really celebrate with any wild abandon. I explain this to Adam. He is exasperated but understands the point. 'Look,' he says, 'I'm happy for you, what more do you want?'

All through the first half, as we cling on to our lead, the chanting continues half a dozen rows behind us at the back of the stands. It's noisy, witty and obscene, often all at the same time. Every so often I see Adam looking back at them, bewildered. Then he looks away again, as if he might be attacked if they see him staring.

In the second half, predictably, Fulham equalise. Adam looks sympathetically at me, rather concerned. He knows how much the Albion mean to me, so I suppose he must be wondering how exactly I'm going to react now we have conceded a goal. He's probably expecting some explosion of grief but I just shrug and smile and he looks back at the pitch again, ever more baffled. Then, right at the death, their goalkeeper fluffs it and we score. I jump about in delight. Adam claps and looks happy. But, unbelievably, Fulham equalise again. 'Why do you put yourself through this?' he asks.

Extra time sorts out the fans from the non-fans. 'I'm off,' says Rob. 'I'll come,' says Adam straight away. As they say goodbye to Sandra, Rob says to her, anxiously, urgently, 'Haven't you got a coach to catch?' She looks at him uncertainly, as if she thinks he might be joking. 'Won't you miss it if you stay here?' he says. 'No, it's a supporters' coach,' she says, 'it won't go without us.' No less confused than they were when they arrived, Adam and Rob leave.

At this moment in Worcester Royal Infirmary, Steve Hayden, who has been following the match on *Sky Sports News*, is left in the dark when the network moves on to something else. He just sits and waits for a text from his dad, who is here, obviously. It is worth the wait. Half an hour later the news is relayed to Steve that Inamoto has scored a blinding goal for us. In the ground we all celebrate wildly. We are through to the next round.

The following day I quiz Adam and Rob about what they made of it all. Adam is honest about his lack of knowledge: 'I just can't follow a lot of it. If there's a handball everybody, as one, shouts, "Handball." But all I can see is a player and maybe, if I'm lucky, the ball somewhere, though I've no idea whether it's a handball or not. I can't even tell whether it's in the goal.'

What he did pick up on was the community spirit. 'When we met beforehand, I was jealous of that. Because it was just like extended family and, more than that, there's a huge range of people you meet. And that's a very rare opportunity to meet different people – the kind of people you wouldn't normally meet. To have those kind of relationships, I'm genuinely jealous of that.

'When Albion scored I did jump up without thinking about it and said, "Yeah!" but then I felt a bit embarrassed because I didn't know what to do with my hands. Everyone else was doing that boing boing thing, jumping up and down, and I was thinking I'm not doing that. I just had my hands clutched in front of my groin like I was in church. I knew I looked ridiculous but I couldn't think what else to do.

'The terrible thing was that the only time we became really emotionally involved was after the equaliser because we didn't want it to go into overtime. And we went, fucking score, anybody. It was more than a game at that point for me and Rob, but only because we wanted to go home.'

For his part, Rob says: 'I really enjoyed the night out and the football but it confirmed to me that I couldn't do this for pleasure, regularly. I thought I understood that you were a fan of a football team. I thought I understood what it was to be a fan of a football team, but absolutely, fundamentally, what I discovered yesterday was that I do not understand it. I don't know what drives you and the other people to go week in week out, to spend those hours doing that. I can't see how anybody could dedicate that much time. You're the busiest man I know and yet you still find all that time for the Albion.

'I gave up five hours of my life to go and that felt like devotion to me. Five hours at a football match in the last fifteen years, I felt was more than enough. To go from that point and realise that you and those people you were with go all the time . . . well, I'm just miles away from you. And it's not like a fad, something you're doing this autumn, it's something you've done and will do all your life. It's unfathomable to me. I kind of thought I knew you, that you are a West Brom fan, but I was shocked to see what that actually entails.'

As I mull over Rob and Adam's bewilderment, a truth about fans' devotion to their teams suddenly comes to me: until now I have always juxtaposed the passion we have for our teams with the rest of our lives. I (and, more often, my wife) have asked why I care so much, why I get so down, when I have so much else to be grateful for. In the same way, I looked at Val Ball and wondered why she, who has been through so much, still cares about the Albion.

But I've been looking at it through the wrong end of the telescope, as it were, because our love of the Albion doesn't exist alongside the rest of our lives. No, it is all part of the same experience. So, for Val, the win against Arsenal is all part of the same life story that began in what is now Poland, nearly ended prematurely somewhere near Danzig, and finished up in West Bromwich. It is the same with Steve Hayden: when his heart broke at the realisation that he wouldn't be at Man City it was the ill-health keeping him away that he was grieving about, too. So it is that his family don't talk about his recovery per se – it's only seen in terms of if and when he will be well enough to see the Albion again.

When I get home I try to explain all this to Jane, but she's sceptical and, in my desperation to get the point across, I end up confusing myself. But, later, lying in bed, I realise that for me, Val, Steve, Gurdial, Nathan, one-legged Kev and everyone else, our love for the Albion is a kind of distillation of everything, good and bad, that we've been through in our lives, everything that we are. I'm not sure why we feel like that, but I'm sure we do.

Sunday, 30 October 2005, Newcastle at home

Sam Allardyce is our main guest on *Match of the Day 2*. It's all a bit peculiar: this time last week Sam was breaking my heart managing Bolton to a 2-0 victory over us. Now we are watching the Albion together. I know he is good friends with our manager so I'll have to keep my observations about tactics to myself. In fact he tells me that after beating us last week he went to a party with Bryan Robson and Steve Bruce, Birmingham City's manager, who also lost that weekend. Must have been some do.

Les Ferdinand joins us, our other pundit. He used to play for Newcastle but he used to play for loads of other clubs, too, so I'm not sure where his loyalties lie. Normally I would just be pleased to be in such exalted company for the afternoon but as it's the Albion playing I could be watching with anyone.

It is an appalling game. Newcastle score at the start of the second half, a great goal by Michael Owen. I say nothing. Sam says nothing. 'Great finish,' says Les. Then we have a succession of chances and contrive to miss them all. After the best of these is fluffed by Rob Earnshaw, Sam says, without malice or pleasure, 'That's it. You're fucked. You've had it.'

He's right, of course. We concede again. I go upstairs to do *606* and by the time I have shambled to the studio it's 3-0. Now I have an hour's football phone-in to get through and, since there are no other Premiership games to talk about today, I can't steer the calls on to any other subject. Newcastle fans come on to say they have been playing like Brazil. No one says the score flatters them a bit and it's not a point I can make without it sounding like sour grapes and an abuse of my position. But eventually I lose the plot and say, 'Look, let's swap Michael Owen and Robert Earnshaw, play the game again, and see who wins then!' A facile point, but it makes me feel a little better.

Five

The sort of player fans love: Jeff Astle – 361 appearances, 174 goals

Saturday, 5 November 2005, West Ham away

My daughters are playing with some teddy bears they have stuffed in one of the kitchen cupboards. I hear Evie whispering something to Sian: 'Go on, go and give that one to Daddy.' Sian, who is nearly three, obediently brings me a little white teddy bear with the Albion's club crest on it.

I bought them this teddy as part of my carefully planned but spectacularly unsuccessful brainwashing programme. Neither of them has taken much notice of it before, but now it turns out that Evie at least does understand its significance. This makes my heart sing. Evie is five and this is only the fourth signal she's ever given that she might cave in to the intense pressure I've put on her to care about the Albion like Daddy does.

The first three were as follows: she once pointed at the thrush on the club crest in the stained glass window above our front door and said, 'That's Albion bird'; in my local, she spotted the QPR strip pinned to the wall and said, 'That Albion?'; but, most impressively, a couple of months ago she was telling her mother about a game of football they'd had in PE at school. One team was called Chelsea but Evie's team was called Albion. And Albion won.

Now, heartened by her gesture with the teddy, I ask if she wants to go to see Albion today with Daddy – she's nearly six after all. 'No,' she says.

The omens were never good. She was born on a Saturday, by Caesarean section, on 18 December 1999. The Albion were at Ipswich. Jane said that if we won that day, and it was a boy, I could call him Cyrille. As it turned out Evie was a girl and the Albion lost 3-1, had two players sent off and there was a fight between our goalkeeper and our centre half.

I have arranged to watch today's game with Paul Perry and his son Liam. Paul was suggested to me as someone I could talk to about being, like Nicola Rhodes, priced out of the game. He goes to all the home games but has had to stop going to most of the away matches. 'It's a shame because we just enjoy the day out. We like to get to the ground early and go to the shop and that. Not the town, just round the ground, like, and talk to the other fans.'

I asked him if he was coming to this game. 'No, can't afford West Ham. Won't go to another away game until Christmas.' I always suspect that people who can't go to games, for whatever reason, are secretly relieved. If I can't go to, say, Bolton, because I'm at work, a part of me is rather grateful that I have been spared the time and the trouble and don't have to feel guilty about it. So, I tested Paul out: 'I've got a couple of spares for West Ham. You can have them. Do you want to come?'

'Yes,' he said, before I even finished the sentence, 'we'd jump at the chance.' It was only then that he thought to mention his son is visually impaired.

Liam is eighteen and has a sister with the same condition. He tells me what it is but I've never heard of it and certainly can't spell it. He is sitting between me and his dad. He tells me about his first game. He was six years old and it was before he could wear contact lenses so his sight was very poor indeed. 'We sat very close to the pitch but that worked against me because I couldn't see anything at all and then suddenly there would be lots of action right up close. I was quite frightened.'

We are at Upton Park sitting behind the goal way to the left of it, at least five yards outside the touchline, so this isn't a great position for him. Standing over the ball to kick off for us are Kanu, who is very tall, and Robert Earnshaw who is extremely small. 'They look ridiculous next to each other, don't they, those two?' I say, nudging Liam. My voice trails away as I check myself, remembering that Liam almost certainly can't see that far. Luckily, the crowd noise crescendoes and drowns out my stupidity.

Liam joins in with all the chants, which surprises me for some reason. He can't see a lot of what is going on but he can hear it and he can participate in a way that he couldn't if he wasn't here. But the sight of him seeing only a vague milky greenness and singing blindly into it moves me.

Paul doesn't exactly commentate for Liam; he disguises his commentary as punditry. Instead of reporting that X is trying to get the ball to Y but gives it away to Z, he says, 'We're struggling to retain possession here.' Liam nods. Liam says he just needs to get a vague idea of the shape of the game. His dad helps him do this. 'And sometimes I have to be told when we've lost the ball.' So it falls to Paul to keep breaking the bad news to Liam that possession has been lost.

West Ham, attacking our end – the only end Liam has a hope of seeing – have lots of chances to score. One corner after another comes across and begs to be put into our goal but all the chances are spurned. After one such near miss, amid the cacophony of relief from our fans and frustration from West Ham's, I attempt irony: 'That nearly went in.' Liam smiles and nods.

On the way to the toilet at half-time, I edge past an attractive young woman with curly hair and a woolly hat, and a good-looking bloke about the same age as her with long floppy hair. I smile at them. He shakes my hand and nods to the younger woman: 'This is Jeff Astle's daughter,' he says proudly.

Dawn's dad, Jeff, was probably our greatest ever player. Between 1964 and 1974 he played 361 times for us scoring 174 goals, including the only goal of the 1968 cup final against Everton. I never saw him play but I have been told so many times about how he used to hang in the air before he headed the ball that I can almost see him there, hanging in the air.

Dawn was born just before the final in 1968. 'The first match I remember watching me dad play in was his testimonial and I'd be about six. It was an all-stars team, I think, because George Best was playing. I remember we sat in the directors' box and my grandma put a rug around me legs.

'Dad used to get so much attention here. At home games he was always inundated and he never used to walk off. If there was somebody there wanting an autograph, he'd wait 'til he'd done them all. At the time it annoyed me a bit 'cos I didn't want to miss the start. He seemed to have just as many people round him as the current players. It was odd really because he hadn't played for us for twenty years. But I didn't realise how special he was to the fans, to be honest, until he died.

'Towards the end he didn't go as much – he'd been weaned away from it because of his illness. By the end he didn't even know who he'd played for, bless him. He was surrounded by all his football stuff, his England caps and cup winner's medal and it meant nothing to him.

'We used to dread people asking us how Dad was. We used to lie and say he was busy, or watching in the directors' box or something. What nobody knew was that for probably four years before he died we always suspected that his illness was due to heading a ball. We dreaded certain people who'd always come up and ask how he was. And we'd always say that he was all right, knowing damn well that he wasn't. Which we felt awful about but we had to do it to protect his dignity. It was horrible.'

Jeff Astle died on 19 January 2002. The neurologist, in Dawn's words, said, 'When I examined the brain of Mr Jeffrey Astle, it resembled that of a boxer. On the death certificate it says "Industrial Disease".'

It was late on that Saturday evening when the news broke. I was at the end of a long night out in Birmingham when I was called by a producer on Five Live's Edwina Currie show. There I was, outside a restaurant in Birmingham, discussing with Edwina Currie of all people the passing of a man who I met only once and never saw play but still felt close to. 'He used to hang in the air,' I said to her. She made sympathetic noises.

The following day we were at home to Walsall, a match that Jeff's widow and three daughters watched on the telly. 'We knew there'd be a minute's silence but I was just praying that nobody would shout out. I was so on edge. We were all sitting thinking, Oh God, I hope nobody shouts, and it was just immaculate. I taped the match. You could have heard a pin drop.

'And then we scored and Jason Roberts lifted his shirt up and there was a picture of Dad on his T-shirt. We burst into tears, we did. Later on I put the radio on in the car. It was the phone-in with Tom Ross and everybody was phoning about Dad, not about the match. I pulled over and I was listening for a good quarter of an hour, twenty minutes. And I thought, God, people were nearly in tears on the radio and they were saying we wonder how his family are. And I just felt that I needed to tell them that we were listening and we just appreciated everything they were saying. So I called in myself. I spoke to Tom Ross. And tears were streaming down my face when I spoke to him. I just needed to let the fans know that Dad loved them as much they loved him, because he did. He really, really did.'

Listening to Dawn, an email I had from a fourteen-year-old called Danny Grainger comes to mind. I dig it out later:

my whole family were deeply saddened by Jeff passing away so we decided to pay our tributes to him by going to his funeral me and my dad John made the trip to a small place in

Derbyshire called Netherseal or maybe Netherseel I'm not quite sure. But the problem was it was on a school day so I had to miss the day off school, so as moms do she phoned in saying I had a sore throat, we got there and stood out side and the speeches were said the songs were sang and then a central news reporter came up to me and asked if I would like to be interviewed I half murmured yes because I was a bit shy but I was worried if my school teacher would see me if they actually put me on the program on the evening, in the end I did the interview and I enjoyed it and told them what I knew about Jeff but when I got back to school the following day and I was collerd at school by many frantic pupils asking about my day they had all seen me on central news and my teacher she just said sarcastically how's your sore throat Danny. She had got to be a wolves fan. Another thing which happened that day which I didn't no whether to laugh or cry about was when Jeff's coffin was being brought out my dad was crying I said dad you didn't cry that much at Grandad's funeral and my dad replied with his albion scarf round his neck and tears in eyes 'but my dad couldn't head the ball like the king.'

At the end of that season we were promoted. Ahead of the last game, against Crystal Palace, a friend of mine, Bryn Law from Sky Sports, sent me a photograph of Jeff to keep in my pocket for good luck. And so many people around me that day were saying Jeff was watching and that it was all for Jeff.

'I heard them saying that around me, that it was all for Jeff,' says Dawn. 'And at another game we had to win, a bloke who sits near my eldest sister, who didn't know who her dad was, he just kept saying, come on, come on, let's do it for Astle, do it for Astle. We never thought for a million years we'd get in the Premiership, but to do it and him miss it you just felt gutted for him, you just wished that he was there. He'd have been punching the air and all sorts. Even now when I'm there I don't sit where we used to. I could never sit there again.

'My kids were mascots not long after Dad died. It said in the programme that Jeff Astle's grandchildren, Matthew and Taylor, were the mascots. And this woman who sits behind me taps me on the shoulder and says, is Matthew Jeff Astle's grandson? I said, yeah, and she said, bloody hell, I didn't know that. And within a minute it was like wildfire all around us. Anyway, a couple of minutes later the same woman patted me again and said, that must mean he was your dad! I said, yeah! and she said, bloody hell I didn't know that!

'But it was incredible, that moment, as they ran on as mascots. And seeing Matthew, as little as he was, completely unfazed. He ran straight to the Birmingham Road End with his hands above his head clapping just like it was his stage, just like his granddad. And I thought, If my dad could see this now. It was really emotional. I cried my heart out all match.'

We could do with an Astle on the pitch today. Shortly after I return to my seat, West Ham score. It's at the other end so Liam can't see it but the noise tells him what he needs to know. I feel his shoulders slump. Thence begins a spell of pressure from us that any neutral would assume might result in a goal. But we know different. Their fans start to goad us. Someone behind me shouts, 'Fuck your bumholes!' back at them. We all laugh. We lose.

Walking away from the ground, there is desperation everywhere. One bloke walks with me for a while and says over and over again that our players lack compassion. 'It's compassion they need,' he shouts repeatedly, banging his chest each time he says it. I'm sure he means passion rather than compassion but an image comes to mind of our manager demanding more compassion from the team. 'Come on, boys,' Bryan Robson could shout, 'have compassion, for God's sake, those fans of ours can't take much more of this shite.'

Back at home normal rules apply: betray any sign of my misery relating to the Albion and Jane will, quite rightly, come down on me like a tonne of bricks. She breaks the news to me that Evie wants to go to the firework display in the park. I have tried to take her before but on each occasion the noise has scared her witless and I've had to bring her home. This time, though, she says she'll be fine.

When we get there she spies a load of giant cuddly toys to be won. I spend about ten quid trying to win one by lifting a plastic duck out of some water; but no joy. I then spend another tenner throwing balls at a stack of tin cans. Knock them all down and you get as big a teddy as you want. Again, no joy. By now my little angel has become hysterical.

So, finally, my best shot: a dartboard on which you can score nothing, one, two, three or four. Four darts for a fiver and if you score eight there's a big teddy for you. I throw four darts for five points. No teddy. A man watching nearby, with a nasal, posh voice says: 'I think you've done about as well as West Brom today.'

'Worse,' I say, scowling miserably without looking at him. He probably thinks me very rude. I don't care.

My encounter with Dawn Astle and the memories it has brought back of her dad's passing have me thinking about how death bonds us to our clubs. The Astles are obviously a special case given that Jeff was a club hero, but many of us, it seems to me, are supporters partly out of loyalty to those we were close to and have lost. If I was to turn my back on the Albion, I'm sure I would feel the disappointed gaze of my granddad on my back for evermore.

At any great or terrible moment in the club's history my thoughts have been with my granddad; Martin, who I sit next to, will always be thinking of the seventeen-year-old son he lost; Val and Sue Ball will be thinking of Cyril. The spirits of all those Albion fans who came before us hover above the ground waiting for their names to be called in our hours of joy or need.

Mindful of all this, I seek out the club chaplain to sit beside at our next game. Ken Hipkiss, or the Rev as everyone knows him around here, has been club chaplain for years. He's in his fifties.

His dress is always as neat as the moustache he sports. You would think him a bit of a Lothario if it wasn't for his determinedly benign demeanour.

Saturday, 19 November 2005, Everton at home

I arrive early and wander around the ground half an hour before kick-off. The floodlights aren't even on yet. I fall into conversation with a woman in a wheelchair called Tracey. She is probably in her fifties. She has a pink blanket over her knees and new-looking Timberland boots in the same colour. She has a woolly hat on, on the front of which is the legend, 'Albion 'til I die'.

I have a small, very small, idea of what it is like to watch the Albion from a wheelchair. For most of the 1990/91 season, I had a broken leg. This was arguably our worst-ever season. On the last day we were relegated to the third division for the first and only time in our history.

Most relegation seasons feature an embarrassing defeat in the cup and this one was no different. In January we famously lost at home to Woking in the FA Cup. Woking were many, many divisions below us, but still beat us 4-2. A player called Tim Buzaglo scored a hat-trick. Our fans hid their shame and anger away in a huge show of sportsmanship, carrying the chap on their shoulders around the pitch. I watched miserably on from the corner with my many (permanently) wheelchair-bound friends.

Now, right in the corner where I used to park my wheelchair, I am recognised by a large man sitting in one. He well remembers the old disabled area because that's where he used to stand as a St John Ambulanceman.

'So why . . .' I venture gingerly. He gets my drift instantly.

'Oh, I had a stroke,' he said, before adding: 'I've been coming here since 1947.'

That was the year Danny Stokes's dad brought him to his first match: 'I don't remember much about the early days but when I was at school my idol was Billy Elliot. He always had an Austin Atlantic sports car, the one with the headlights in the bonnet. I got to know him and he let me ride in his car. I really got to know Billy; he was my idol. And we played the Wolves and they crippled Billy Elliot, they broke his ankle. I was sure it was Billy Wright who did it, but I can't be sure now. But after that he never got his speed up again because he was really quick on the wing. And I've hated the Wolves ever since.'

Danny was an ambulance driver for thirty-six years before he had his stroke. I ask him if he fixed it so he always worked the ground on match days. 'That's correct,' he says.

'Wasn't that against the rules?'

'Sometimes it was without pay,' is all he says, grinning.

I dimly remember him from my year in the disabled section. I always suspected that the ambulancemen secretly prayed for players to get injured. They would sit very still during the game, even the ones, like Danny, who were supporters – as though it might be somehow unseemly to leap about in their fluorescent uniforms. But when a player went down they'd perk up a little bit and if he stayed down they would stand up. They'd mass right by the corner flag and wait for the referee to call them on. Then they'd be off.

Danny reels off a list of players he stretchered off in his time like he is describing trophies in his cabinet. 'Alan Gilzean, Jimmy Greaves, Tony Brown, Jeff Astle, Jackie Vernon. I also helped with the tall chap who swallowed his tongue.'

'Colin West?'

'Colin West. I ran on with the oxygen. I hadn't had a stroke then.'

Danny's stroke happened on a Tuesday night in 1996. 'I'd just come home from work, six till two I was on. I went to bed and when I got up next morning, well, I couldn't talk and I couldn't move down the right side. It frightens you at first. You think you're talking properly but you're coming out all gobbledegook.

'Luckily, by virtue of the fact that I worked on the ambulances, I didn't have to go through casualty. And I knew what was happening from experience, but you still don't really understand what it is and it's really, really frightening. And I found people don't talk to you. They talk sort of over you. They'd say to the wife, ooh, he looks normal, doesn't he? And it was so frustrating that I knew what they were on about. My friend's daughter's a speech therapist and she came round every night. She helped and I ai' too bad now.'

I ask him if he felt any differently about the Albion after his luck changed – with bigger things on his mind did he still care as much? 'Before I had the stroke I used to get really ratty. I'd come back to the car, throw the programme in the boot and say I ain't going to come no more. But since I had the stroke I thought, Well, if this is what we've got to do, if this is all we've got to lose by, then OK.

'I still love the Albion, though. Even if we were in the third division I'd go, but that Liverpool thing about life and death and football being more important. Well, it ain't, it ain't. But it does give you something to look forward to. It's fantastic. All right, some weeks it's pouring and there's rain running down my nose and we're losing, but I still love it. And in that corner you've got your real disabled, the real young ones. They're absolutely fantastic.'

Danny humbles me. He considers himself the luckiest person ever: lucky to have been an ambulanceman when he had his stroke because it got him seen at the hospital quicker; lucky to have a friend with a daughter who's a speech therapist; lucky to be old and disabled rather than young and disabled; and, above all, lucky to have the Albion.

I find the Rev sitting high up in a corner of the ground. I squeeze in between him and his daughter Julie: 'All my kids are Albion fans,' he says proudly.

I ask him how he thinks we'll do today. 'I fancy us,' he says,

114

'but, then again, I always fancy us.' He says this in the same way he might tell me he believes in God but can't supply any firm evidence of His existence, except Ken is totally sure about God in a way he can't be about the Albion.

It is quite difficult to pin Ken down on the interface between football and scripture. I once quizzed him on the subject for a rather serious-minded piece I was trying to write for the *Independent*. 'Have a look at Hebrews 12,' he said. 'With all these witnesses to faith around us like a cloud, we must throw off every encumbrance, every sin to which we cling.'

'Not quite sure I'm with you, Ken.'

'Well, throwing off every encumbrance is like getting changed before you run out, isn't it?'

He also pointed me in the direction of Acts 13.3: 'After they had fasted and prayed they placed their hands on them and he sent them off. You see,' said Ken triumphantly, 'even in them days if you raised your hands it was a red card!'

It's just before kick-off. The Rev nods towards our front two, Horsfield and Ellington. 'It's the first time he's paired these two together,' he says.

I see an opening now for an ecclesiastical joke: 'He never stops fiddling does he, Robson? If he'd been in charge of the twelve apostles, he'd have tried thirty-six blokes out in the job.'

There is something in his laugh that suggests he thinks I'm a bit of a smart-arse.

Before we know it, it appears that we are playing rather well. We're attacking the end the Rev and I are sitting in.

'What do you think, Rev?'

'We're doing all right.' Pause. 'I don't mind saying it,' he adds, realising he's committed the cardinal football supporters' sin of tempting fate.

'You're not superstitious, are you, Rev? I thought that was against the rules.'

He shrugs. 'Day off,' he says.

A cross goes in from the right, just in front of us. Phil Neville of

Everton clearly handles. 'Penalty!' the Rev and I roar in unison. No penalty is given. To our right, in the Smethwick End, are the noisiest of our supporters. Their language is ghastly. The Rev seems torn between dismay at their apparent godlessness and pride that they're generating so much noise on our team's behalf. 'I used to be one of them,' he says, 'until I saw the light. It's just part of life, I suppose.'

On the pitch we are still the better team but it's all gone a bit quiet. I ask the Rev what his gut feeling is.

'We'll win this,' he says.

'If we win this,' I say, 'I'm going to church in the morning.'

A moment later Nathan Ellington is brought down on the edge of the penalty area. Penalty given. As Ellington himself steps up to take it, I wonder if the Rev is silently praying. I decide he probably is, despite himself. As Ellington scores, the Rev leaps up with both fists clenched and lets out a deep, even pagan roar from the very depths of his soul. The Smethwick End bounce up and down for a bit then, as usual when something good happens, they sing 'The Lord's My Shepherd'. 'I taught them that,' he says happily.

For the second half I walk around to the East Stand to sit with my Sikh friends, the Super Singhs. Gurdial's here with Jadeen, Jeevan and Joshan, her son, who I have not met before. All of them are fortressed up against the cold. I ask Joshan if we're going to win. 'Won't lose, might draw,' he says grimly. Such battle-hardened realism in one so young.

Their father works abroad in the oil industry and is away for weeks at a time. I ask the girls when he is next back. They think carefully, look at each other, and Jeevan says, 'Just before Man City.' The family diary obviously runs from August to May and is calibrated not in weeks and months but in fixtures.

The Smethwick End chant for the East Stand to start singing. Nobody really responds. Gurdial reaches across me to poke Joshan quite firmly: 'You heard them, Joe,' she commands. 'Go on – answer them.' Now that's what I call parenting. The poor lad, half frozen to death, murmurs along with whatever song the East Stand is trying to organise itself to sing.

To everyone's delight, we then score. It's 2-0, and it really does look as if we might win this. Everton are hopeless. Gurdial and I are relaxed enough to fall into quite a serious conversation about religion, her relationship with the rest of her family and so on. She speaks quietly and earnestly, occasionally pausing to shout 'Look at that, ref!' or 'Well done, Ronnie!'

Nathan Ellington then scores again. A beautiful goal curled in with his left foot from the edge of the penalty area. We are going to win. I hug Gurdial and tell her I want to be Asian, preferably Sikh. She laughs. I leave early, loving the luxury of being able to leave the ground with the game in the bag. And deliciously we then score a fourth.

Sandra texts me: 'Fanfuckingtastic.'

The Reverend Ken Hipkiss texts me, too: 'See you in church in the morning.'

Sunday, 27 October 2005, Middlesbrough away

Frank Skinner calls. He can't get up to the game and it's not on Sky, so he asks if he can come in to watch it with me. As ever, he is beside himself with optimism. I take him into the *Grandstand* production office away from the *Match of the Day 2* people. This is personal and, as against Bolton, we need to be on our own.

Early on Frank surmises, quite correctly, that we are the better team. I agree with him, but if we're performing well it only makes me think how much more painful it will be when the opposition score. Frank, on the other hand, not unreasonably, sees it as a good thing that we're playing well.

'We're the better side here,' he says happily, tapping my knee.

'I know,' I reply miserably.

Almost straight away, Boro score. Practically their first attack of the game. Frank curses. I, as usual, feel only relief. Now we don't have the draw to hang on to, I can relax a little bit, but we then equalise. I'm a bag of nerves all over again. And early in the second half, we manage to score again. I just want to go out for a walk and come back at the final whistle to see what happened. I can't bear to watch us spend the next half an hour throwing it all away. 'Don't worry,' says Frank, 'we'll score again. They'll have to come at us and there'll be gaps at the back.'

Fortunately the agony doesn't last long as Boro are awarded a penalty, which they score. From this point I am absolutely 100 per cent convinced that, with twenty minutes left, we will go on to lose this game. Frank, of course, remains totally convinced we will score and win. 'I'm not just saying it,' he says, with his hand on his heart, 'I really honestly believe it.'

Boro bring on two substitutes, one of whom is Jimmy Floyd Hasselbaink, a prolific goalscorer. 'Shit,' I say.

'Great,' says Frank, 'more gaps at the back.'

But we hold on. 'I'll settle for that,' I say.

'Could have won,' says Frank. The final whistle has changed everything: he's the unhappier of the two of us now.

Wednesday, 30 November 2005, Manchester United away in the Carling Cup

This is Man Utd's first home match since the death of George Best, one of their greats.

Oddly, it was against us that he made his debut forty-two years ago, and most of the players from that game will be here tonight. On the train to Manchester, it occurs to me that I am looking forward to seeing a game of football. This is because, under the circumstances, the result doesn't really matter. For once, I'm feeling relaxed.

A tall, good-looking bloke walks through my carriage, grim-faced. I recognise him as Calum Best, George's son. I catch his eye and, somewhat absurdly, try to convey my compassion by winking at him. He manages a weak smile.

I meet the usual crowd in a pub near Piccadilly Station. As usual, the conversation is sucked in the direction of Nathan's sexploits which he is happy to recount with a mixture of pride and shame: 'She was in her fifties. Widow. Got a lovely big house in Kingswinford. Semi-detached. Her daughter had just had her twenty-first birthday. When the daughter saw me, she said to her mother, who's that? What do I say to that?'

'Are you sure she didn't ask, what's that?' says Sandra.

At Old Trafford our fans are as keen as theirs to pay tribute to George Best and have turned up in numbers. I chat happily with several of them and, as ever, it feels like we're all part of a big happy family. But then a large swarthy man nudges me as he walks past and says, 'Adrian Chiles!'

'Hello, mate,' I smile.

But he's not smiling. He points his finger at me says, quite angrily, 'Cheer up you miserable fucking cunt.'

He is obviously sick and tired of me moaning and groaning about the Albion on the telly. I don't really blame him, but I can't bear to be criticised by one of my own. Someone has recently posted something on one of the chatrooms describing me as a part-time fan. I wanted to cry when I read it. I had the poster's email address and composed a mail inviting him to call my wife and ask her how much of a part-time fan I am. Wisely, probably, I decided against sending it.

The commemoration of George Best gets underway. From high up in the away end, I look down at Calum Best standing in the line-up of his dad's former team-mates and the former Albion players George made his debut against. He looks even lonelier than he did on the train.

Our fans chant, 'There's only one George Best.' Their fans applaud us. There's nothing better to warm the cockles than two lots of fans setting aside their enmity to sing from the same hymn sheet. But about two seconds after the minute's silence, our fans chant, 'We are Albion, we are Albion.' This doesn't seem quite right, somehow. Their fans respond with chants of 'United, United,

United.' After each 'United', our lot chant, '*Shit!*' No offence really intended or taken. To everyone's relief, it's business as usual.

I've arranged to meet a lad called Dale, one of the hard-core chanters who so alarmed my friend Adam at Fulham. I want to see how exactly you get to lead the chanting, how you decide what to chant and when, and why some chants are taken up by everyone and others never get going at all. Dale's coach is late so we agree to meet at half-time In preparation for this, I pay more attention than usual to our chants. As soon as the match kicks off, we loosen up with 'Proud to be a Baggie' to the tune – absurdly, when you think about it – of 'If You're Happy and You Know It'. This segues seamlessly into 'Bryan Robson's blue and white army'.

'The Lord's My Shepherd', our anthem, is followed by my least favourite, a tuneless number pioneered, I think, by Liverpool where you just slowly repeat your club's name over and over again. No one's quite sure, incidentally, why we sing 'The Lord's My Shepherd'. The most plausible explanation I have heard is that some fans started singing it at a Sunday match when they were introduced in the eighties. Oddly, or perhaps aptly, it's a funeral hymn, which pleases me because it means it can be sung with real feeling at my funeral.

Thrillingly, we win a free-kick in a promising position and celebrate the fact with an upbeat 'Come on you Baggies', followed by another 'We are Albion'. The free-kick's wasted and there's silence for a few minutes until United have a goal disallowed. We advise their fans to 'Sit down, shut up'. Some among our number choose to accompany this with masturbatory hand gestures.

United win a penalty, score it, and then score again from open play, so by half-time the match is a lost cause. The singers I'm meeting know it's not going to be easy. Dale and his mate Rich, having arrived late, have had to watch the first half from the seats ('Our actual seats', as he puts it) they've been allocated. They are bang in the middle of the away end which is hopeless for the choirmasters. They need to be right at the back where the other singers will have gravitated to as well. Word has reached Dale by text from another singer that there are spaces available there.

'We've got our work cut out,' says Dale grimly. Then, addressing Rich and a young woman and her boyfriend sitting just behind them, he says, 'Up the back?' Like marines waiting for the order to break cover, they nod imperceptibly and silently move up the stand to take their command positions on the higher ground for the second half.

It turns out there are enough seats available there to accommodate the City of Birmingham Symphony Chorus, but for the moment we are just five. As the match recommences far below us, they briefly review their singing season. 'Boro wasn't great,' says Rich. 'And this is going to be tough,' adds Dale. 'But Fulham was something else,' they both say, almost in unison, 'a one-off.' 'Great acoustics,' recalls Rich affectionately.

All of a sudden, as if bidden by some hidden signal I've not been party to, they both leap to their feet and roar, 'Baggies!' The couple sitting in front of us jump, startled by this outburst. Shyly, I leap up and try to chime in with them. Then we pause. Like hunters on safari listening for the sound of our quarry, we cock our heads and strain to hear if anyone else has joined in. Miraculously, they have. With renewed vigour we roar again: 'Baggies!'

Again there's a response from elsewhere but it tails off very soon.

'It fades away so quick,' says Rich sadly.

They have another go: 'Come on you Baggies!' Again, rather bashfully, I join in. Once more, the same words echo back at us but the moment they start to fade Dale and Rich try to keep the noise up by changing chant: 'Albion, Albion, Albion,' they incant, furiously clapping their hands. We keep this up for about a minute. I can see the woman in front, a little frightened, trying to catch a glimpse of us out of the corner of her eye.

But soon silence falls again. 'Dead, innit?' says Rich. 'Need a goal,' replies Dale. Dale, who's twenty-two, works in a call centre for a utility company, which he says is OK. He grins and nods when I ask him if he has ever sung so hard the night before that he's been unable to take any calls.

Rich is twenty and struggling for money. He had an apprenticeship with a painting and decorating firm but packed it in. He has no idea what he wants to do. He went five years without missing a game but now money is short so he can't get to every match. He says his dad and his brother help him out 'because they know how much it means to me'.

After a period of silence, the two of them suddenly strike up again: 'Oh, when the stripes. Go marching in. Oh, when the . . .' Percussion is provided with fierce clapping of hands. Somehow, between breaths, Dale manages to explain that, 'If you get this one going, it's really good.' And it lasts longer than the other chants. Soon, though, it's just the two of them doing it. Then just one of them, Dale, who slumps back into his seat.

Rich says to him, 'Have you got the drink?' I suspect this is in reference to some hooch they have smuggled in but Dale just pulls out a half-empty bottle of Sprite. They handle it like medication, taking sips to soothe their overheating vocal chords.

Man Utd score again. Three-nil. Irony is the only option now. Dale and Rich spring up and launch into 'We're going to win 4-3.' But they sound doleful. Sung without spirit, without bags of ironic enthusiasm, it just doesn't work. 'United!' chant the United fans. 'Shit!' we respond, reflexively. But soon our 'shits' die away and the home fans' territory is their own again.

Somebody starts up with 'We support our local team!' A jibe at Man Utd fans who hail from everywhere. They've heard it before and clap sarcastically. I hate that song because it smacks of desperation. And hypocrisy: I – like all football fans – can't help deploring Man Utd fans who aren't from Manchester. But if I come across an Albion fan with no connections in the area, from Dublin or Kent or wherever, it's all I can do to stop myself from kissing them full on the lips.

We get a consolation goal. 'Easy! Easy!' chant Dale and Rich.

As the match peters out, my boys muster themselves for one

more chorus of 'Albion, Albion, Albion,' then sit down. 'That'll be it now,' says Dale. And there are no more songs. The final whistle goes and we applaud wearily.

All football fans love a great atmosphere in the ground but it is only very few who actually join in with most of the singing. And it's only a tiny minority of them who have the guts to take it upon themselves to initiate the noise, to get the singing going. On countless occasions I've been terribly proud at the noise our fans have made but never once, in thirty-two years, have I started – or even tried to start – a chant.

Dale and Rich look despondent. Neither the result nor the chanting has gone their way. I tell them how vital they are to us, and how I suspect that any clown can get the singing going when we're winning. It's nights like this when they're really needed. They nod appreciatively.

Six

Steve Clare (left) and Danny Stokes at the Albion

Saturday, 3 December 2005, Fulham at home

We ought to know better but we are all hopeful. I travel up with a Spanish-Moroccan man I know. Younos is married to Claire, who looks after our children when we're at work. He has got several degrees but, probably because his spoken English isn't the best, ended up working as a postman. He's been to a couple of matches with me before and I have found myself loving him for speaking of the Albion as 'we' not 'they'. Anyone who uses the first person plural when talking about West Brom is all right by me.

He's yet to see us win, but his nascent faith remains intact.

My leg's been hurting after doing too much running this week. I mention this to John Simpson, West Brom's press officer, who, though it's only fifty minutes from kick-off, asks Nick Worth, the physio, if he could possibly have a look at me. Since the players are out on the pitch warming up, Nick is happy to see me. John leads me backstage down a long corridor and, to my alarm, through a door marked, 'Home Dressing Room'. In there are Nick and his assistant, two masseurs and the kit man. Ashamed of my intrusion, I stammer, 'Oh, sorry, I didn't mean to come in here.'

'Well, fuck off, then,' suggests one of the masseurs, mildly enough.

Nick presses my shin in several places, manoeuvres my foot about and asks a few questions. He diagnoses shin splints. 'Rest it a few days and you'll be fine,' he says.

I'm relieved it's nothing more serious but, under the circumstances, I am more than a little ashamed as I make my way to the disabled section, where Danny Stokes has promised to introduce me to other disabled fans, especially a lad called Steve he told me about on the phone. 'Steve,' he warned me, 'is in a terrible state, arms spraying about everywhere, but an amazing kid.'

Steve Clare duly arrives, pushed in by his mum and dad. As I worried would be the case, I simply don't have the words or actions necessary to interact with Steve. His twisted arms flail about and his head moves from one contortion to the next. He is happy to see me, I think. I grab his hand and squeeze it.

I shake hands with his dad, Ivor. He looks to be in his sixties and is very neatly turned out. I want to ask him a question about Steve but can't find a way of doing it without referring to Steve in the third person. 'What's wrong with him?' is the question I want to ask, obviously. Instead I go for 'How old is he, er, how old is Steve?' I've used the third person anyway. Stupid. His dad tells me he is thirty-five.

'And how long have you been coming up here together?'

'Since he was four or five – I used to carry him in on my shoulders. 'He wasn't so bad then,' says Ivor, 'he was smaller and he sat in the ordinary seat. But there wasn't so many disabled there then.

'No, no,' says Steve's mum, 'not so many.'

'No,' agrees Ivor.

'There was only a small corner,' she says.

'Only a small corner,' agrees Ivor.

Steve has cerebral palsy. His mother is called Marie which makes her Marie Clare. She is an attractive woman and there's something youthful about her hairdo which I can't quite put my finger on. She speaks incredibly quickly. When I ask if she gets fed up with people staring at Steve, she says, 'I must admit – and I'm not proud of this but I don't care – I always say something. Even sometimes little kids if they do it, because after all they do see plenty of people in wheelchairs these days, it isn't a novelty, because it's not like the old days when they were shut away in homes. I just say to them, you can turn away, he's not got two heads. And I wait for the mother or father to say something, but they never do.

'Funnily enough, when we've been on holiday or gone out we've made lots of friends through Steven. They'll come and talk to him. They all say what a likeable fella he is.'

'And he's interested in whatever people say,' adds Ivor.

'So when we've been away we've always made friends right away,' says Marie.

A few weeks later I visit the Clares' semi in Wednesbury. *Sky Sports News* is on the television. Steve sits in a little leather chair. His feet point inwards and he writhes around more violently as he thinks of things he wants to contribute to the conversation.

'Anything like this, he gets fidgety,' says Ivor. 'This is just the frustration. Normally he's not, like, quite this bad.'

I ask why they thought to take Steve to the Albion in the first place. Marie says, 'We just thought it's time to go. And he liked it but he was afraid of the noise and it took us, oooh—'

'Months,' says Ivor.

'Months,' agrees Marie. 'It took months for him to adjust but when he did he really loved it and never looked back. After that he's never not wanted to go up to West Brom. Have you, Steve?'

'No,' Steve just about manages to gasp.

'Was it a bit frightening?' I ask him, aware that I have been unable to stop myself from sounding like I'm addressing a child.

'Yeah, yeah,' squeaks Steve, moving his head from side to side.

'The sound . . .' says his dad.

'When you're like Steven,' explains Marie, 'the sound is just at a different level. Their hearing's very acute. He can hear everything. It comes over much louder and he was afraid.'

'Yeaaaahhh,' shouts Steve again.

'He just got used to it. He loved it,' says Marie. Steve is making noises all the time now. I ask him how old he was when he went to his first match. He shouts something in reply. 'Seven,' says Ivor.

'You were same age as me, then. I was seven,' I say, 'and I've been miserable ever since.'

Steve roars with laughter, literally helpless with mirth, shifting violently from side to side.

Marie shows me some of Steve's memorabilia collection. There are photos of him with players, some of whom are club legends; others came and went and probably never think twice about their time with us. There is a photograph of Steve with Lee Hughes and Andy Hunt crouching next to his wheelchair. It must have been taken about ten years ago. Lee Hughes is now in prison; Andy Hunt is living in Belize; Steve is still here, though, with his Albion bits and bobs. There's a signed photo of Ray Barlow, a fabulous star of our 1954 cup-winning side, and one of Shaun Murphy, an Australian international who came and went, and once got himself some bad press for being honest enough to admit that he just played for whoever paid him.

There is a pennant from the seventies, signed by our players, and a puzzle of a photo of the hopeless team managed by Alan Buckley. And there's a cheap trophy, like I once won at school for a seven-a-side competition. It is inscribed, 'Steven Clare. Loyal Supporter of the Year.'

And there is a green flat cap in a polythene bag, along with a picture of Jeff Astle. 'That's Jeff's hat,' says Marie. 'He was always very good with Steve. We used to see him a lot on away trips. And

127

we got to know the family quite well and when he died they gave us the cap. It's the one he used to wear at the matches.'

Jeff Astle's cap – Dents, the Finest Quality – lies there on the arm of the sofa as we talk.

I ask Steve what his highlight is, what his favourite match is. His dad answers for him: 'You've got to go a few years back,' says Ivor.

'Talk to Adrian,' says Marie gently.

Steve grunts something.

'Cyrille?' suggests Marie.

Steve, getting more agitated all the time, resorts to spelling out a name: 'L. . .A. . .U. . .R. . .'

'Laurie!' says Marie, 'Cyrille and Laurie Cunningham.'

I take it that Steve is trying to say that he loved all the matches in the late seventies and early eighties when Regis and Cunningham were playing, but his dad, probably anxious that I am losing patience, thinks he's got the wrong end of the stick. 'He's on about the best match, Steve,' he says, 'or what's your happiest moment.'

Steve's struggling terribly now.

'Go on try, Steve,' says Marie. 'What about Swansea when we went up?'

'Yeah, yeah,' gasps Steve.

But Marie keeps pushing him: 'That's me, what about you, Steve?'

Steve tries to say something else but then gives up.

'Swansea,' says Marie again, almost to herself as if she is suddenly lost in the memory. But then she makes another suggestion: 'What about Bradford away? We had to get everybody to help carry him. Ivor'd had a bad back and we thought we couldn't go. But he said we just had to go . . .'

'Yeah, yeah,' shouts Steve, waving his arms a bit.

'We had to get all those hefty blokes to help,' continues Marie. And we go on to fondly remember Igor Balis's penalty. Steve claps with joy at the memory. Marie says of Balis, 'I've never seen anybody like him. I don't know how he kept his head. He was marvellous, literally marvellous.'

At this moment I can't decide who is actually most marvellous: Ivor, Marie, Steve or indeed Igor Balis. It's a close call. 'Bradford . . .' says Marie again, as wistfully as she said Swansea a few moments ago. For a moment we're all lost in thought, but then Steve suddenly explodes into life, desperate to say something. The harder he tries, the worse his diction gets. His mum and dad focus intently on trying to understand him. In the end Marie says, 'Spell it.'

'V!' bawls Steve.

'V,' say Ivor and Marie together.

'A!'

'A.'

'L!'

'L.'

'Val, val, val,' they both repeat thoughtfully. Suddenly Ivor has it: 'Valencia!'

'Valencia,' says Marie to me.

Steve probably has a thousand things he wants to say about our UEFA Cup victory against Valencia in 1978 but, as ever, he will be able to articulate hardly a thing. I wonder if the kindest thing now would be just to leave him alone as he is finding it so frustrating to respond. Then again, if everyone took that view nobody would talk to him at all. So I press on, this time asking them all which game made them unhappiest.

'Well, I think that's hard to say,' says Ivor. Marie, still in a UEFA Cup frame of mind, goes for the quarter-final tie we earned by beating Valencia. 'Red Star Belgrade, when we did get knocked out,' she says.

I tell them that was on my eleventh birthday and I cried on the way home. And I remember my granddad putting his hand on my knee and telling me I shouldn't cry because 'football is like life: you've got to take the rough with the smooth'. This was sound advice, except that I could tell he was close to tears, too. Steve makes agonised sympathetic noises at this tale.

I explain how miserable the Albion make me, how they affect

my whole life. Steve laughs. 'It's the same with him,' says Marie. 'I mean, although he's disabled, it don't make him feel any better about the Albion. He still gets as down as any able-bodied person.'

I ask how she tries to bring him round when he gets fed up. 'You have to talk to him and say, well, you've got to keep a sense of proportion. But it's days, sometimes it's days,' says Marie. 'He keeps on about it Saturday, Sunday, Monday. Starts to wear a little bit Tuesday, then he's building up for the next match. He's like you really, Adrian.'

I ask if he can write things down. 'Yeah, yeah,' says Steve. Marie says, 'He could do it, he couldn't physically write, but he could press the button on the thing. The computer's not working, though – he broke the keyboard. But if we could sort it out, he'd write you what he thought. You'd be amazed. He's done it at college. You see,' she says finally, tapping her temple, 'it's all in there.' She pauses, before laughing in an ashamed way and saying, 'Mind you, I'm surprised what does come out sometimes. He was really annoyed with the ref one time and he was trying to say something, really struggling, and then suddenly it just came out.'

'What did?'

'He just suddenly shouted it.'

'What?'

'Wanker!' she says, and laughs.

Back at the Fulham game, another lad in a wheelchair arrives, also called Steve. He's pushed in by his dad, Joe. Steve has cerebral palsy, too, but his disability is different in that he looks more stable but somehow less animated as he grins up at me. Again, I examine his dad's face for evidence of years of agony, frustration, misery, bitterness and so on. But there is nothing of the sort there. He's only anxious about the game: 'How're we going to do today, Adrian?'

I walk away from Steve and Steve and their fathers, beside

myself with admiration for them. I feel selfish pleasure at my own health and even more absolute desperation than usual for us to win, for their sakes. I watch the match from my usual seat. Younos endears himself to me by jerking involuntarily when we come close to getting a scoring opportunity. And he claps in all the right, less obvious, places: for a good bit of ball control, an intelligent bit of defensive work. He knows his football.

In the match, though, more or less nothing happens until just before half-time when their captain is sent off. We celebrate, but somewhat half-heartedly. The man in front of me says, 'We've had it. We're hopeless against ten.' We all agree but secretly believe we will now go on to win easily.

In the second half it quickly becomes clear that we won't win easily; then we realise we're actually finding it very difficult to win; then we're all quite sure it will be a draw; and finally we're rather relieved not to lose.

Saturday, 10 December 2005, Manchester City at home

A fan's support for his team can manifest itself in many ways. For some, just being there is enough. For others, mementoes and memorabilia can play an important part, whether it is Steve with Jeff Astle's cap or Vic Stirrup with his tickets. These are physical mementoes and we all have them to a lesser or greater extent, even if it's just an old programme or scarf. And we all have numbers in our minds, too; much loved and reflected upon statistics long committed to memory, effortlessly. I can't remember what I did last week but I can tell you exactly where I was when Graham Harbey scored the one piledriver of his career fifteen years ago.

Before our next home game against Manchester City, I'm back in the Sportsman in West Bromwich and again bump into John Mitchell, the bloke from Evesham who can remember exactly in which minute every goal is scored. He asks me what I'm drinking and I ask him when it was exactly that Middlesbrough equalised against us three weeks ago. He thinks. 'Sixty-seven?' he suggests, a little uncertainly. Then, emphatically, as he hands me a half of mild: 'Yes. Sixty-seven.'

Later, as I queue at the bar, a large man with curly hair in a Man City shirt taps me on the shoulder. He is delighted to be in this pub, Ray says, and he claims to be absolutely delighted to meet me. I never know quite how to respond to such kindnesses and often say something clumsy. Here I elect to point out that the Man City shirt he's wearing might result in him getting his head kicked in as I'm led to believe many of our headcases frequent this establishment. 'I know,' he smiles, unconcerned.

Embarrassingly, he then goes on to express his love for me in some detail: 'I fookin' love *Match of the Day 2*. I watch it in bed, though, 'cos it's on so late, in't it? Every Sunday night I say to my wife, I say, I'm going to bed to watch my Adrian.'

'I hope you wear pyjamas.'

'Nope,' he says happily, 'don't wear a thing.'

Moving through the crowd, I grin at a group of three blokes. I hear one of them say to the other: 'That's him off Sunday night *Match of the Day*.' Then there's an explosion of laughter and one of them turns to me. He looks like he's in his mid-thirties. His face is quite red and shiny. He exudes happiness laced with anger. 'Did you hear what he said? Did you?' he demands, pointing at one of his mates. I shake my head. Another explosion of laughter spurts out of him before he says: 'He just said that you don't do proper *Match of the Day* 'cos you ai' fookin' good enough!' All three of them roar with laughter and the one who said I wasn't good enough says it again, to my face this time: 'Well, you ai', am you?'

'Too close to the truth, mate,' I say gamely.

So far there is no malice in any of this by the way: it's a Black Country thing. Humour being the best form of attack and defence. But then the guy with the shiny happy face says, 'What's that Graeme Le Saux like?' Before I can reply, he tells me what he thinks Graeme Le Saux is like: 'He's a cunt. He really thinks he's somebody. I'd like to get him and fucking have him.' As he says this he bends over, so his upper body is at right angles to his legs, and executes sharp jabbing punches into the thick, smoky air. 'He's a right cunt, isn't he?' he says, straightening up, a little breathlessly.

'Actually,' I say carefully, 'he's one of the nicest blokes I work with.'

'Oh,' he says doubtfully, 'is he?' Then, more defiantly: 'Well, as a player I thought he was a cunt.' His fist starts clenching up again but his anger is melting away.

Then he notices the half of mild in my hand: 'Look at him, drinking an half! Richest bloke in the fookin' room and the tight bastard's drinking a fookin' half.' The three of them are once again beside themselves with mirth, clutching each other as if the power of the comedy might otherwise cause one of them to float away. I try to join in but the lad's now in full flow: 'Look at the way he sticks his little fookin' finger out as he drinks. He's posh, ai' he?'

I have my notebook with me and I resolve to spend a bit more time with this bloke. I take his home number – 'I ai' got a fookin' mobile. I ai' as rich as you!' His name is Dean Smith and when I ask what he does he says, 'Put "Fabricator" down.' I'm not quite sure what a fabricator is or whether it is indeed what he does. 'Window fabricator,' he explains.

'I'll give you a call,' I say, moving away.

'Just get me on your fookin' programme,' he shouts after me. 'I've got a fookin' suit,' he says, straightening his imaginary lapels.

I wait at the bar to buy John the mushroom man a drink. As I wait to get served, I hear Dean the fabricator say to someone: 'He's off the telly. I think he's a fookin' pervert, though, actually. He's written all our numbers down!'

There is one number that is particularly special today and it belongs to Dave Watkin.

Today is his 750th consecutive game – an unbroken run that began on 1 April, Easter Monday, 1991, with a 2-1 win over Swindon. That is remarkable enough, but the statistics that go with this feat are equally extraordinary. As it stands, after 749 games, he has seen us score 980 goals. He has also, incredibly, seen us concede 980 goals. Furthermore, he's watched us lose 275 times and win 274 times. So, thrillingly, if we win today, after 750 games it will be precisely all square in terms of games won and lost. All that effort, though: 750 games just to end up all square. Wins cancelling out defeats, defeats cancelling out wins, the joy of every goal scored nullified by the misery of every goal conceded. Dave says he's wondered what the point of it all is but, then again, haven't we all?

Dave thinks his first ever match was a 4-0 home win against Everton on Saturday, 15 March 1958. Through the sixties, seventies and eighties, Dave followed the Albion home and away, not going to every game but only missing one if it was absolutely necessary. His 750-game run encompasses the best and worst of the last fifteen years. The ninth game was the defeat at Bristol Rovers that relegated us to the third division for the first time ever, but 112 games later we were back in the second division (by now known as the first division) after winning the play-off final against Port Vale (Game 121).

That's nearly as far as the run went, though, because on the morning of Game 122 Dave broke his leg playing for the supporters' team West Bromwich Albion Strollers at Barnsley. Yet he managed to limp to the ground before getting it plastered that evening.

By now Dave was keen to keep up this unbroken run but there was a problem: Game 145 was an Anglo-Italian Cup tie at Fiorentina. He went to that one with friends, but if he was to make Cosenza away (Game 147), he would have to go on his own. He went, but even then there was a hitch: 'Albion had announced the game would be an evening kick-off but it was played in the afternoon. By sheer good fortune I turned up at the ground in time to see at least part of the action, joining a crowd of just 139. I think this was the point where I resolved that having overcome so many problems I must keep the sequence going as long as possible.

'In October 1994 I was involved in a serious car accident in France. I broke several ribs, my collarbone and a finger. However, the insurance company arranged to get me home and I was back the evening before the next game, which was home to Sunderland (Game 190). My brother Phil delivered me to the gate and, perhaps fortunately, as I was in no state for boinging, Albion lost 3-1.

'Our next foray into Europe came in 1995/96. A visit to Salernitana (Game 236) via Rome passed without incident, but the final match at Brescia (Game 254) was quite eventful. There was a blizzard and we won with a ninetieth-minute goal from Bob Taylor when the ball trickled over the line like a giant snowball. After the final whistle, the players had a snowball fight with the fans.'

After Game 596 it must have all seemed worth it for Dave as we were promoted to the Premiership, but it was 135 games later before we really had anything to celebrate again, with the great escape on the last day of the 2005/06 season – Game 731.

It's not just since 1991 that Dave's been keeping count: 'I've built up a significant historical archive covering all Albion's results in the League, FA Cup, League Cup and Europe from 1883 through to the present day. I've written macros which allow me to analyse the club's record against any opposition in any of these competitions.' In other words, ask him how we've done down the years against a particular club and within a couple of keystrokes he'll have the answer for you.

I don't think the players know about Dave's run, but we start well and by half-time we're 1-0 up. I make my way round to the disabled section in the corner, where I'm spending the second half. Steve Clare is here, but not in his wheelchair. He's sitting three rows back in a proper seat. I grab his hand to shake it but find myself sort of squeezing it instead. He lets out a screech of greeting.

Here, more than anywhere else in the ground, it feels like a real group outing. The refreshments are in full flow. Steve's mum Marie presses a hot drink into my hand. 'It's fudge chocolate,' she says. Another chap, Mick, who is looking after Danny, the former ambulanceman with stroke damage, has a flask of something. 'Is it legal?' I ask. He smiles. It's mulled wine. 'Just need some mince pies now,' I say. Steve's mum shouts to an older lady behind and a bag of mince pies is produced.

I tell them this is the first time I've watched a match from this spot since 1990/91, the season we were beaten by Woking in the cup and were relegated to the old third division. 'You better bugger off, then,' Mick advises.

I get talking to Joe Male, whose son is the other Steve with cerebral palsy. He tells me he has been coming since he was nine. 'And I'm sixty-two now so you can see how long I've been going up. That was the Ronnie Allen days. My family were Albion supporters, but I was the only one who used to go to the ground.'

'So how come you went?'

'I don't really know. I just used to go up. I was an only child, so I should think I've always been a bit of a loner.'

Joe has also got a daughter called Julie. 'She's a bit worse than Steven,' says Joe. 'She can talk to you a bit but she's more physically disabled. She's older by two years, born in 1964. Steve was born in 1966. It's cerebral palsy, brain damage in effect.'

I start asking a question but abandon it before I've got to the end of the sentence: 'So what happens to your son when . . .'

Joe immediately grasps what I've had the temerity to ask: 'Well, what we're hoping is that when we eventually depart, and we go to that great wondrous away game in the sky, we're hoping that they'll continue to live in the house and have support coming to them. People would come into the home and they'd actually live here with them, if you know what I'm trying to say.

'I first brought Steve up here when he was sixteen because he just started asking me when he could come.'

'So by the time you took him to the Albion,' I ask, 'you'd gone past the stage when you were worried about people staring at him?'

'Oh yes. I don't give a bugger about that, no. He just loves the

Albion. He loves it. His bedroom's a shrine. He's got all the bed-clothes, the Bob Taylor signed picture on the wall. He's got everything, you know.

'He's at a centre in the day, and when he comes home he likes his television, especially when there's a match on. He does puzzles, writing. And he has a little computer upstairs which he has a tap into. Mentally he's not as well as other people are but he does his best. And we encourage him to do as much as he can. He's obsessed with the Albion.'

Joe's a full-time carer now: 'I was made redundant and was getting towards sixty and obviously too old to be applying for much. When I was at the Jobcentre they realised I was actually looking after two disabled, and they put me on a book. It suits me because as they get older it's got a lot more difficult and my wife, she's got osteoarthritis, so I'm glad I'm here to support the family.'

I ask him how he stays so cheerful. 'Well, I get damn upset when they lose, the same as you do, I suppose. Of course, the dog has a sore backside for a couple of days but apart from that—'

Astonished, I cut him short to explain that I didn't mean the Albion, rather how he kept so cheerful with his life in general. 'Adrian,' he says, 'if you sat down and thought about it, you would cut your throat. So it's best to be the other way.'

I badly want to express my admiration for him but struggle to come up with a form of words that won't be patronising. By the time I've thought of something, Joe has long lost interest in anything but the match. Far away at the other end, we see Andy Cole hoof the ball wide. The desperate yelps of pain the Man City fans make suggest he should have scored.

It's noisy here, right in front of the Birmingham Road End, and Joe's Steve, sitting right in front of me in his wheelchair, tries to join in the chanting. It's the first words I've heard him utter. His voice is kind of squeaky: 'Come on, Albion!' and 'Come on, you Baggies.'

I sit next to Danny's wheelchair-pusher, Mick, with whom I got off to a slightly bad start. We talk a little, and he's already beginning to thaw when we score a fantastic goal from a great cross right in front of us. Mick and I leap to our feet, embracing each other. I clasp Steve by the shoulders. He grins up at me.

We hold on, and win. They have Andy Cole sent off. Joey Barton, who has a skirmish with our Ronnie Wallwork, is taunted by nearly everyone in the ground. His brother has just been sent down for murdering a black lad in Liverpool. Twenty thousand people sing, 'Where's your brother gone?' to the tune of 'Where's your mama gone?', the first line of 'Chirpy Chirpy Cheep Cheep'.

At the final whistle Mick stands up to go. As he walks away, with quite unspeakable tenderness he bids Steve goodbye and quickly strokes his chin. The other Steve, meanwhile, is lifted out of his seat by two stewards and carried back to his wheelchair.

Outside, as luck would have it, I bump into Ray, the big friendly Man City fan who watches me in bed with nothing on. He looks no less happy then he did in the pub before the game. 'We were rubbish, you murdered us,' he beams. 'See you tomorrow night,' he winks as we part company.

My phone buzzes with a text. It's from Sandra. 'Fanfuckingtastic.' I'd forgotten about Sandra. She wasn't here today. Selfishly, her husband has taken her to Prague for the weekend. It's the first home game she has missed since she can remember. I call her to hear that, happily, they found a sports bar but, unhappily, though it had Sky Sports on, there was no sound, because a load of Germans wanted the sound up on a Bundesliga game. 'So every time it went live to the Hawthorns, we couldn't hear what they were saying.'

I ask how she feels not being here now we've won. 'A bit odd, I suppose. Jealous, really,' she says.

I never mind having missed a game once it's over. Although I dread, really dread, not being there, once it's done and dusted I'm fine. If we've lost, I'm glad I wasn't there; if we've won, I'm so happy I don't give a toss about anything; and if we've drawn, it's somewhere between the two.

Dave Watkin goes home happy. And I, too, draw joy from such beautiful numerical symmetry. A reminder: though, irritatingly, we've scored two more goals (982) than we've conceded (980) in Dave's 750 consecutive games, we've drawn 200 of them, won 275 and lost 275.

Later, ruminating on the massive coincidence that Dave's numbers seem to represent, it dawns on me that it isn't necessarily so remarkable – it's just that Dave knows what his personal score is because he, for reasons he can't fully explain, has been keeping count. The fact is that we all have a personal score with the teams we support.

My first game was 27 April 1974, a 1-1 draw with Luton. I recently chanced upon an article about that game in a Luton Town programme. Luton won promotion that day and Eric Morecambe was thrown in the team bath. A crowd of 13,227 were there, this article informed me. My eyes fix on the last digit. If my granddad and I hadn't gone that day that last digit would be a '5' instead. There we are, my granddad and I. Even if only in that one attendance figure, statistically we're forever part of the club's history.

But since that day, how have I done as a fan? I call Dave, and Dave gets busy. Obviously I can't remember all the games I have attended, so I just ask him to count every match from that Luton game in 1974 up to and including today's famous 2-0 triumph over Man City. I'm fascinated to hear the result because I, like most football fans, consider myself hard done by by my club. I feel unlucky, but am I?

Dave is soon back in touch. Counting from that 1-1 with Luton, we have played 1573 matches. I wonder how many extra heartbeats the stress of those games has caused me. Of those 1573, we have lost 564, which is five, just five, short of the number of games we've won. Why does it feel like we've lost five hundred more than we've won? Even more incredibly, we've actually scored 2046 goals, twenty-two more than we've conceded. Rejoice.

Dave tells me that my Albion supporting career actually

peaked nearly a quarter of a century ago on Saturday, 2 May 1981, when we beat Spurs 4-2. 'It was on that day that the positive gap between Albion wins and defeats was at its widest.' Do you know, I felt sure at the time that win was a bit special. Finally, I know why.

Seven

Mark Reynolds, NZ, you can run but you can't hide

The Christmas period is a critical phase of the season. This year we are playing five times in sixteen days. The pressure on players and coaches is intense, but I don't feel very sorry for them as it's just as great on fans. We have to put families first, yet it is difficult to be fully festive when it's possible our teams will make or break their seasons, and, possibly, our hearts, with a good or bad run.

The pressure on me starts early. I am offered three tickets for a children's carol service at the Royal Albert Hall.

'Great,' I say, 'when?'

They are for the Saturday before Christmas. The Albion are at Portsmouth. What would be the right thing to do? Take my children to a carol service they'd really enjoy or take myself to a football match I almost certainly won't enjoy? I go to Fratton Park.

Before this I pay Vic and Brenda Stirrup a visit at home. There are cards and bits of tinsel and a tree. Brenda makes some tea and heats me up a mince pie while I get Vic's full life story. He has had a season ticket since 1925. In 1937 he and his dad cycled to Stoke to see us play. 'It was a twelve-hour round trip,' says Vic. 'We lost 10-3. Had a new goalkeeper called Light.'

Vic and his dad before him had a newsagents and sweet shop, 'So money was never a problem. Mind you, the prices were different then.' I ask if his dad missed many matches. 'Not when he was alive, no. He used to miss away matches sometimes.'

Once Vic got going on his endless run of games, his dad was left minding the family business. 'He looked after the shop and we had a lady who worked there, too. The matches I missed were Nottingham Forest, after I had my hip operation. I would have gone to that but I needed to be in the directors' box and the secretary, Mr Evans, couldn't get me a ticket. I still went up the reserves though. Other than that, missed two at Ipswich and two at Norwich.'

I ask him if it's significant that four of the five games he missed were in East Anglia, but he just mutters something about the lady who minded the shop being off sick.

'The year 1935 was a bad one,' he remembers. 'We got to the cup final but lots of tickets were sent back because the manager didn't play Arthur Gale. He'd scored in every round.' We lost to Sheffield Wednesday.

Soon war got in the way. 'I was in the Dorset Regiment when I first enlisted. I'd been there about twelve months and they were asking for volunteers to man merchant ships when they came into port. And when they were ready to sail, they'd take you off and put you in barracks. It went on like that for about three or four months. And I said to my mate, Dubby his name was, I said, Dubby, I think this is a good thing this is. So we volunteered.

'Well, it was all right for six months. Then one day the carpenter of the ship came into our cabin and started measuring up. We still had all our own army kit and our own rifles. He said, I've got to find somewhere here to put a rack up for your kit and your rifle. I said, what's that all about? I shall only be on a couple of days. He said, oh no, I'm afraid you're coming on every trip with us now.

'I didn't come home for about four or five years. I kept in touch with the Albion, though. I got a diary somewhere where I used to put down how they got on. We got it over the radio, or in letters. They used to play everybody in those days, in the war.

'When I got back, the first thing I did was renew my season ticket. Oh, it was great. It was then I really started following them. Me and me dad used to go, we had four season tickets. Me dad, me mum, me and me oldest brother. Then Mum and Dad stopped going, but I carried on.

'When we went away we'd go mostly by train. I'll never forget when we used to go to Sunderland or Newcastle. We'd catch the ten past ten train from New Street on the night and used to arrive in Newcastle about six o'clock next morning. We used to do that regularly.'

'What did you do on the train all night?'

'Sleep,' he says.

'One time we drew Gateshead in the cup but we played it at Newcastle. And it was the time the king died. When we got to Durham we could see all the flags at half mast and I thought, Well, we'll get there and the match will be off, but the match was played anyway.'

'Who did you go to that match with?' asks Brenda suddenly.

'Meself,' says Vic. 'But as soon as I come out the station at Newcastle, this bloke shouted to me, "Are you that Vic?" It turned out he was from round here and used to come in the shop, but he was living in Newcastle at the time.

'I often used to get back late and be in the shop at four in the morning. I used to go straight into the shop sometimes.'

It was after the war that Vic got together with Brenda. 'She lived opposite the shop. I used to see her in the pram,' he says quite warmly, though it's an odd thought, young Vic and tiny Brenda in a pram, getting married one day.

Brenda says: 'I was only two when we came to live in this road. The shop was already there then. I'd grown up with that shop, so he watched me grow up from a little one really, you know. I don't know, we gradually got together.'

'Did you know he was an Albion fan?'

'Oh, yeah, everybody knew.'

'My wife's never complained since we got married,' says Vic appreciatively. 'Mind you, we didn't get married until I was in my forties. At Smethwick Council House. Had to postpone it 'cos the Albion were a-playing. Put it off from Saturday until Monday week.' Brenda looks at him, apparently without malice.

I ask if she ever gets fed up with it. 'Well, I do sometimes because it seems that Saturday and Sunday nights I just sit here on my own, you know. Not as we do anything when we're in but I do sometimes think, Oh, here we go again. But that's only since the kids have grown up and gone. It didn't matter when they were small because the house was always full of them. I'd just go as far as I could walk with the pram or down the park. Luckily we'd got parks by us. So we just used to go. My mum only lived up the road so I spent a lot of time up there, you know, when they was little.'

I ask what her parents thought of Vic. 'Not a lot sometimes,' says Brenda with a little snort. 'My dad used to say he shouldn't be going off all the time, he should be at home with the kids. Sometimes on a Saturday I had the three kids and I still had to go and sell the *Sports Argus* outside the pub.

'Occasionally I did mind being left on my own when I didn't even know where he was. 'Cos he'd go from the shop and I knew he was going to a football match but then I'd think, Where is he? And I had to get the paper and have a look where they were play-ing to find out whether he was home or away.'

Vic seems to have tuned out of the discussion a bit. Anxious not to have provoked an argument between them, I say I suppose that in those days men went to the football and women just looked after the kids. That was the way it was.

'Yeah, that's the way it was,' Brenda says. 'But I suppose as the children grow up and do their own thing, you get left, like, don't you?'

'All in all,' I say to Vic, 'you've got away with it one way or another, haven't you?'

'No, she's been very good. Very good indeed,' he says kindly.

'Daft, I suppose,' says Brenda.

'I've seen it in her face sometimes,' says Vic.

'But you just ignore it?' I say.

'That's right,' he sniggers. But Brenda laughs, too.

I ask Vic if he has ever gone through a phase of thinking why's he bothering.

'No, no. Never.'

'No,' agrees Brenda. 'He's never thought like that. Football's got a magnet, hasn't it?' She almost seems to be apologising for him, as if it's something the poor man just can't help.

I ask Vic what'll keep him away from the matches, then? 'A wooden box,' he says. Brenda laughs and says, 'Sometimes he's been ill. Oooh, he's been dying here. Men. They get a cold, they've got pneumonia. And he's been here going, oh dear, I'm miserable, and I always tell him, you'll be better tomorrow. And come the next day, he's off to the match and he's been a dying duck here on the Friday. Always better by the Saturday.

'Now that's what bugs me,' she continues, getting into her flow now. 'When he's sitting here and he'll say, I dunno, I've got to go all the way to Newcastle, all that long way in the coach. And I say, who says you've got to go? Who's dragging you to that coach and putting you on it and saying you've got to go to Newcastle?'

She has raised her voice but Vic is grinning like a naughty child, ashamed but proud.

'Who is dragging you?' she demands. 'Yourself, that's who!'

Vic sniggers and Brenda rolls her eyes and laughs.

145

Saturday, 17 December 2005, Portsmouth away

This is down as a must-win game. You have many 'must-win' games when you're at the bottom. Last season every other game seemed to be a 'must-win' game, most of which we lost. A week after one 'must-win' game, my Auntie Barbara said to me that she'd heard we 'had to win' that game. She was puzzled because, though we hadn't won the game, as far as she could see nothing had changed. There had been no actual, tangible punishment for not winning. I tried to explain but ended up confusing myself as to why it was we said we 'had' to win this one even though it didn't matter conclusively in the end that we hadn't.

Almost a year on, though, we all agree that this is a must-win. We are six points ahead of Portsmouth who are third bottom. They have their old manager back, Harry Redknapp, and might now go on a little winning run. But if we win, we'll be nine points ahead of them. We've got to win. And I've got to be here.

Comfortingly, I am surrounded by friends. Next to me, Yvonne: the slightly built middle-aged lady who I met on the coach to Man City for the first game of the season. At the end of the row behind: Dale the singer who bust a gut at Old Trafford. As usual, he's screaming his head off. Two rows in front: Nathan, who was probably having sex with a woman twenty years older than him somewhere in the Black Country only twelve hours ago. A tap on the shoulder – it's Vic Stirrup; four feet eleven inches of frozen pensioner grinning happily out from under his hat. I know I should be with my family, but these people feel more like family all the time.

We control the first half and come nowhere near either scoring or conceding. The language today is really terrible, worse than usual. Darren Carter, scorer of the wonder goal against Arsenal two months ago, is a substitute. As he warms up right next to us, one of our number shouts at him, quite slowly and very clearly, 'Sit down, Carter, you useless cunt.' It's otherwise quiet so the poor lad must hear this, but he doesn't flinch. I ask lovely, demure, petite, mature, shivering Yvonne if she ever notices the bad language, or does she just not hear it. 'I heard that,' she says quietly.

At half-time a blind bloke I know is led past me towards the toilet. 'Haven't created a single bloody chance,' he grumbles in a tone as bitter as the weather. I see Jadeen Singh, too. She is so cold she's almost unable to speak. She goes for a hot chocolate but the queue's too long. She queues for a pee instead. I ask Nathan if he got his leg over last night. 'No,' he says, 'unusually I didn't. I did get a call from a woman in Pensnett at half-two but I told her I couldn't be bothered. Had an early start. She offered to come and pick me up actually.' So for the same reason my kids didn't get to a carol concert today, a woman from Pensnett didn't have sexual relations with Nathan.

Second half. It gets colder. We make a defensive mistake and concede a goal right in front of us. We get worse. We lose. Terrible game, terrible ground, terrible result and terribly, terribly cold. Another must-win not won, or even drawn, but lost. Sometimes God moves in mysterious ways, but in this case He didn't. I really should have gone to that carol concert.

Christmas Day is a good day. For minutes at a time I forget to worry about what kind of tonking we are going to get at Old Trafford tomorrow. The fixture list is a daunting sight this Christmas: after Manchester United on Boxing Day, we play Spurs at home. Then we're at Anfield on New Year's Eve and then there's a derby against Aston Villa on 2 January.

Boxing Day 2005, Manchester United away

I have to leave home at 8.30 a.m. My going has been the subject of tense negotiations for several weeks. Jane has only given me permission to attend on the understanding that I give a firm commitment never again to go to a football match on Boxing Day.

It's crazy. I have no hope of a result but, for that reason alone, it seems especially important that I should be there. To miss it would be like not visiting an ailing aunt at Christmas. It's times like this the Albion need me.

Many others feel the same away. On Christmas Eve I called Stan Pagett, who I know struggles to afford the away trips. Stan, who's fifty, told me that as well as working nine to five at a manu-facturing company, he also works nights at a call centre to soften the blow of ticket prices. And he has done so for nine years. I really, really love the Albion, but would I work nights as well as days for nine years to afford to go? Er, no.

If you have had to struggle that hard to afford the tickets, then how on earth do you cope with disappointment on the pitch? I devote an awful lot of time and emotional energy to the Albion and I feel incredibly miserable and angry when they let me down. If I'd been working hard days' nights to scrape together the money to watch players who then didn't seem to be trying for me, I'm not sure I could be responsible for my actions. When I offered Stan a spare ticket for this match, he accepted it without a moment's hesitation. 'Do you not want to check with your family first?' I asked. It is Boxing Day, after all. 'No,' he said, 'I'll have it.'

I drive to the Hawthorns where I'm going to pick up the coach. Dave Holloway, the coach king, is sweating profusely with the stress of it all, but finally we are all aboard and on our way. Our driver's name, deliciously, is Mr Pastry. I ask Dave what the Albion means to him. He shrugs and says: 'Everything.'

He went to his first match when he was seven in September 1970 and by the time he was in his teens he was going regularly. 'In February 1976 I missed the home game against Bristol Rovers because I got the flu and my mum wouldn't let me go. But I haven't missed a home game since. In fact Vicky, my missus, was born in seventy-seven, so I actually haven't missed a home game in Vicky's lifetime.

'My ambition was always to go to all forty-two league games in a season. It used to be forty-two, remember? Lovely number, wasn't it? And in '83/4 I thought because I didn't have to work Saturday mornings, right I'm going to do it. I went to the away games on the coaches and at the end of the season they said to me they didn't have anyone to run the travel next season and would I have a bash at it. So I thought about it and said, yeah, go on, I'll give it twelve months. And I'm still here.'

I remember seeing Dave's name in the programme when I was a teenager. He was always in there as Dave 'Mammoth' Holloway, the man you needed to call if you wanted to be at the away game the following week. With such a name, and such a role, I much admired him from afar, especially as I hardly ever went to those games.

'Thanks very much for that,' he says when I remind him of the Mammoth bit. 'It was from school and word got out that that was my nickname, so when they picked a name for the travel they called it Mammoth Tours after me. But we dropped it in '95 because we sort of became part of the club and you can't call the official supporters' coach Mammoth Travel, can you?'

When I ask him if he's had any travel trouble he looks for some wood to touch and says, 'Had the odd bump but nothing really bad. Millwall used to be the place. No matter what time you started out you always missed the first twenty minutes. Sunderland's the bogey ground now, coach six caught fire on the way there this year.

'I get really pissed off when we lose, though, and really, really pissed off when people start cancelling. In about 1990 we played Newcastle at home midweek and we lost 5-1. Then we were playing Ipswich on the Saturday and I had so many cancellations. I started getting really, like, shirty with them. And when I was on the way to Ipswich I was thinking I'd just love to come here and win and that lot would have missed it. But we didn't, we lost 3-1. I hated that.'

Organising the coaches serves a valuable psychological purpose for Dave: 'The thing for me is I am a worrier, right, I really worry about the Albion but I can't worry about two things at once. So, having to worry about the coaches, I don't worry about the Albion. I've done it now for twenty-one years but every match day I wake up with butterflies, not about the football – that's up to the players – no, I worry about the coaches. I just want the coaches to be spot on because I take it all personally. They're my babies.'

The partially sighted lad I was with at West Ham, Liam, and his dad Paul, are coming to Old Trafford, too. Paul tells me that they left home quite sure we'd get stuffed. Then, on the journey to the ground, they decided a draw might be possible. Now he is just beginning to wonder that maybe, maybe, we could actually win.

I sit next to Alan Cleverley. Also on board are the father and brother of our Danish full-back Martin Albrechtsen. The brother looks the image of our player. He doesn't take his headphones off during the entire journey. Laraine Astle, Jeff's widow, sits a few rows behind. And there are the Rimmer brothers: Roger, who was the club doctor for many years, and his brother, who is also of advancing years. They keep their coats on for the whole trip and look thoroughly content.

A video is shown, highlights of a famous victory we once had at Old Trafford – our last win there almost exactly twenty-seven years ago to the day. As every Albion fan knows, we win 5-3. Each time we score, Alan takes out an old-fashioned wooden rattle and waves it about. He says we're going to win today with a late goal. He always thinks we'll win. He knows nothing.

As the coach gets closer to the ground, we edge through thickening crowds of Man Utd fans. We look at them in wonder; they look at us in wonder. They simply can't understand what it's like to support a team as crap as ours. We simply can't understand how they can support a team like Man Utd and be taken seriously. How can we know they mean it? How can we know they're for real? And how can they begin to understand our motivation? We baffle each other; we quite pity each other. Alan looks out of the window and then at me and says, with the quiet satisfaction of a man who knows he speaks the truth, 'One of our wins is worth

150

twenty of theirs.' Precisely. In this context I start to feel rather sorry for them.

An Asian family stand just near the turnstiles. There are three blokes and a little kid, about nine years old. The kid and two of the blokes are clad in obviously newly purchased Man Utd regalia. The bloke who isn't in Man Utd kit tells me he is an Albion fan, but points at his son and says, 'He isn't, he's Man Utd.'

'What went wrong?'

'Don't know,' he says, shaking his head sadly. 'I took him to nearly every game one season and after one time we lost he just came home, went into his bedroom, threw his shirt on the floor and said, "That's it, I'm not supporting them any more."'

I'm ashamed to feel some loathing for the poor child, but I also have a grudging admiration for his good sense in realising that Albion would bring him more misery than joy. I can't help thinking of all the trouble it would have saved me if I'd done the same thing at his age.

Dale is inside the ground talking to his parents, Jim and Chris. The tickets to this match are his Christmas present to them, and they seem happy about it. I ask him if having his folks here will cramp his singing style. He nods sheepishly. Then I ask Jim if he used to sing his head off when he was Dale's age. Jim nods sheepishly, too.

My seat is just in front of Vic Stirrup's, and Danny Grainger's here as well, the lad who told me about his dad crying at Jeff Astle's funeral. Danny and his mate Tom, both fourteen, have come up on their own on the coaches with us. They tell me how they play football and do refereeing but how they couldn't do much more of either or it would get in the way of the Albion.

The match kicks off and United control the game. One of our best players, Paul Robinson, a full-back, is deployed to man-mark Wayne Rooney, one of the best players in the world. For a short time it seems to work, but then Robinson is stretchered off with concussion. Shortly afterwards United score.

151

The atmosphere becomes unpleasant. A kid in front of me keeps standing up, his young face twisted with rage. He makes obscene gestures at the whole body of home support generally and, apparently, certain individuals who he has established eye contact with. He keeps jabbing his fingers at them, calls them cunts over and over again and gestures to them that they might care to step outside. Goodwill to all men.

Suddenly everyone turns around to watch one of our lot at the back being dragged out by several policemen. Something gets thrown into the home fans. Then, just before half-time, they score again and calm descends. In the interval some spirited drinking takes place and drifts on well into the second half. The Super Singhs are all here. Gurdial, who is rapidly becoming one of my favourite people in the world, buys me some beer. I tell her about the Asian lad I met outside who ditched the Albion at the age of seven. Gurdial looks at her daughter and says, 'I would have given him a good hiding.'

Some more Asians appear – Gurdial's cousins. They are really quite drunk. One of them, her cousin's son-in-law, says, 'I'm keeping quiet', and shows me his mobile phone. On it as a screensaver is the Manchester United club crest. In the Gents a bloke spots me as he turns away from the urinal. He smiles but as he goes to shake my hand he thinks better of it, withdraws his hand, and goes to wash and dry it, before returning to complete the formalities.

By the time I finish this conversation, another bloke has spotted me. He's very big and very drunk. In one movement he turns away from the urinal and without ceremony, hand-washing, or even zipping up his flies, he gives me a big damp hug.

I consider not watching the second half. How much more rewarding would it be just to hang around here with hundreds of others drinking beer and eating lukewarm pies? Many people take that option, but I go back in. I find myself a seat next to a bloke with what I take to be his daughter sitting on his lap. She is no more than eighteen months old. She's well wrapped up against the cold and is sucking on a large bottle of milk. She stares at the match without interest.

I ask her father how often he brings her. 'Usually,' he says.

'Doesn't she get fed up?'

'Fidgets a bit sometimes.'

Man U score again. All hope is gone now for sure.

For some reason the coaches' police escort doesn't materialise, so it takes us ages to get away from the ground. Dave says it's normally more fun on the coach when we've lost. 'I do find that winning tires you out more than losing, 'cos you're usually hanging on for the last half an hour or so and it knackers you up, doesn't it? One of the best trips we ever had was when we lost 5-0 at Charlton. We had a great day out. And we've had some wins when nobody says a thing on the way back.'

I am sure he's right, but on this journey nobody says a word. It is eight o'clock by the time we get back to the Hawthorns. It's nearly ten by the time I'm back home in London – eleven hours after I left. I'm quietly grateful I'll never again be allowed to attend a Boxing Day football match thanks to the agreement I struck with my wife. I hope she enforces it rigorously.

Wednesday, 28 December 2005, Spurs at home

I travel up with Garth Pearce, my good friend who interviews film stars for a living. He's from the Black Country but now lives in Berkshire. We meet at a hotel off Junction 4 of the M40 at High Wycombe. He gets out of his BMW and into my Volvo. He smells expensive, as usual. Even his breath smells expensive.

Garth once interviewed Pamela Anderson in Los Angeles at the very same time that we were playing Birmingham City. He could think of nothing but the Albion. He credits the considerable success he has had in his life to the club. 'For example,' he says, 'without Derek Kevan I would never have passed my eleven-plus.

In 1958 I went to my first Black Country derby, Albion versus Wolves, with my dad and Uncle Fred. It was supposed to be a treat before the big exam. Wolves were then the best team in the country. The ground was packed. It was 1-1, the game was virtually over and I can remember Uncle Fred saying, "At least this is one of my draws on the coupon." Then the Wolves right-back passed back to the goalkeeper, Finlayson. The pass fell short and Derek Kevan, my personal hero, slipped in between them to wallop the ball into the net from about eighteen yards. We were right in line with it, so as soon as he struck it I knew it was a goal. The final whistle went within a minute. For the next few days, I floated into a state of self-belief I've never quite recaptured. I supported the champions of the Black Country and anything was possible. I remember going in to the eleven-plus exam the following Wednesday saying to myself that if Derek Kevan can score in the last minute to beat the Wolves, then I can pass my eleven-plus and get to grammar school. I did.

'About ten years ago I sat next to big Kev at a supporters' club lunch. I recounted this little tale and his golden goal. He said he didn't remember a thing about it.'

Tonight it's freezing cold and there appears to be no prospect of a result. Several key players are out injured and everyone winces and/or rolls their eyes when they hear the team news. All hope is comprehensively abandoned. I go into the supporters' club in what is somewhat absurdly branded the Banqueting Suite of the Hawthorns pub next door. Everyone who makes eye contact with me seems to be saying the same thing about the Boxing Day game at Man U: 'Fookin' shit, wor' it?'

'What about tonight?' I ask.

Hopeless shrugs all around.

There is a fan called Mark from Guildford who often drinks in here. He's got a proper south-east accent and no connection with the Midlands at all. 'So why do you support us?' I ask.

He shrugs.

'Well, you must have some idea.'

'To be honest, I think it's 'cos when I was a kid they just used to lose all the time, so I felt sorry for them.'

Tonight we're all feeling sorry for ourselves.

Emma calls. She is a teacher in a prison in Worcestershire. Every time I have spoken to her before a home game this season we've won – against Arsenal, Everton and Man City. Now we speak again and, ludicrously, I feel a bit more hopeful.

One-legged Kev is having terrible trouble with what he refers to as his stump. He's looking ahead to the Aston Villa match next Monday with as much venom as everyone else is looking back at Man Utd. 'Hate the Villa,' he says, 'hate 'em. Fookin' hate 'em.'

I'm meeting Steve Hayden in the ground. Since being diagnosed with leukaemia two days before the start of the season, this is only the third game he's been to. The chemotherapy and radiotherapy worked but also shot his immune system to pieces so he got pneumonia. They've been bombarding him with drugs to help him through that but it has taken for ever. Now, finally, it looks like he is past the worst of it and can go for the bone marrow transplant that should cure him.

He can't be in the pub now because he's been told to keep away from smoke. His dad has got him and a friend seats in a box and I join them there. I last saw him two and a half months ago and I'm frightened of being shocked by his frailty. I fight my way through a fug of smoke in the corridor to get to the box.

Steve is taller than I remember, probably because he never stood up for very long when I was with him in the hospital. And now there is much more colour in his cheeks. I'm relieved for him, and myself, I suppose. I tell him I'll be back for the second half as my dad's come tonight for the first time in ages and I'll sit with him for the first half.

My dad is a lapsed fan. He was passionate once but now just kind of looks out for us in a disinterested way. He finds my commitment to the cause rather pathetic, I think.

'I remember going during the war,' he tells me. 'I think they played Birmingham City. And then I started going to all the home games with my father. He'd sit me on the wall and stay with me until half an hour before the kick-off, then he'd go up to the back.'

'So you went to every home game?' I ask. I'm incredulous really that he was so keen because now, even though he always asks how we've got on, it never seems to noticeably affect his mood.

'Every home game, yes, I loved it,' he says.

'So why stop?' I demand. 'Why haven't I stopped?'

'Well, we moved house, I married your mother, I was working on Saturday mornings, and didn't really want to get the car out.'

So, in short, he couldn't be bothered to go any more. Why is it that I've always been bothered to go? 'Well, you've got the passion for it, haven't you? Just like my father. I suppose I can't have had the passion and that's the end of it.'

I work out that he stopped going when he was about twenty-seven. As I am desperately close to forty, I suspect that the moment has now passed. I ask him if he thinks my feelings are rather silly. 'Well, yes,' he says, 'but you've got the passion for it.'

What about the cup finals?

'Never went to a cup final, your granddad had the ticket.'

'Quite right,' I say.

'Why?' my dad blurts, quite indignantly.

'Because he had the passion and you didn't,' I say. Harsh, I know, but it seems to me that my granddad was the more deserving case.

'The other thing,' he says after a pause, in a confessional tone, 'is that I didn't like losing.'

'But who does?'

'No,' he continues, 'I really hated it; it made me miserable.' And then, rather darkly, he adds, 'I didn't like the person it turned me into.'

Blimey. My father the axe murderer; it's a sobering thought. Perhaps it's for the best that he did stay away.

As we kick off against Tottenham the abuse, as usual, starts to fly about from all sides. Someone calls Edgar Davids a cheating twat when he pretends he's been fouled in the penalty area. The chap behind us shouts, 'Spurs – you're a fucking disgrace.' Dad laughs as if it's all good-natured stuff, as he might at a pantomime audience booing and hissing and shouting, 'Behind you.'

This irritates me, but maybe he's right. Maybe that's the best way to view all this nonsense: as mere pantomime. On fans' websites reference is often made to the 'banter' between opposing fans but it always sounds more menacing than banter to me. You'd have to be deaf – which my dad more or less is, actually – to miss the genuine seam of hatred running through the whole business.

His football vocabulary is stuck somewhere in the late fifties or early sixties. When we execute a neat sequence of passes in the Spurs penalty area, he gets a bit excited and says, 'Ooh, good one. Good one', with each pass completed. Another nice move has him saying, 'Good 'un that was. Good 'un.'

At the other end someone gives the ball away in our penalty area. 'Oh my gawd,' he groans, 'oh my gawd.' Then we have a near miss: 'Ooh, bloody hell!' exclaims Dad. He's like an extra in a crowd scene in a film about football as it used to be played.

Another Spurs player takes a dive in the penalty area, but the more vitriolic the abuse gets, the more Dad laughs at it – although his laugh's becoming a little hollow as he realises that a lot of those around us really do mean it.

Losing concentration a bit, he starts to drop in bits of domestic news from the home front. Just as we mount an unsuccessful little attack, he tells me that a friend of the family's is now out of hospital. I grunt, trying to convey my interest in and gratitude for this news. Then he tells me something about some building work that is going well. Then we score. And I'm thrilled to see that he has not lost the knack of celebrating a goal. He's on his feet, cheering and clapping his hands.

At half-time, on the way up to Steve's box, I look at the Albion and Spurs supporters milling around in the Smethwick End of the ground. They're now apparently oblivious to each other. There is no sense at all that five minutes ago they were exchanging vile abuse. Perhaps my dad's right to see it all as mere banter. After all, if it was more serious then why would it stop just because it was half-time? The more I think about it the more this peaceful interval seems to give the lie to the nastiness before and after it. It's actually rather ludicrous that for this fifteen-minute period everyone gives the obscene language and gestures a rest and goes for a pie or a piss or just a quiet chat instead. Did anyone ever get done for violent conduct or bad language at half-time? I doubt it. Suddenly all the passion and torment's started to feel a bit synthetic.

But as if to remind me that genuine baser instincts are in play, once in Steve's box I'm appalled to find that the other lad in there, Steve's mate, is a Spurs fan. I just can't bear sitting with anyone but my own. Then I remember that there are, arguably, more important factors in play here than tribal loyalty. I ask Steve when he'll be going in for his transplant. 'The Sunday after Reading,' he says. The day after that game, then, the first Saturday of the year, Steve's life will be saved by a bone marrow transplant. But for the moment I can feel life and goodness being breathed into his blood cells simply by virtue of him being here. He just can't stop smiling. The box feels almost as hermetically sealed as the isolation ward he's been in for the last four months. 'I'd love to be out there in the fresh air,' he says, 'but this'll do.'

Throughout the second half we talk about the Albion and about leukaemia, chemotherapy, anti-bacterial drugs, anti-fungal drugs, bone marrow and associated topics. This running dialogue about his fight for life makes it difficult to suspend disbelief about the game. What with all these reminders that football isn't about life and death, it becomes quite hard to pretend that it is.

I am reminded of a scene in *When Harry Met Sally* when Billy Crystal and his mate are at some sports event talking about love and marriage and deep and meaningful things. They continue this discourse as a Mexican wave goes round. When the wave comes round to them, they stand and put their arms in the air without breaking the conversation.

Steve is telling me how exceptionally severe his case of pneumonia has been when he suddenly groans, 'Oh, Greening, how much time does he want on it? Just put the cross in.' And without a breath he continues: 'A lot of the doctors congratulated me. They said that some patients who'd had it as bad as me didn't survive.'

I have a moment, only a moment, to take this in before we score again. Incongruously, Steve and I dance about embracing each other, celebrating nothing but the goal. His survival is insignificant at that moment.

After Spurs have kicked off again and the singing has died down a bit, Steve says, 'Kanu is just brilliant when he's playing well. They've had to wait until I'm strong enough before they do the transplant or the operation would kill me. I would die.'

The Reverend Ken texts me. He can't be here because he's in East Anglia for his daughter's wedding: 'no signal on my phone. this is my daughter's no. any score yet? Ken.'

I text back: 'Winning 2-0. Half an hour left. We're doomed.'

But we win.

Emma calls again. Speaking to her before the match seems to have done the trick once more. I tell her I've got her number saved in my mobile as Mystic Emma. She laughs and promises to call again before the Villa game on Monday.

It's late now, driving home, but I need to share my joy with more people, so I call Mark Reynolds in New Zealand. Mark, a nurse, lives in a little fishing village called Raglan near Hamilton. He has been in New Zealand for eight years and is married with two children. He's really happy there, although he does miss the Albion. Having said that, part of the reason he's so happy is precisely because he is where he is.

He told me once: 'I was really passionate. For years I went home and away. It was a massive part of my life. It still is, but in a different way obviously. Back at home life used to be dictated by the Albion schedule. My wife used to get really pissed off with it. She's happier now. I'm happier now – my life is better. It's better because this is a great place to live but it's also better because I'm so far away from the Albion.

'Drink got to be a bit of a problem. My life was going in a completely different direction. I was getting to the stage when away games were just a huge booze-up. I really don't miss that travelling home when you've lost. On your way there you've got that nice looking-forward-to-it feeling. On the way back when you've lost it's kind of . . .'

' . . . miserable?'

'Miserable. I still like a drink, don't get me wrong, but it's much more under control now.'

I said he should advertise in the *Evening Mail* or the match-day programme: 'Leave the Albion behind. Sort yourself out. Start a new life in New Zealand.' The idea appealed to me. It might be the best way to get the Albion out of my hair; it might be the answer. 'It didn't feel like the answer last season when we survived,' he said. 'I so wanted to be there. I was so happy, though, I just cried and cried.

'I've got Sky so see all the games. Even get some of them live. It's really weird. I'm watching them live and my brother's texting me from the ground. For Saturday afternoon kick-offs, it's usually about three in the morning here. I always go to bed as normal on Saturday night but in the early hours of Sunday morning I wake up automatically. If it's a big game, I wake up for kick-off. If it's not such a big game or we're not doing so well, I'll wake up for half-time. My wife calls it my secret life.'

Tonight Mark's wife answers the phone. His brother and sister-in-law are over, so they watched the match in the morning and now the two brothers are out playing golf. 'He's chuffed to bits,' says Mrs Reynolds, sounding genuinely pleased for him.

Rev Ken texts me again: 'Brilliant.' And from Sandra: 'Fanfuckingtastic.'

Saturday, 31 December 2005, Liverpool away

The fixture list has been kind to me for the last match of the calendar year. Each June when it's published I scan it anxiously, worrying not about the results but about how I'm going to swing it to get to the games. This one has been a doddle, though, as Jane's mum and dad live in Liverpool and she can hardly turn down the opportunity of visiting them. Also, on Monday we're at home to Villa, so we can go to that one on the way back to London. Great.

I have two tickets for the Albion end at Liverpool. I was hoping Jane wouldn't want to come. She was raised a Liverpool fan and used to go to Anfield with her dad Ray, though more recently she has supported the Albion with me. Now I couldn't bear the thought of sitting in the away end with her. If she so much as clapped a Liverpool move, I would, I'm ashamed to say, hate her for it. And she would probably get fed up with our fans chanting abuse at scousers.

Alan Hansen has helped me out. He's got me two tickets with the home fans. Problem: this means I'll have to sit with Liverpool fans. Unthinkable. Thankfully, though, Jane's dad, twenty years after he stopped going, has decided he wants to come. And Alan's said he'll pick them up. Maureen, my mother-in-law, is impressed. Jane says that her dad 'wouldn't be impressed if you told him Bill Shankly was coming to pick him up'. Before I leave for the game, I ask Ray if he has ever had a lift off a European Cup winner before. He has a think, shakes his head, and says he hasn't.

I get the train into Liverpool from Crosby to meet some of our lot. As I am walking from Central Station to the pub they're in near Lime Street, a young chap walks past me. He gives me a thumbs-up and says, 'Hello, mate. You're that cunt off the telly, aren't you?'

'Yes,' I say.

In a Wetherspoons aircraft hangar of a pub there is a smattering of football fans among a majority of blank-looking shoppers. Sandra and Kate are here, and so are Nathan and Pete the former fireman.

'Nathan only had an hour and half's sleep last night,' says Sandra, raising her eyes.

'I think I might have fallen asleep on the bog,' says Nathan, by way of clarification. 'I lost two hours somewhere.'

'You'll never guess what else he did,' says Sandra.

'What?'

'It's horrible. It's nothing to do with sex.'

'Go on.'

Kate winces.

'Well,' begins Nathan.

Kate buries her head in her hands. 'I can't bear to listen to this again.'

'On the way home last night,' he continues, 'I needed the toilet, so I went in an estate agent's doorway.' He looks at me happily, with the usual mixture of shame and triumph on his face. I still can't quite see what the fuss is, but then it dawns on me: 'Not a number two, surely?'

He nods.

I meet Rich outside the away end. I called him yesterday to offer him my spare ticket. I last saw him at Old Trafford when he and Dale were trying, in vain, to get the singing going. Having given up painting and decorating, he can't afford to go to many away games. So, the day before New Year's Eve, I rang to offer him my spare ticket. 'Yes,' he said, without hesitating, 'I'll have it.' Twenty-four hours before the New Year's Eve celebrations start and he is dropping whatever plans he hasn't made to somehow get on a bus to Anfield and watch the Albion lose. It's his top priority.

When I told Jane about this conversation, and how sorry I felt for him, she said, 'The trouble with you is that you only ever seem to feel compassion for people who happen to be Albion fans. Why don't you start a charity for distressed throstles?'

I hand Rich the ticket. He asks, evenly, 'How much do I owe you for this?' I know he can't afford to give me anything; he knows I know he can't afford to give me anything; and we both know the deal is that it's his for nothing.

'Nothing at all,' I say, 'happy new year.'

I take my seat between an anxious looking Rich and a black bloke who, it turns out, is a prison officer called Bernie. He has a little boy on his knee. Bernie's parents are from the West Indies, 'one from Grenada, one from Trinidad. My granddad – he's seventy-five or seventy-six now – came over in the fifties. So he must have been one of the first. Mum came over when she was twelve.

'It was a school pal of mine who got me started on the Albion. One of the first matches I can remember was when we played Millwall and had to turn around a three-nil deficit in the League Cup. Oh God, they were fighting on the pitch and everything was playing up. We scored five on the night. I was thirteen, I think. A year later I started saving up my paper round money to go, and used to go on my own.'

Bernie is, I think, the first black West Brom fan I've ever really met. This is pretty odd given our proud record of introducing black players to the British game. It's a point I make to Bernie. 'Well, you say that, but I think they should get an Asian playing now and just exploit it, because there are just loads around West Brom.

'As a young kid, the truth of the matter is that the racism was there but it was on the surface. Does that make sense? Whereas nowadays I believe that there's still quite a bit of it going round but people are frightened to say it. They weren't frightened to say it then. Certainly at the Albion, because we had Cyrille and so on, I didn't hear it a great deal. But I remember going to watch the Villa, because I was just mad for football, and hearing it there and thinking, Oh, we don't hear that at West Brom.'

His son lives in Hull. 'He was born there,' explains Bernie. 'I met his mother in Ibiza. I was playing away, if you know what I mean.' I make some rather macho understanding noises as if I've played away a bit myself. Somehow Bernie's managed to keep his son following the Albion. 'He had a bit of a wobble when he was about five, saying, my friend supports Man Utd, can I have a Man Utd top? and so on. I said, son, you can have any top you like but

I won't buy it for you. And to be honest that was the last of it. And since then he's been very much Albion.' Bernie might use the same tone of voice one day to explain how his son struggled at school for a time but found his feet eventually.

Bernie is a prison officer working in the gym at Her Majesty's Prison Birmingham. It's in Winson Green, so is known simply as 'the Green'. As with most middle-class white boys, something fearful and fascinated stirs within me whenever I pass a prison. And I used to pass the Green an awful lot when I was a kid, as my dad's scaffolding business was just round the corner.

I worked at the firm for a while with a huge man called Ray Povey. Raymond William Anthony Povey. He was easily the hardest man I have ever associated with. He looked a bit like Kevin Keegan's bigger, badder, taller, stronger, more-tattooed older brother. He lifted a twenty-one-foot scaffold pole like it was a snooker cue. He'd been in the odd bit of bother in his time but, in his own way, he was magnificent. And he was my mate.

One day, out delivering scaffolding, Ray was telling me what a big Albion fan he was when he first spent time in Winson Green and how he had a picture of Colin Suggett on his wall. Since then I've never driven past the place without worrying there's some poor Albion fan incarcerated there – barely two miles from the ground, yet so far away. Villa and Birmingham fans, of course, I couldn't give a monkey's about.

I ask Bernie if the inmates know he is an Albion fan. He's got this incredible laugh, by the way, that goes a bit like this: 'Hee hee hee hee hee hee hee hee.' The 'hees' come out very quickly, though, like out of a machine gun.

'Hee hee hee hee hee hee hee hee,' he says. 'When I was at Belmarsh they used to call me West Brom! They all know. If there's one thing they know about me, they know I'm an Albion fan. It doesn't cause problems, it's good banter. If you've got a good relationship with them, it's good banter.

'At the moment we've got a few of them in – when we played the Villa last year, there was quite a bit of trouble and at least eight or ten from each side got sent down. Most of them were still in when we next played Villa, betting Mars Bars with each other on the game. That was quite amusing.

'There's one Albion fan we had in, now I know you shouldn't stereotype people, but he was the most unlikely kind of football fan, let alone an Albion fan. When we beat Tranmere five, he'd obviously been released and we spotted each other. His son was there with him. He was boinging and his long dreadlocks were going all over the place, and I just thought, That's quality.'

'So what was he in for?'

'Oh, a few attempted murders, I think, but he never got done for 'em.' Pause. 'Hee hee hee hee hee hee hee hee, I sounded pretty blasé about that then, didn't I? But then again, he is an Albion fan.

'In the nick, as soon as it gets to three o'clock, the fans have got the radio on and if it's a big game, a night game, they'll start banging the doors to celebrate.'

'I'd love to come in and listen to a game.'

'Hee hee hee hee hee hee.'

Later, I write to the governor, seeking permission to go in one Saturday afternoon. When he read the letter, he probably went 'hee hee hee hee hee', too, but his reply advised me, in so many words, to get knotted.

'Anyway,' says Bernie, as though I wouldn't want to come in anyway, '90 per cent of all prisoners are Birmingham City fans. They're all blue noses. They've all had trials for Blues as well. Crap, like, but they always say they've had trials.'

'Well, they've had trials all right, but not those kind of trials,' I say.

'Hee hee hee hee hee hee hee.'

Meanwhile, in Crosby, a large car has pulled up outside my in-laws house. Inside, you can smell the tension. Jane and her dad have been milling about, feigning nonchalance, for ten minutes. Upstairs Maureen, who's long had a thing for Alan Hansen, has spent the morning tidying the house, even though he won't be coming in. She admires him from the bedroom window as he gets out of the driver's seat and holds the door open for Jane and her dad to get in. Jane later confesses that, at this moment, she was so afraid Ray would say something daft that she gave herself a bout of diarrhoea which lasted well into the new year.

Alan, to Ray's consternation, has a very poor sense of direction. Although he has lived in the area for donkey's years, he can't find his way from Crosby to Anfield. Jane later points out that if it was her mum unable to navigate this route, she would come in for no end of flack from Ray. But, here and now, it is his very great pleasure to point Alan Hansen, football legend and television star, the right way.

When they arrive at the ground, they are given strict instructions by Alan to leave their seats as soon as eighty-five minutes have elapsed, and make their way to the Hillsborough Memorial to meet him and Kenny there. 'Kenny?' queries Ray, tremulously.

'Dalglish,' says Alan. 'We're giving him a lift home.'

Jane's bowels loosen once more.

In the first half Liverpool attack the Albion goal at our end of the pitch relentlessly. Harry Kewell is marked out for special attention by our fans, his wife having recently appeared on *I'm a Celebrity, Get Me Out of Here!* She did so with Cannon and Ball. Hence someone has come up with the idea of singing, to the theme of the kids' programme *Rosie and Jim*, 'Cannon and Ball – shagging your wife.'

Improbably, Liverpool fail to score. At half-time everyone looks at each other and puffs their cheeks with relief. It's going to be a long second half.

We all concentrate hard on the clock, praying we can hang on for an impossible draw. Away to my left, Nathan is spending a lot of time on his feet chanting and carrying on. He spots a Liverpool fan going to the toilet and gets quite a few people chanting: 'We know where you're going.' He quickly changes tack to something along the lines of, 'You're going for a wank!' This elicits a smile from the bloke. Liverpool score. We're not going to draw after all.

166

Rich is getting more and more worked up. His body and face contort a little with every demonstration of our incompetence. 'Why the fuck doesn't he play a team that could fucking win?' he demands of me, the manager, himself and anyone else who might be listening.

We lose. Other results go against us, too – Everton fluke a 1-0 win at Sunderland and Fulham contrive to lose at Portsmouth, so we slip down to fourth from bottom. We all get the feeling that 2006 isn't going to be a barrel of laughs. Frank Skinner sends a text: 'Why don't we just attack the big teams? We never "contain" anybody. Stupid fuckin Sunderland didn't help either. Or Fulham. Happy new year, by the way.'

Rich, who looked to me very much as if he had had a thoroughly miserable afternoon, texts: 'I'd just like to thank you once again for the ticket, it's highly appreciated and very thoughtful of you. All the best, Rich.'

On the train back to Crosby, I call Jeff Farmer, one of our directors. I always bleat to him when we lose. 'Samaritans,' he says when he answers my call. And Jeff normally does cheer me up with a few it-was-always-going-to-be-tough thoughts, a couple of laments about our bad luck and some optimistic predictions about forthcoming fixtures. When I hang up, a Liverpool fan sitting across the aisle smiles supportively and says, 'You won't go down, you'll be fine.' I'm so grateful to him I want to rest my head in his lap and sob.

When I get to my mother-in-law's, she says that they were listening on the radio and my girls were supporting Liverpool. I know it shouldn't but this puts me in the very blackest of moods. Although they don't know one team from the next, the very thought of them supporting anyone but the Albion is almost as awful a thought as them calling someone else Daddy.

The night is young. New Year's Eve with the in-laws. I love them but I want to go to bed. Some friends of mine from Neath in South Wales ring up to wish me happy new year. Their teenage kids are wonderful but one of them comes on the phone and starts telling me how crap West Brom are, as kids do. He means no harm because he probably can't imagine that any grown-up is daft enough to take it as personally as I do. But I seethe. I'm in bed by eleven. Disgraceful, really.

Monday, 2 January 2006, Aston Villa at home

I can cope with my in-laws being Liverpool fans. I certainly would struggle if they were Villa fans, though. I really hate Aston Villa. When I was a kid I remember even considering it an affront that they wore their claret and blue kit on our pitch. To lose to them was to make the prospect of going to school on Monday quite unbearable. I have been watching the Albion for thirty-one years and never recall actually seeing us beat them. Last night I couldn't sleep for worrying.

We drive down from Liverpool with the kids. On the way, a text alert pops up on my mobile phone. It's from Mystic Emma. It says: 'Call me before the game and we'll be all right.'

'Who,' demands Jane, 'is Mystic Emma?' I explain it's someone I've got to know and when I speak to her before a home match we always win. Jane rolls her eyes, but only at the absurdity of it. She's not the jealous type.

We meet my dad in West Bromwich. He gets into our car and takes the kids back to their house, leaving us his car to drive there after the game. A masterpiece of organisation, I'm sure you'll agree. As we cross the bridge over the M5, Jane thanks me for bringing her out on such a delightful stroll.

Jadeen texts me: 'I feel sick so nervous.' Her mum texts: 'Ohh oh god oh god oh god oh god oh god oh god oh . . .!' In the press room Bill Howells of Birmingham's *Evening Mail* is deathly pale. He is the Aston Villa correspondent for the paper but a massive Albion fan.

Outside the ground, I meet Rosie Ellis, daughter of a former vice-chairman of West Brom but, astonishingly, now married to

Peter Ellis, a director of Aston Villa and the son of the chairman Doug Ellis. With her husband, she's just been in the boardroom on the other side of the ground, taking advantage of a boardroom pass to berate our chairman about the blanket no-smoking policy being brought in next season. Knowing our chairman, he will not have been impressed.

She is smoking when we meet. In her fifties, Rosie is an attractive woman in a fun-filled, flirtatious, chain-smoking kind of way. She's wearing boots, jeans and a complicatedly constructed, expensive-looking coat with lots of woolly balls all over it. Her daughter Sarah, a medical rep, is with her: 'More into rugby,' says Rosie of her, apologetically.

I ask how her husband will behave in the unthinkable, but hardly unlikely, event of Villa winning. 'Will he be gentlemanly about it?'

A huge sneer covers Rosie's face. 'He'll pretend to be charming,' she says, 'but he won't be. He'll be nice at first, then he'll just drop things in like, "I must say, Clement isn't up to much, is he?" Stuff like that.'

'And what about you? If we win and the boot's on the other foot, will you be ladylike about it?'

'No,' she says flatly, shaking her head.

Rosie has been an Albion fan from the moment she could speak. 'The first thing my dad taught me to say was "Daddy" and the second thing was "I hate Villa".' I ask what he would have made of her marrying an Aston Villa director. 'Not much,' she says.

'I suppose I started going when I was nine. Alan, my brother, went when he was about four, but girls didn't go then. We were a solid middle-class family. Dad was a surveyor by profession but he was an old-fashioned entrepreneur really. He'd been going to the Albion with his uncle since he was four. His ambition was always to go on the Albion board and when he finally got there Mum started going, too.

'He died in 1970 when he was fifty-three. He had a heart attack.

169

I was nineteen. It was awful but actually it was about his fourth heart attack and, amazing as it sounds, two of them had been at Albion–Villa matches. No wonder I hate the Villa so much.

'So then Alan and I got season tickets. I don't think I could have stopped going. It felt wrong to stop going. The only time we thought about not going was during the Sean Flynn days.'

Sean Flynn was a local lad who ended up playing for the club he supported. He ran around a lot, getting unusually red in the face as he did so. Once, after fluffing a straightforward pass, he dropped to the floor and did five press-ups. We loved him for that. And he loved us back because he loved the club. So I'm sure he would be terribly upset to hear his name used as a byword for a dismal period in the club's history.

'It's just so important to me, being here,' says Rosie. 'It is very powerful. It's almost like going home. I feel more at home here than anywhere else on earth. And people still call me Rosemary James, which I really like. It's my maiden name. They're as much my family as my family, really.'

I ask how her previous husband dealt with her love for the club. 'Well, I've had three actually,' she says. 'My first husband was an Albion supporter and that was great, but I split up from him and ran off with the second. He was a rugby man and wasn't interested in football and we just went our separate ways every Saturday. He didn't know anything about football, didn't understand it, never watched it. I think it was better because there'd be no point me coming home in a sulk – it meant nothing to him.

'Then I was on my own for about eight years until I met Peter and apart from the fact that he's Villa, he's very, very nice. He's a lovely man. His job doesn't really come between us. What really worries me, though, is that we play Villa close to the end of the season and they could put us down. I just can't imagine how I'd feel if that happened. What is so difficult to say is that when he goes out to watch a match, I always say, Bye, best of luck, but I really want him to lose 'cos I hate them – not him, the club.

'My dad, he wouldn't have discussed football with my husband and wouldn't have liked his father any more than I like his father, but that would have been all right. It probably would never have happened, though, me and Peter, if Dad was alive.

'When my dad came home from the match, if we'd won, he'd take us all out to dinner or give us ten pounds to go out. If we'd lost, he'd lock himself in his study and we'd have to pass his *Argus* under the door.'

I try to imagine what exactly Jane would do if I behaved like that. If we've lost, she watches me like a hawk. Just one glum look, one snap at the children, one sigh, and I am toast. I always spend the journey home preparing myself to pretend to be happy. I warm up my face and try to lift the corners of my mouth to form a smile – it's a position my face is very rarely in on a match day. I then try to keep this fixed until such time as it is acceptable for me to go to bed. As I climb wearily into bed, I wipe the smile away and thank God the day is over. I try not to focus on the chances we've missed or the goals we've given away. I begin to prepare myself for the panic I'll feel when I wake up in the morning and remember how we did yesterday. Lost? We didn't, did we? Oh no.

How much better to be Rosie's dad who just shut himself away and didn't talk to anyone. I ask Rosie if she considered that kind of behaviour acceptable. 'Well, I suppose we all felt the same really. Nobody felt like talking to anyone else. He was the best father on earth, my dad, because he was a bit naughty. I never went to a speech day in all my schooldays because it was on a Wednesday and there was always a match. He used to write me a note every year to get me out of it so I could go to the Albion. I was the only child in the whole school who never went to a speech day and I thought that was incredibly funny.

'My mum thought it was all rather silly, but she adored him. I come from one of those families where we all smiled at each other and said how lovely we all were, except when we lost, when we were all vile. Mum used to go, too. That was the only time she swore. If we'd lost, she'd turn round and say, "Shit." And that was the only time I ever heard my mother swear. She died in 1986.'

The match begins. We miss a sitter and they miss several. It becomes apparent that they're miles better than us.

Our Martin Albrechtsen is clattered by Villa's Gareth Barry. 'Bastard,' says Rosie quietly. 'Little shit. I hate Barry. Mind you, I hate them all.'

As Villa come ever closer to scoring, a furious goalmouth scramble results in injuries to two of their players. With them lying in our penalty area, Rosie expresses her pleasure: 'Good,' she says, 'best thing we've done all game. Pansies. Mind you, they do play in pink. They're cheating bastards, aren't they?'

'To be fair,' I say, 'they are playing absolutely stacks better than us, Rosie.'

'Yes, they are,' she admits. 'Bastards.'

At half-time it is generally agreed that each and every one of us would settle for a draw. Frank Skinner is having none of it. He sits a few rows in front of Rosie and is happy to provide me with some positive thoughts about how all the signs are that it might be our day, given the number of chances Villa have missed. And he says how good it is that our players aren't panicking. His girl-friend isn't feeling well, so has gone to sit in their car. I tell Frank I'd like to join her there.

The second half starts and Villa score immediately. Their fans erupt. Rosie looks at them darkly and tells them, with feeling, to fuck off. She lights up what I make to be her seventh cigarette. Almost to herself, she keeps up a steady stream of invective: 'Pricks . . . pansies . . . bastards . . . wimps . . . hate them.'

Her daughter Sarah, to my right, is no less desperate for a goal from us, but she betrays her lack of experience as a supporter by shouting, rather shrilly, 'Come on, West Brom!' over and over again. Somehow it doesn't sound right. You tend to shout for the Albion rather than for West Brom, but I'll let it pass, especially as we then contrive to score. I hug Sarah and her mother, though it takes me a while to get a firm grip on Rosie. She's more concerned with yelling, 'fuck off', and furiously waving a V-sign at her husband and his fellow Aston Villa directors hundreds of yards away from us in the opposite stand.

We are now, albeit briefly, the better side and it seems not entirely impossible that we could win. But Villa score again, a disputed free-kick having led to a disputed penalty. Despair. We press hard for another equaliser without creating any decent chances. Rosie has her face buried in either her hands, her scarf or a cigarette. When, almost mercifully, the final whistle goes, I tell her I'd rather be me than her tonight. She smiles evilly, lights her tenth cigarette and says, 'Don't worry about me, I can be vile.'

Back at my parent's house I wallow in desperation. But then mum tells me about an old friend of ours being slowly killed by a brain tumour. This, shamefully, bizarrely, cheers me up because it puts the Albion defeat against Aston Villa in perspective. I think about what Rosie said: 'Don't worry about me, I can be vile.'

A couple of days later I call Rosie to find out just who's been most vile to whom. 'After the match I went up to the boardroom and I was excessively rude to three Villa directors and I think I was rather rude to our chairman, too. Peter wasn't too bad. It would have been too much for me not to have had a slight smirk if the result had been the other way round, therefore why should he not do it. But, ooh, I could still kill him, even though he was better than the other directors. I haven't really spoken properly to him yet. I will do, I suppose. He's going shooting tomorrow, so I might be quite nice to him then when he gets back.' She pauses, then says, 'Yes, there are guns in the house, which is always tempting.'

I find myself wondering what, if anything, I would tell the police if Peter Ellis were to have a nasty accident and they saw my number on his wife's phone.

Eight

'Earnshaw – I can fucking *spunk* harder than that!'

Saturday, 7 January 2006, Reading at home in the FA Cup

The first Saturday of the year used to be one of the big weekends of the football calendar: the third round of the FA Cup. But with the Premiership being the financial be-all and end-all, it's not quite like that any more. Unless your team's absolutely mid-table with no chance of promotion or relegation, you'll probably swap a win in the cup for a win in the next league match.

Neither side has any appetite for this game. Reading are miles clear at the top of the Championship and thinking only of promotion. All we care about is surviving in the Premiership. The worst possible result would not be to lose but to draw. A replay would be most inconvenient for both teams. Especially us.

My younger daughter is being christened tomorrow and the club chaplain Ken 'the Rev' Hipkiss is doing it. In point of fact, it's not a christening, but a dedication. In his church they are of the opinion that a child shouldn't be formally brought into any faith until he or she is old enough to make up their own mind. But the important thing to me is that the club chaplain is doing it because Sian is an Albion baby if ever there was one.

She was conceived the day after we first got promoted to the Premiership in April 2002. I can't be sure our promotion improved my fertility, but I wouldn't be surprised. The next time we were up for promotion, Jane was on the radio and, asked about our chances of going up, she said: 'It mustn't happen; the last time they got promoted I gave birth nine months later.'

To celebrate the occasion of Sian's dedication, I've hired a box for today's game, for Jane and me, and the three godparents and their spouses, and the Rev's come along, too. Apart from the Rev and me, there is not an Albion fan among us. Peter Allen, Jane's co-presenter on Five Live, is a lifelong Spurs fan but these days watches them only from his armchair. Schadenfreude is his middle name and, though he won't admit it, he is hoping for a Reading win today.

This soon starts to get on the Rev's wick as much as mine. I ask Peter if he has ever been punched by a vicar. Peter says the Rev wouldn't do a thing like that. The Rev smiles and says: 'Oh yes, I would.' He looks heavenward, clenches his fist and pleads, 'Just give me five minutes, oh Lord, to sort this bloke out.'

Peter's wife Rowena is full of enthusiasm for the whole thing, but clearly hasn't seen the inside of a football ground for many years, if at all. She asks if she is allowed to put a bet on Reading winning. I tell her she's free to as long as she doesn't collect her winnings if it does come to pass.

Lucy, another godparent, asks her husband Adam, a Portsmouth fan, what he thinks the score will be. I'm talking to the Rev at the time but I still hear Adam say, '2-0 to Reading.' Adam's one of the nicest people I know yet homicidal thoughts flash through my mind. How *dare* he sit there bold as brass in my box at my club and airily announce that Reading will win.

When the game starts there isn't room for the Rev and me to sit in the seats in front of our box, so we sit a short way away in front of another box, one peopled entirely by Albion fans. We are much more comfortable here. It is a dire game. Both sides miss a decent chance – ours is sheer slapstick as Nathan Ellington stands on the ball in front of an open goal right in front of the Reading fans. They sing: 'That is why you're going down' to the tune of 'Bread of Heaven'. I nurse a deep hatred for them.

At half-time Peter smiles cruelly at me. Adam suspects, correctly, that I'm annoyed with him, too, because Portsmouth are winning at Ipswich. I tell everyone how upset I am that I have brought them all here, paid for a box with lots of food and drink, and yet it seems to me that they would be quite keen for my beloved team to lose. They insist this isn't the case, but I know it is.

The second half starts. At my suggestion, the Rev and I swap seats – I tell him that a change in formation for the second half is often a help. He says, in his most benevolent vicar's voice, 'Don't worry – we'll be all right.' We are both soothed by this, although then he adds: 'We'll be all right as sure as I'm riding this bike.' I've not heard this expression before but I get his drift. Sure enough, we are not all right. A suspect penalty gives us the lead with just a few minutes left but then an equally suspect penalty gives them an equaliser. A draw – precisely what we didn't want.

The dedication is the following morning. Ken has warned me over and over again that his church is 'not some beautiful thing with stained glass windows and stuff'. I've told him it sounds just fine. It turns out to be a small modern building that looks like a community centre or village hall. The elevated section of the M5 thunders overhead and industrial decay is all around. God's love isn't immediately apparent.

But inside the Bethel Christian Fellowship, the love of God is in abundance. Every member of the congregation – in Ken's words, 'humble Black Country folk, lovely people' – seems to greet each one of us personally. One of them, Ron, shakes me warmly by the hand. 'Welcome,' he says. It's only clerics who ever greet you with the single word 'welcome', isn't it? Then he asks, 'Were you there yesterday? Terrible, wasn't it?'

'Oh, you an Albion fan?'

'Fifty-five years,' he says with a mixture of pride and regret.

I ask if it's harder to have faith in the Albion than it is in God.

'Much,' he says.

Sunday, 15 January 2006, Wigan away

I am at work and watch the match with Mark Demuth, editor of *Match of the Day 2*. He's hoping for an Albion win almost as much as I am because he knows how miserable I'll be to work with if we don't get a result. We have a big away following at Wigan, partly because the club has laid on forty free coaches to get us there. But Nathan, Pete, Sandra and a friend of hers have taken the train anyway. The coaches might be free but they are also dry. As the camera lingers on our supporters, I feel envious and rather lonely. I want to be with them.

The match starts and I'm soon moaning about how we are going to lose. Mark, bored with my grumbling, says, 'You're doing all right. Shut up.' Only then do I realise that this first-half performance, while hardly barnstorming, is reasonably competent. Neither team looks much like scoring, but we are marginally the better side. Then, just before half-time, our huge, lovable, born-again Christian of a defender, Darren Moore, barges Jason Roberts over and, as he has already been booked, is sent off. With more than forty-five minutes to play, all hope of a win is now gone. I smile triumphantly at Mark. 'There, told you so.' I am so pleased to be proved right.

It reminds me of when I was a student and a terrible hypochondriac. I was always at the doctor's. My parents and friends used to despair of me. I would dream about being diagnosed with something horrible. How lovely to be able to come home and say, 'There, I told you so – I'm terminally ill!' I suppose one day I'll actually be able to do that. Can't wait.

Meanwhile at Wigan, where we're terminally certain to lose, Bryan Robson takes off Nathan Ellington, who we bought from Wigan, and replaces him with a defender, Martin Albrechtsen. The Wigan crowd cheer their former favourite off the pitch, delighting in their cruelty. Our fans believe our other striker should have been taken off – the older, slower but more experienced Kevin Campbell. Accordingly, they chant that our manager doesn't know what he's doing. At this point, it later turns out, Nathan and Pete have simply walked out of the ground to register their discontent: 'Well,' says Nathan, 'I was disgusted at the substitution and I wanted some beer – I had a taste for it by then.'

Unaccountably since we're a man down, we start the second half much the better team and, astonishingly, our substitute scores, his first for the club. I stand up, shake my fists and sit back down again. 'That's it, we're fucked now,' I say to Mark. He rolls his eyes.

I get a text from Lee, an old friend: ' . . . and now thirty minutes of hell.' When I was little I used to fantasise about being able to have power over time: to stop the clock when Albion were desperate for a goal, and speed it right up when we were trying not to concede one. Now, supposedly grown-up, I wish no less fervently for the same thing.

In fact I use it in reverse: if I am in a situation when I want time to pass quicker or slower, I pretend I'm watching the Albion. For example, if I'm out running and have decided to sprint for three minutes, I pretend we are 1-0 down with three minutes left on the clock and pressing for an equaliser. Time then travels really fast. Conversely, if I'm running late for an appointment, say I have only three minutes to get to a studio, I imagine we're 1-0 up with three minutes left and the opposition are about to score. Time lingers on.

Wigan are on top but not creating that much. They hit the bar and have a free-kick well saved. We miss a golden opportunity to score again. I deploy a number of time-management techniques. Instead of praying for the ninety minutes to be up, I take just one minute at a time. So at sixty-seven minutes I pray for us to reach sixty-eight without conceding. This works less well if, as I do now, you have sight of the seconds ticking by on the clock in the corner of the screen. Apart from anything else, it means that you don't have to watch the football, you can just watch the clock instead. I try, inwardly, to cheer every passing second. That way I have sixty things to celebrate every minute! This novelty soon palls.

On one of the dozen or more plasma screens in front of us, Sky is showing some Australian rugby league. I try looking at the clock on that screen instead. This doesn't help much, though the time it takes me to calculate the difference between the two clocks is time well spent. It has, albeit momentarily, kept my mind off the terror at hand.

I look back at our clock. Still twelve minutes left. It's like those dreams where you're attempting to run and just can't get going. I try watching something other than the football on the other screens. ITV is showing *American Idol* and I am guiltily thankful for the precious seconds during which I'm diverted by the sight of a rather overweight girl being reduced to tears by the judges.

The dying moments. By now I have run out of diversionary tactics and have to focus on the game. I'm almost starting to believe that we will win when there is a goalmouth scramble – at our end, obviously. The ball squirts to the right corner of the six-yard box where Jason Roberts is advancing unopposed towards an empty goal. My buttocks tighten, but then relax as I accept that he must score. In a nanosecond I look at the clock, realise that there is no time for them to score a winner and console myself that a draw isn't a bad result. But at the conclusion of this nanosecond, just as Jason Roberts pulls the trigger, our Polish goalkeeper,

Tomasz Kuszczak, launches himself across goal, his arms aloft, his mouth agape. Incredibly, he saves it.

Mark, agog, gasps: 'Fuck. Ing. Hell.' And laughs.

The final whistle goes and the world seems an altogether happier place.

Text messages flood in: From Sue Ball, daughter of Val Ball (née Grubbe): 'Fanflippintastic.' From Sandra: 'Fanfuckintastic.' Frank Skinner: 'I hope you got those positive thoughts. Truly brilliant victory. Joy, joy, joy. X.' The Reverend Ken is enjoying the Sabbath more than usual: 'Got no voice left 4 tonight. Can't wait to watch motd2 tonight. Bet u don't stop smiling.'

In Wigan Nathan and Pete watched the entire second half in a pub called the Seven Stars. 'When we went in they asked if we'd been locked out of the ground. Locked out? I said. Walked out!' In there, according to Nathan, it was empty apart from three 'tasty' barmaids and a bloke slumped on the bar with his head in his hands. 'He woke up,' said Nathan, 'saw us, smiled, bought us a drink and then went back to sleep.'

Garth Pearce calls me to say he's got 2500 words to write tonight on Gwyneth Paltrow and it's going to be a breeze. Elena, who until Bradford in September hadn't seen the opposition score against us, is in touch. I ask if she saw the Pole in goal's fantastic save. 'Of course not,' she texts.

From New Zealand, Mark Reynolds emails me: Just a quick note to celebrate our first away win. It was on telly of course, but I didn't set my alarm, just my video recorder. Thought if I slept through it I'd just watch it later. Woke up at the exact moment the match started. Texted my brother who was watching it in Indonesia! Had to drop a pill to get to sleep afterwards I was so wired. (OK, I know I know, we'll lose to Sunderland now!) Anyway, Up the Baggies! Mark.

My mind goes back to what Alan Cleverley said at Old Trafford on Boxing Day: 'One of our wins is worth twenty of theirs.' How true. What joy would an away win at Wigan bring Man Utd fans? None. Tonight, as West Brom fans the world over go to sleep (or in

Mark's case wake up) with smiles on their faces, I almost feel sorry for fans of Manchester United, Chelsea, Arsenal and any other club that has made a habit out of winning.

Tuesday, 17 January 2006, Reading away in FA Cup replay

A match neither side wants to play and most fans can't be bothered to watch. Graeme Le Saux expresses an interest in coming. I tell him he's welcome, but I won't be sitting in the press box, and if he wants to sit with me, he'll have to sit behind the goal with all the Albion fans. And he'll have to pay for his own ticket. I ask when he last paid to watch a football match. He thinks, then says, 'Never. Will I get any stick from your fans?'

'No,' I say, 'don't be silly.' As I say this, I recall the bloke in the pub miming how he'd beat Graeme half to death. I call Dave Holloway, our coach-organising mastermind, and ask him if he thinks my friend will be in any danger.

'No,' he says, 'don't worry. There's no idiots going.'

'No idiots?' I say. 'Midweek, everyone's skint after Christmas, and yet they're going to take the afternoon off work to watch a match they don't care about. And you say there are no idiots going?'

'Well, there's two kinds of idiot, isn't there?' says Dave. 'There's our kind of idiot and there's the violent kind of idiot. There'll be lots of our kind there but none of the other.'

Nathan, Sandra and Kate are coming down by coach. I call Nathan to find out what time they'll be arriving.

'I think the coach leaves West Bromwich at two o'clock,' he says.

'Two? You'll be outside the ground by four. What you going to do for four hours.'

'Oh, I think we're going to a pub first – in Newbury.'

'Do you know which pub? And why Newbury?'

'Don't know. Sauce is organising it.'

'Who?'

'Sauce.'

'Sauce who?'

'Dunno. Just Sauce. I've only ever known him as Sauce.'

I ring the man called Sauce. He runs a coach service independent from the one Dave lays on. Black Country Travel, as he calls it, puts on at least one coach for every away game. He takes me through the itinerary: 'We leave Cradley Heath at quarter past one and pick up at various places, and then leave West Bromwich at two.'

'And I understand you're going to a pub.'

'Yes. In Newbury.'

'Do you know what it's called?'

'It's in the middle of the town. It's either called the Something Hatchet or the Hatchet Something. I can't remember. Anyway, it's in the middle of the town.'

I arrange to meet them there and then he'll squeeze me, and my bladder full of lager, on board for the last leg of the journey to Reading. There is a question I have to ask. 'Do you mind me asking why you're called Sauce?'

'Well,' he explains, 'my name's Tkaczuk – t-catch-uk – and when I was at school in the sixties no one could say it. But they could say ketchup. And at the time I think there was an advert on the telly about ketchup sauce and I've been called Sauce ever since.'

Sauce has been an Albion fan for over thirty years. 'The first match I can remember being taken to was Bobby Hope's testimonial, in 1970, I think. What done it for me, though, was when my mum, who wanted to see George Best play, took me up against Man Utd and I think we won 4-3 and Tony Brown scored a hat-trick. It was about seventy–seventy-one.

'By the time I got to about eleven or twelve, I was getting to as many games as I could. To 1985 I didn't miss a home game. Then I had to work nights and I missed a couple. I went eighty-six to about ninety-eight without missing a home game. When my father died, I missed a home game that weekend. I don't think I've missed one since. That was Wolves at home and we won 2-0 on a Sunday. My dad died on the Thursday night, no, it was a Friday night, as I remember.'

I ask him, as delicately as I can, if beating the Wolves made him happy even though he'd just lost his dad.

'It was a strange time for me. My wife says, why don't you listen to it on the radio? Bit weird because my dad had no great love of football. In fact he hated it, he didn't like it at all.'

'What did he think about you going?'

'He hated it. He just had this thing in his head that, like, it . . .' Words keep failing Sauce on this subject, but he presses on: 'Well, one of the reasons he hated it was that it dictated my lifestyle. I wouldn't do certain jobs when I left school 'cos I didn't want to work Saturdays. Then it was, like, you know, well, what's the matter with you? I could understand it now, but I couldn't understand it then.

'I was offered a job when I left school which involved working Saturdays and I didn't take it because I'd have to miss the Albion. It was with an electrical company in Dudley. Of course this thing haunted me for years because the chap who took the job eventually ended up running the place and by the time he was twenty-five, he got a company car and was on twenty-five grand a year and I was still working in a factory, you know. But I didn't have to work Saturdays, so I was happy.'

'One time we were playing at Norwich. The coaches used to leave about 7.30 in the morning, which meant I had to get the ten past six bus from our estate into Dudley, then get the seventy-four to West Bromwich. I got up late and missed the bus. Dad, I said, need a lift. He wouldn't take me. So I couldn't go. I didn't speak to him for about six months.'

'Did we win?'

'I can't remember,' says Sauce miserably.

Sauce speaks of his early years watching the Albion as he might about taking his first drink, or losing his virginity. To him it was a rite of passage: 'While I was still at school we had the FA Cup semi-final defeat against Ipswich. There was twenty-five, thirty thousand of us down at Highbury and, as a lad growing up . . . them years, you're breaking away from home.

'My first trip down to London ever, on my own, was to watch the Albion play at Leyton Orient. We drawed nil-nil. I think it was a Tuesday night. April seventy-six.' There is a hushed reverence about his voice now. 'We drawed nil-nil with Leyton Orient. I was three weeks off my fourteenth birthday. They were running a coach from Cradley Heath. I just happened to see a notice in the window of a shop that said, Leyton Orient vs West Bromwich Albion coach departs, whatever time it was, three o'clock in the afternoon or something. So I run back home to get some money and I run back to Cradley Heath and just got on the bus and went.'

'What did your parents say?'

'Er, I didn't tell 'em.'

'Well, where did they think you'd gone?'

'I didn't tell 'em.'

'Weren't they worried about you?'

'Yeah,' he laughs.

Sauce's memories of the occasion overwhelm any sense of guilt: 'It was such an adventure,' he remembers with wonder. 'I'd never been to London before, I don't think. It was certainly the first time I'd made me own arrangements to get there. We drawed nil-nil with Leyton Orient,' he says for the third time, like it's an incantation, like the words 'nil-nil with Leyton Orient' possess some magical power.

This sounds ridiculous to me at first, but then I remember what I was like at that age. If I'd had the balls to go to London to see us draw nil-nil with Leyton Orient, I certainly would have told everyone about it the following day. The difference with me would have been that my mum would have summarily removed my balls the moment I arrived home, so I would have been telling everybody the score in falsetto.

I put it to Sauce that Black Country Travel has a reputation for being the hard-drinking wing of the travelling supporters' club. 'No more than, say, Tividale Travel,' Sauce replies defensively. 'They're of a similar ilk to us. They go early and stop and have a drink in a pre-booked pub or club. We organise the pub over the internet, though there are pubs we go to on a regular basis. Because of the laws governing sporting events, we have to stop at least ten miles from the ground.

'Sometimes we turn up on spec and drop off in the town centre. Other times I'll actually book somewhere or phone a working men's club. I tend to do that if there's three or four buses 'cos I like to keep them all together. If you go to the town centre with two hundred people, you've got to try and round them all up when you want to leave and if they're in one place, it's easier.

'Touch wood, we've never had any trouble. I don't think we've been anywhere and not been invited back. Which I think is a testament to the supporters, to be quite honest. The majority of our lads are a bit rough and ready, but they just like to drink and they like to go to the football and they like to go home. We don't go looking for trouble. And they're all blokes aged between twenty-five and fifty. We're not talking about a busload of youngsters here, no jack the lad kids straight out of school who want to fight the world after two halves of lager.'

I know what he's saying, but surely, I say to him, there must be times when locals have come in looking for trouble. Sauce answers as if he has thought about this many times. 'Well, we're only there an hour and half, don't forget. And the way I look at it, if we turn up anywhere with, say, three buses, 150 people, they've got to have 160 blokes to beat you. You know what I mean?' Put this way, I suddenly understand why Sauce is never going to get much trouble.

He sees meaning in what he does beyond the humdrum reality of fixing up drink and transport for a load of West Brom fans. 'It's like an extended family to me. Bear in mind some of the lads who go on the bus, I've known them since the late seventies. There's some from Cradley Heath who I went to junior school with. If somebody's not there, it's, like, well, where's Dave? Where's so and so? It's like a family, looking out for each other.

'Having said that, I enjoy the break in the summer – I like the last game of the season when I drop everybody off and I can throw the phone in the cupboard, and the book that I do all the bookings in, I throw that in the cupboard, too.'

The pub in Newbury is called neither the Something Hatchet nor the Hatchet Something. It was until recently called one of those things, but now it's been rebranded the Berkshire Tavern. It is the cavernous kind of place that would be heaving on a Friday night, although now it's more or less empty, bar a coachload of Albion fans. Fifty people might make a fifty-two-seater look full but they don't make much of an impression on a giant, screen- and fruit machine-filled pub in Newbury.

A publisher friend is with me. The commissioning editor of this book, funnily enough. Tom's tall, friendly and studious. He can talk about anything from politics to jazz to Bob Dylan to York City's back four. I've told him all about Nathan on the way here. As luck would have it, Nathan doesn't disappoint. No sooner have we sat down than he tells us the following story: 'Had a good day last Saturday. Me and some of the lads from West Bromwich went down to Worcester for the day. We hatched the plan at half-time at the Villa game 'cos we knew there was no game, with us being at Wigan on the Sunday. They're good lads – some of them have been in a bit of trouble in their time – but they're good lads.

'Anyway, this woman I know from Wednesfield rings me up on the way back. I was on the train. Says she wants to see me. I said, I can't, I'm on the train from Worcester. There's no direct service. I can either go via Smethwick or via the Hawthorns.' (I love Nathan for the way he includes bizarrely prosaic details in his anecdotes, like the time he told me that a woman called Tracey who he was sleeping with stabbed her ex-boyfriend 'a couple of Tuesdays ago'.)

'Anyway,' he now continues, 'she says, never mind that, can't be bothered, I'll pick you up from the station. As we went into the house, she says, look it's just for sex. Then, when I got on top of her, she said, you can't come inside me. But it was too late. It was all done in ten minutes and off she went. I went to the pub and shagged somebody else later. Well, I presume I did. I can't really remember.'

Tom blinks nervously but does a fairly good job of not looking too aghast, though I wonder if I can see a little bit of condensation forming on the lenses of his studious little specs. Overcome with embarrassment, I go to the bar to help Sandra with the drinks.

'You'll never guess what he's just told Tom,' I say.

'Oh no, he never has, has he?' she says, burying her head in her hands.

A very drunk man, possibly a down and out, staggers into the pub. Blinking in confusion at the proliferation of blue and white shirts around him, he lurches to the bar. By some unseen signal the young Polish-sounding barmaid summons the Bet Lynch-like landlady. She, not without compassion, turfs him out. Meanwhile we talk, play pool, drink, laugh, moan, wander around aimlessly. In its own rather unambitious way, it's heaven.

At about six o'clock Sauce puts his empty pint glass down and stands up. Everyone else does the same and files out of the pub. Mysteriously a burger van has materialised in Newbury's market square. Some of our number, apparently reflexively, form a queue there.

The rest of us, reluctant to risk a bollocking from Sauce, follow him to the coach. Those arriving late, munching on dodgy looking burgers, munch more quickly as they approach as if to destroy the evidence. Some of them throw their wrappers on the floor. This is behaviour I normally find intolerable but, as ever, I'm blinded by love for West Brom fans and put their behaviour down to drink and tragically poor upbringings. Sauce mutters a couple of obscenities as they climb on – about lateness rather than tidiness – and we're soon on our way.

*

At the ground, the Madejski Stadium, we do a full circuit in order to admire the place. I've met John Madejski, Reading's owner, and he seems a really good bloke, but I do wonder how rich and fantastic I'd have to be before I consented to having a building named after me. And not only the stadium, there's the Madejski Hotel next to it as well, and the Jazz Café. 'Jazz Café!' snorts someone. 'Fucking Jazz Café? What the fuck's that all about? It's a fucking football ground. Jazz Café! Cunts.'

We file off the coach. I have to wait around outside the ground for Graeme Le Saux to materialise. Vic Stirrup taps me on the back. He's with Old Les, weaver of the 'Great Escape' rug. I ask Vic how he is. 'Not so good,' he says, 'gone blind in one eye.' Whether Vic's telling you he's got a cold, gone blind, or his entire family have just been wiped out by some mystery horror virus, his tone is always matter-of-fact. 'Gone blind in one eye,' he repeats, 'just went suddenly. Got to see the doctor tomorrow.'

'Did you think about not coming?' I ask, but Vic ignores the question.

Les looks at Vic, nods at him and winks at me: 'He's trying to get in at half price now.'

Vic smiles.

Les then assumes a graver tone of voice. Pulling me to one side, he whispers quite urgently: 'I've got something to ask you.'

'What's that, Les?' I respond, wondering what on earth could be more serious than Vic's loss of vision.

'Would you', he asks quietly, 'accept a carpet from me?'

'Of course I would, Les,' I say, touched beyond measure, 'of course I would.'

Les and Vic, aggregate age 167, one half-blind, the other planning to weave me a carpet, make their way into the ground.

By now a couple of quarts of Newbury lager are settling in my bladder, but there are no toilets outside and Graeme still hasn't shown up. I go back to the bus, where Sauce is talking to the driver. 'Can I pop back on here for a slash?' I ask.

They nod, but as I get on board again, Sauce shouts after me, 'I hope you ai' having a shite 'cos there ai' no paper. You'll have to use your hands.'

When I come out, Sauce's bravado has suddenly deserted him and he shyly asks me for a photograph. He gives the camera to the driver, who is wearing very thick specs and gets in a bit of a muddle. He's got the camera upside down and back to front. Exasperated, Sauce says, 'You've got it the wrong way round.' Peering suspiciously down at the contraption, the driver turns it the right way and squints through the viewfinder. 'He can't see a fookin' thing,' says Sauce to me, 'and he's got to drive we home, the cunt.' The flash flashes. The picture is taken.

Graeme appears, looking a little furtive. This is all new to him. Anxious to get the transaction done and dusted, he pulls a wad of money from his jeans. It's as though, six months after he retired from professional football, it is only now when he hands me twenty quid for a ticket to see a more or less meaningless cup replay between Reading and West Brom, that he truly knows it is all over.

I needn't have worried about him getting any stick. A small crowd soon gathers around for photos and autographs. We sit in the fourth row, right by the corner flag. At pitch level it's hard to work out the shape of the game because our usual perspective is from a position high above the halfway line, where the main television camera is located. But for Graeme this is just fine – after all, as a player he's watched most of his football from pitch level.

Within ten minutes we score, far away at the other end of the pitch. We all jump up and, fractionally after the rest of us, Graeme does, too. He claps his hands uncertainly and smiles, not quite sure how to celebrate.

As usual he spots things on the pitch that elude me completely. He is particularly interested in our young full-back, who is getting his senior debut. Jared Hodgkiss is nineteen but at five foot six inches tall he's a bit short for the job. 'You watch,' says Graeme, 'Reading'll just keep pumping high balls towards him because they know he's new and they can see he's short.' And Reading do

189

exactly that. It's a cruel game. But Hodgkiss deals quite well with everything thrown at him. 'He's doing all right here actually,' says Graeme.

Hodgkiss gets into a bit of a tangle with a Reading player on the touchline but somehow comes out with the ball and passes it down the line to Jonathan Greening. 'He did well there, didn't he?' I volunteer, but Graeme's not so sure: 'He did well to win the ball,' he says, 'but a decent player would have passed it to Greening's right foot – he's right-footed, so a ball to his left foot is going to take him longer to deal with.'

Now we score again. And this time Graeme rises to his feet in time with the rest of us. 'Job done,' I say to no one in particular and instantly regret doing so. High up behind us, I see Nathan on his feet, beaming with happiness, chanting abuse at the Reading fans to our right. 'Two-nil to the Premiership,' everybody sings, some pointing fingers at our adversaries.

At half-time we're still two goals ahead. 'What do you think?' I ask Graeme. 'Next goal wins,' he says. We all gulp. We know he's right.

In the second half Reading are all over us and score twice. Their fans now sing at us: 'Premiership? You're having a laugh.' But nobody is laughing where we sit. Graeme looks straight ahead, rather sheepishly. Nathan, who's joined us, shouts some abuse back. Occasionally he just leaps to his feet, gesticulates wildly in the direction of the Reading fans and yells, 'Fuck off!' Then he sits down again.

In extra time Leroy Lita scores his third goal of the evening. The crowing of the Reading fans becomes intolerably loud. We are going to lose. With about three minutes left, we win a corner, to be taken right in front of us. We roar with approval. Could we equalise and take this to penalties, after all? But Robert Earnshaw, our pint-sized, under-performing and totally pissed-off striker, just strolls over to take the corner. Strolls. And as our roar of excitement turns to one of derision he seems to go even slower.

This is going to have to be some corner if he is to redeem himself. He steps up and more or less passes it gently to the Reading defender at the near post. Nathan, against stiff competition, is first to his feet: 'Earnshaw – I can fucking *spunk* harder than that!' Graeme laughs in an appalled way and says, 'I'm off, want to miss the traffic.'

The following morning I've agreed to appear on Radio Berkshire to talk about the match. The presenter, Andrew Peach, is good but I've already taken against him because he's an Aston Villa fan even though his family are Albion. And his co-presenter sidekick, though a competent broadcaster, really annoys me. Andrew says on air that, 'She's been a loyal supporter of Reading for, ooh, must be about ten minutes now.'

'Not true!' she squeaks in the typical smoke-too-much, stay-up-too-late voice of the zoo-format radio dolly. 'I've been to every game this season! And it was sooo funny last night, yeah. We were all singing "Premiership, you're having a laugh", it was hilarious.'

'Yes,' I say, 'that's exactly what it was. Hilarious.'

Saturday, 21 January 2006, Sunderland at home

On paper, after a demoralising cup defeat, a game against the Premiership's bottom team is just the job. Needless to say, I just can't see it like that.

'Do you realise', someone says to me in the press room, 'that Sunderland have lost the last ten games?'

'No,' I reply, knowing at that very moment Sunderland will not lose today. We have simply no chance whatsoever of extending the run to eleven straight defeats. We will put a stop to Sunderland's rot. Nobody ever extended a calamitous losing sequence at the Hawthorns – apart from us, obviously.

Ticket prices have been reduced to a pound for children in a bring-the-family, give-the-children-the-bug idea. Today I am sitting with Lilwyn, who I met at Sian's naming ceremony. 'She', Rev Ken had said, pointing at her, 'is mad. Really, really mad. Don't sit next to her at the match, whatever you do.'

When I called earlier in the week to offer her my spare ticket, Lilwyn admitted she found the whole experience so nerve-racking that she rarely went to matches any more. She counselled caution: 'Ooooh, do you know what you're letting yourself in for?'

This I had to see. I meet Lilwyn outside the ground. She has a neat club hat and scarf combination on to fortify herself against the cold. The scarf is wrapped around her mouth and she nibbles away at it nervously. We are still twenty minutes from kick-off and not in sight of the pitch, but she keeps clenching and unclenching her fists. I ask why she gets into this state. 'Because I love it,' she says. 'I just love it. I'm not nervous, just excited,' she says, worrying away at the threads of her scarf.

As the players' names are read out she cheers each one and, though I'd say she's in late middle age, Lilwyn claps like a teenager with her hands high above her head. When the game starts she makes a series of extraordinary noises. One of our midfielders puts a ball through that momentarily looks as if it might lead to something. 'Wah, waah, waaah, *wah*,' says Lilwyn, the volume rising and falling as the threatened run on goal fails to materialise.

The noise gets louder and more frequent until, as we pass the half-hour mark, it's an almost continuous hum of assorted vowel sounds that rise and fall and sound more strangled the closer the ball goes to either goal. '*Oooooooohhh*, aaaaahhhh, *eeeeeee*, eerrrrr, aaarrh.' I make no noise at all, I never do. I just brood and suffer in silence. I don't think that's particularly healthy because inwardly I'm making noises just as anguished as Lilwyn's.

The continuity of Lilwyn's vowel sounds is only broken when a goal looks certain to be scored. 'Quick, *quick*,' she shouts suddenly at our defence but the ball squirts through them. 'Oh, dear me, dear me. Aw, they're going to score!' she wails, burying her face in her chewed up scarf. But Sunderland don't score and neither do we. It's a truly rubbish game of football and the only thing that has been generating any tension for me is Lilwyn's sound effects. The second half is so bad that even Lilwyn goes quiet.

Eighteen minutes from the end Sunderland score. It's an own goal that comes via a double deflection off two of our players. Desperation hangs like a fog in the air. Lilwyn, her spirit now broken, is silent. She chews forlornly on what's left of her scarf. We lose. 'Kids for a quid?' says someone as we file out. 'They'll have to pay them more than that to come next time after that load of shite.'

On the way home I feel desperate. We are surely heading for relegation if we can't beat the team that loses to everyone. I text the word 'help' to the Rev Ken. Almost as soon as the text is sent, my phone rings. It's Ken. There is urgency in his voice. 'What's up, mate? Why do you need help?' He sounds alarmed and I feel ashamed. 'Oh, nothing, Ken, just the Albion.'

'Oh, right.' Momentarily he sounds as if he might be annoyed, but then he sighs and says, 'Yeah, terrible, wasn't it?' We wallow in each other's despondency awhile.

I stop, as I always do, to get a coffee at Warwick Services on the M40. There's usually a bloke there on the till called Julian. 'Lost?' he says to me with a raise of his eyebrows. He can tell by the expression on my face.

On Sunday morning Vic Stirrup calls with an update on his eyesight: 'I still can't see out of the one eye and,' he says after a slight pause, 'I can't see out the other eye now either.'

'So you can't see at all, then?'

'No.'

I make a weak and predictable joke about how he didn't miss much yesterday. He laughs bleakly and tells me he is off to see the specialist in a couple of days. We chat for a while and I finish by asking what he's doing today. 'I'm going to the eye socket,' I hear him say.

'The eye socket?'

'No,' he says patiently, 'the ice hockey.'

Tuesday, 31 January 2006, Charlton away

There is something darkly ironic about the fact that the man who has seen more football matches than anyone I know is having problems with his eyes. This is only the sixth game Vic Stirrup has missed since the Second World War. I call him in the morning. He is just recovering from the operation. 'The doctor says I've got to lie down flat. No pillow. And I'm only to get up for ten minutes a day to walk about a bit.'

I ask him if he can see anything.

'Only what I could see before the operation. Not much. They said it would take six to seven weeks to get better if the operation had worked.'

As delicately as I can, I ask Vic how he feels to be missing the match. 'Not really that bothered,' he says.

I call Rich to offer him a spare ticket I have for tonight, but he already has one. He tells me his coach is leaving West Bromwich at two o'clock this afternoon. I tell him Sauce's is leaving at eleven – for an eight o'clock kick-off – to allow plenty of time for drinking. 'They'm terrible that lot. I don't know how they do it,' says Rich, admiring but disapproving.

My next call is to Andy Thompson, music-industry bloke from Kent. He's a no-show: 'I've cracked. I just can't do it. I can't. I just can't raise the enthusiasm. I'll try to get my head together for Saturday. I just don't think that twat [Bryan Robson] knows what he's doing.' I'm minded to have a pop at him as I think of poor Vic banned from coming by his doctor, and impoverished Rich, struggling down regardless. But Andy sounds so desperate that I don't have the heart to try to make him feel any worse.

Sauce's coach left the Black Country this morning and has dropped off at a pub in Shoreditch, miles away from Charlton's ground. The place is called the Albion. However many times I go, the sight of it always gladdens my heart. In an unremarkable street in east London, surrounded by what looks like social housing, sits a pub bedecked in blue and white with a giant club crest beaming down at the confused locals.

It is all the work of Dave Chapman. I find him sitting at the bar, tapping authoritatively along to a Neil Diamond tune coming from the jukebox. Dave was born in the East End but his family moved to Kent when he was six weeks old. 'My dad worked for Warner Brothers pictures. One of the perks he got every year was two cup final tickets and in 1954 he took me to the Albion's final against Preston. I was six. All I remember is the noise and the colour, mostly the colour. And from that minute every magazine that had West Brom in it I'd buy. It was ten years later, when I was sixteen, that I had my first trip to the Hawthorns. And that was it. I was hooked and still am.'

Dave took over the pub, then called the Duke of Sussex, in 1998. He changed the name straight away, in what I've always taken to have been a moment of madness. It turns out, though, that there was a shrewd marketing method in his madness: 'I was twenty-five years in the music business. When we laughingly decided on retirement, we bought the pub. And I thought, Well, there's that many boozers round here we've got to do something to catch people's attention because it's in the backstreets. I knew everyone around here is nuts about football, but if I called it the Arsenal pub everyone would hate me. And I thought, Sod it, if I put a West Bromwich Albion pub here they won't only not mind, they'll think I'm completely nuts and will all have to come and see what it's about. And that's exactly what happened.

'The reaction has changed over the years. When we first came, the Albion were struggling and it was all just good humour. But then after a while, when the pub was established, the Albion seemed to have become everybody's second team. Be they Arsenal, Tottenham, West Ham or whatever, now the next result they look for is the Baggies and they are pissed off when we lose.'

The pub is always packed on match days because Dave screens

games via satellite feeds, usually from the Middle East. Ironically, the success of the pub means he can't get to many Albion games. 'Only about ten a season,' he says morosely.

I ask where Sauce is, but I'm told that he's gone on a pub crawl 'down Liverpool Street' in a tone that suggests I should really know it's happening, or at least what the Liverpool Street pub crawl is all about. But some of Sauce's fellow travellers are still here. Pete's here. Nathan, with a heavy cold, is in attendance, struggling to get his beer down. He shows me a text from Tracey: 'hi sexy dick my sons birthday today he fourteen do you fancy giving me another?'

'Well, do you?' I ask Nathan. He shakes his head miserably.

Another piece of news from Nathan: the woman from Wednesfield has had an Aids test. Nathan seems amused rather than concerned and the conversation turns to another, older, woman he's got on the go. 'She's forty-eight,' says Nathan, 'I came home with her the other night and her two daughters were shagging upstairs with their boyfriends, so I had her on the sofa. She is not bad looking actually.'

'She's on the turn,' says Pete.

'Like a piece of cheese,' says Sandra.

Pete nurses his drink and looks as amiably half-sozzled as ever. He joins in the conversation but often loses the thread, at which point he returns to his pint and just looks on. The conversation turns to Pete's other great passion in life: northern soul. He's planning to go to Worcester for an all-nighter this weekend. 'Actually,' Sandra confides in me, 'Pete really can dance.' I tell him he's a dark horse and I'm going to call him to hear more. He nods and smiles and tries to say something but gets a bit mixed up again and has a big sip of his pint instead.

In the toilet a large man called Lee engages me in conversation. He has the kind of West Midlands accent that makes me sound like Prince Charles in comparison. He tells me he works in construction and that he follows us 'here, there and everywhere'. He also keeps saying, 'We want them to win, don't we?' It's an obvious enough statement but the way he keeps repeating it, more and more emphatically, makes it seem profound somehow.

Meanwhile Nathan's mood is darkening. On top of his cold and the absence of a woman in his life who isn't old enough to be his mother, he now can't get hold of his nan. He is flapping. 'My mum's in Spain and I don't know what to do. I don't know my nan's neighbours at all.' Everyone reassures him but I'm of a pessimistic disposition – something I blame the Albion for – and quickly envisage myself driving him home this evening when it's confirmed that the worst has happened. As usual I find the thought rather reassuring as, if it did come to pass, I/we/he wouldn't be the least bit worried about the outcome of tonight's match.

Sue Ball is here. She takes a picture of us in the pub, which we all examine. 'Looks like we're out of a mental home on day release,' says Sandra. I get a cab to Charlton with Sandra and Sue. Nathan was going to come but we leave him by the side of the road anxiously tapping into his phone. I call Vic who now, with kick-off approaching, is rather less phlegmatic: 'How are you?'

'Just got up. Now going back to bed.'

'How do you feel about not being here?'

'Terrible, really,' he says without emotion. 'But it's my eyes. What can I do, under the circumstances . . .' he trails off.

'Will you listen on the radio?'

'If I don't fall asleep.' I don't know why he says this because we both know that he won't fall asleep.

Sue and Sandra talk about old times, dating players back in the seventies. Sue tells of going out with John Trewick and dancing with Laurie Cunningham. Sandra remembers her friend Lorraine who chucked Bryan Robson because he was a hopeless dancer.

Word reaches us that, hours before the transfer deadline expires, we have sold Rob Earnshaw to Norwich for more than £3m. There's consternation: firstly that a team unable to score goals has sold a striker without replacing him, and secondly that someone has been daft enough to spend that kind of money on him.

Sue calls home to check her mum's all right. Val's got her next-door neighbour round to put Eurosport on for her so she can watch the African Cup of Nations. She's thrilled to bits because Kanu has managed to help make a goal for Nigeria. This is planet football: a German woman in Wednesbury delighting in the efforts of a Nigerian in Egypt.

In the ground our fans are in fine form. Nathan is in exceptionally good voice considering he has a cold and he thinks his nan's dead. Upon seeing the teamsheet, most of us give up hope of any kind of result because Andy Johnson has been selected in midfield in the absence of Ronnie Wallwork. 'Oh no, not that cunt again,' says a bloke with teeth missing behind me. 'I thought we'd seen the last of him.'

Yet it soon becomes clear that we are going to put some effort in, and even the much-maligned Andy Johnson will have a good game. It was all rather good noisy fun when we were resigned to a beating. Now we're starting to care again, there is a new, anguished gusto in the chanting.

At half-time it's still nil-nil which is good, but not nearly so good as the news that Nathan's nan isn't dead, after all – she just nodded off to sleep for a bit and didn't hear the phone.

In the second half we nearly score and nearly concede, but the match finishes goalless. Everyone is happy to declare this a point gained. I call Vic, imagining him lying there sightlessly taking in the drama of our brave goalless draw in south-east London. The whole thing has the whiff of tragedy about it. Brenda, though, is as breezy as ever when she answers the phone: 'Ooh, hello, Adrian, I'll just get him – he's in bed.'

Vic's too busy being annoyed with the chairman's transfer policy to feel very sorry for himself: 'What's he sold Earnshaw for?' he demands. 'We can't score any goals as it is.'

'But it wasn't bad money for him, was it, Vic?' I suggest.

'What's the good of three million quid in the bank?' he barks. 'It's no good there, is it? It's not going to score any goals there.'

Changing the subject, I ask Vic about his sight. 'I can see the telly a bit murky out of one eye but nothing in the other.' He pauses. 'But what's the good of three million in the bank?' he demands again. I don't have an answer for him.

It's impossible to feel sorry for Vic for long. But I find the same can't be said of Pete Talbot, former fireman, heavy drinker and excellent dancer. Pete's been dancing when I call him a few days later. He's at a northern soul weekend in Torquay. 'I'm full of cramp at the moment,' he says, 'from dancing. Dancing's a release for me, like the Albion.

'You know, my fever, er, fervour for the Albion – it's a funny old thing. I have been able to take breaks. I've taken breaks in it. When you see Sandra and Nathan, I think I'm not half as committed as they are.'

Many times, when Pete's not with them, I've asked Sandra where he is. 'Oh,' she'll often say, contemptuously, 'he's picking and choosing his games, he says.' Picking and choosing which games you go to, though not an unreasonable thing to do, is a terrible sin in the eyes of the really committed.

After a spell as a chef, Pete joined the fire service. 'That's when my passion for the Albion was rekindled. I was twenty-one, it was 1979, the Albion were in their heyday. I used to get all these floating bank holidays, so if you worked a public holiday, you could take it off in lieu. I organised it to take days off to watch the Albion.'

Pete goes through phases of lucidity but then loses his way. Whenever I see him before a game he always seems to me to be quietly, happily drunk. He can't get his words out sometimes and I've always put that down to the drink. It turns out now that I have been wrong about him on many counts. For one thing, he's not happy; for another, it's not for the drink that he loses his thread.

'I was assaulted at work, that's why I don't work any more. I was pensioned off because I had a head injury. Have you ever seen the dent in my head?'

'I don't think I've had the pleasure,' I say.

'I'll show you sometime,' he promises.

'I was on station, it was a lunch break. I was just sitting watching the telly, having a cup of tea. There was this bloke next to me. We were sort of dozing.' With this, Pete's voice cracks and, to my horror, he chokes back a couple of sobs. 'God, he . . . I find it ever so difficult to talk about, to be honest. The phone rang and he nudged me, get the phone, will you, he said. You see, every morning there's a parade in the fire station and you work out routines. As I got up to get the phone I realised that, hang on a moment, he was on phones. And he'd spoken to me a bit sharpish, a bit surly. So I put the phone down, kicked it a bit further away, and said, you, you get it. And he just lost it and hit me on the side of the head with an empty mug. He knocked me out. I was on a life support machine. He got sacked, well, asked to resign. Lots of people rallied around him. I felt alienated by my colleagues. He said he'd tried to wake me and he'd shaken me and I'd accidentally banged my head on the radiator.

'Anyway, I wasn't very well. I still suffer with my speech and my nerves. They offered me my pension and I took it. This was September 2000.'

I tell him how relaxed he always looks to me, with a drink in his hand.

'Unfortunately, that's the problem,' he says. 'A lot of people who've had head injuries become alcoholics, because you really can't understand what's happening to yourself. All the time while I was seeing a psychiatrist I was lying through my teeth, saying, no, I hadn't had a drink.'

'Do you drink too much now?'

'Oh crikey, yeah.'

'Are you getting help now?'

'No no. I just try to think to myself I'm drinking too much here. I wouldn't go to Newcastle, say, on an away trip, because I knew it would be a binge trip. I haven't been to any AA meetings or anything like that. But I know that might be the next step.

'My missus works full time. She looks after people with disabilities. My children are eight and eleven. My job is getting them to school and helping them with their reading. When you're assaulted you're very nervous of everything. You've got to confront your evils.' I take it he means demons but he's stopped dead again. 'It's so difficult for me to talk about it. My kids, they didn't know I was assaulted, by the way, didn't want them to know that there were nasty people in the world.

'I've gone nervous now just talking about the experience. I have to think too hard. I can't formulate my speech very well. The frustration . . . when I get frustrated I can't think. You know, when you have to be forceful with your children and you can't get the words out, that's terrible.

'I've tried loads of things to cope. My passion was running. I started running. All over the place. But now it's tennis. And northern soul, that's another release.'

'But what about the Albion?' I ask. 'Can they really be a help, or a hindrance?'

'Oh yeah,' he replies firmly, 'a help, very much so. Even if we've played badly and lost, it still does take your mind off your problems. It's been a great help.' He pauses. 'Then again, I must say the way we've been playing this season it has got to me, so I'm not so sure.'

Nine

Thailand Albion – Adam Cotton and his passion wagon

Any Albion fan who subscribes to the baggies@yahoogroups.com mailing list will be familiar with the name of a resident of Chiang Mai, Adam Cotton. If he can't watch, he listens to the radio commentary on the club's internet site and writes down what happens minute by minute. This he then emails around the world. That's how he and others like him keep in touch; he has never stopped feeling like he belongs.

Adam watched the Albion regularly until he moved to Thailand in 1981 to run his own small business. He exports butterflies and insects: 'I set up Thailand's first butterfly farm; I sold it in 1989. And I grew orchids for export. Then I had a tropical fish shop in Chiang Mai.'

For fans like Adam, the internet is a godsend. 'When I first went out to Thailand the Albion were in the old first division so our results and a little summary of what had happened would be in the

Sunday papers. But once we got relegated we had to wait until Monday for the results and they sometimes misprinted them. So occasionally we lost when we'd won, and vice versa. We didn't get proper information until the internet came along in the late nineties.

'Sometimes, being so far away, I feel an ache, but in other ways it can be really good. Like for the Palace game when we first went up: there were half a dozen of us in Bangkok who got together to listen on the internet. One guy was over from China; the others were all members of the Thai supporters' club. We went mad when we scored. You're far away but you still feel almost there; you are still part of it.'

Adam sends me a picture of his car, which is a quite magnificent sight. It's a 4×4, ideal for chasing butterflies around the jungle. It is festooned with West Brom stickers and trinkets. 'Until we got in the Premier League, West Brom meant nothing to anybody but now people see it and say, oh, yes, good, West Brom.' Occasionally West Brom fans travelling out here leave notes on the car. They get a right shock when they see it.

'On Survival Sunday I was in the jungle with a German moth collector.' He comes out with this like it's the most usual thing in the world to be in a jungle with a German moth collector, which, for Adam, I suppose it is. 'This bloke had arranged it ages before and I thought, Well, by then it will be over, we'll be down or safe.

'We had to go into the forest to collect moths. When the game was on we were at this light trap and I was humming tunes like "The Liquidator" and "The Lord's My Shepherd". I got back to the hotel late and there was no way to find out the score: no internet and no phone.

'Next morning, though, they had Thai TV on. On the ticker tape thing at the bottom of the telly, it said, in Thai, Southampton 1 Man United 2. Then, in brackets, Southampton relegated. West Brom was the last one of course, and there it was: West Brom 2 Portsmouth 0, and in brackets it said, more or less exact translation, West Brom escape relegation. It was fantastic.'

Back in Chiang Mai Adam was able to get on his computer and drink deeply from the well of joy that was our fans' chatrooms. Wherever you are in the world, these websites become part of your daily routine. The first thing I do every morning is see what is being said by whom and about whom. Contributions fall into three categories: there are those (the majority) who say everything's terrible, those who say everything's great, and the rest just want to buy a ticket, sell one or have some practical query about how to get to, and/or where to drink before, a forthcoming game.

Emails that don't fall into any of these categories tend to stick out. Emails like this one:

'Hello, I joined this group last week & I thought it only polite I said hello. My name's Mart & I attended matches from around 1965 until we got relegated to the old Division 3 under Blobby Gould on a regular basis. That was enough for me & my hard earned cash. I managed to come up with numerous ways of throwing money in the cut & getting more entertainment from it. However my feelings to the Baggies are now like a divorced couple who still can speak, have some happy memories together, but needless to say couldn't live with each other.'

I love the simile of the divorced couple and I'm charmed by the responses to this email. Everyone seems to understand where he's coming from and is happy to have him along. The general tone is, 'Don't worry, Mart, we sympathise, it's OK, you're still one of us.' But amicably divorced or not, this bloke, I decide, is going to come with me to a game as soon as possible.

I call to suggest this but warn him that he might get hooked again. 'I know,' he replies, 'it's like being an alcoholic. I still think it's amazing how I got out of the habit. I was virtually addicted. I went to reserve matches, away matches, whatever. I probably went from about 1978 to that game at Bath in 1991 without missing a home game. Then I just went from one extreme to the other, never going at all. The final straw was Bristol Rovers at Bath.'

Just as 'Bradford' is shorthand among West Brom fans for one of the greatest days in the club's history, 'Twerton Park', Bath City's ground, is shorthand for the low point. Never before had we played in the third tier of English football, but unless we won that day at Twerton Park, where Bristol Rovers were playing their home games at the time, we would probably go down.

My leg was in plaster so my mate Martin wheeled me to the side of the pitch in my chair. Our last away game of the season usually has a fancy dress theme. On this occasion, in tribute to previous visitors to Bath, there was a Roman theme. Branded 'Togas at the Rovers', it involved lots of large Black Country types donning sandals and wrapping themselves in bed sheets. Some of them wore crowns of thorns, too. The historical link wasn't quite clear but – don't be offended by this, please – the suggestion of pain and martyrdom didn't seem inappropriate before kick-off, and certainly not once the final whistle had blown.

Rovers had a player sent off after roughly one minute. For the remaining eighty-nine minutes our eleven players failed to beat their ten. With Leicester City winning at home, we were relegated, but not before a rumour went round that they had conceded and we were safe. I jiggled about in my wheelchair as everyone went ballistic. Then the rumour proved to be false and hundreds of Rovers fans came rushing up the pitch to our end, smiling and laughing and making obscene gestures at us.

Some men, many in togas, decided to fight them. Others just filed away, tears streaming down their faces, togas sagging in misery. I never wear fancy dress for this precise reason. It is all very well being done up like a kipper if you've got something to celebrate, but if it's all gone pear-shaped, you're going to feel a whole lot worse standing there in a comedy wig, or with your face painted, or dressed up as a Roman person.

The following morning my lad came into my bedroom to tell me he'd just heard on the radio that our fans spent the night on the rampage in Weston-super-Mare. 'Disgusting,' I said, but, Good, I thought. I'm not proud of it but a night on the rampage in

Weston might have been just the thing to have eased the pain in my soul.

Still, as I've said, two days later I was at a reserve game to demonstrate my loyalty. Not Mart, though, he'd had enough. Oddly, it wasn't the relegation per se that did it for him. 'Me and this other chap went down there – we'd been home and away all season, you know,' he says. 'On the way back from Bath we stopped up at a service station and had something to eat. It was weird, like we were on a different planet. We couldn't believe what had happened. And as we turned back on to the motorway the team bus passed us. And this chap I was with said, come on, we'll follow them back to the Hawthorns.

'When the coach pulled up at the ground, we was there. We watched them all get off and my mate said, look at this lot here – none of them could give a damn. None of them looked bothered or anything like that, and that was it really. He was right, they didn't look bothered. It was just the last straw, after losing to Woking in the FA Cup. Years of disappointment condensed in that moment.'

The truth is, Mart didn't miss much throughout the nineties, even though we were promoted back into the second tier two years later. I asked him if he's missed it. 'Quite honestly, it didn't bother me. I thought, No, I won't go, and when my mates tried to talk me into it I put my foot down and said, no, I haven't been to a single game, I'll put the jinx on them. I've actually given friends a lift in to catch the coach to a game and then gone home and watched it on the television.'

I ask about other key games in our comparatively successful recent history, such as the last of the 2001/02 season, when we needed to beat Crystal Palace to go up to the Premiership. 'Watched it round my brother's house. He was at the game but he said, go round and watch it at my house. Quite frankly it was probably the worst ninety minutes of my life. The nervousness did get to me. It reminded me, you know, why I stopped going, because I used to think it was actually damaging my health. I'd get so wound up and nervous coming away I had sweaty palms.

If I'd been to the game, I often was grossly upset. I've got so many memories of coming away completely hoarse, unable to speak and going to the pub to recover.

'To this day, it's still always in the back of my mind even if I'm walking round the supermarket or something at three o'clock – I think, It's three o'clock, they're playing. It's always there. I look at the website virtually every day and the *Express and Star* for any news. I still care; I have the blue and white in me. But I've got out of it,' he says triumphantly but somewhat unconvincingly, 'I've got out of the habit.'

Mart agrees to come to the Blackburn match, though he says, 'I think I might have second thoughts.' He laughs as he says it, but there's a quavering tone to his voice.

I fully understand how seeing that shower come back from Twerton Park, apparently not caring less that they broke our hearts, put him off coming for life. To really love your team, you have to suspend disbelief, you have to forget that they will hardly ever win anything. And you also have to forget that none of the players, not one of them, cares about the Albion like you do. Seeing them get off that coach with smiles on their faces was the moment Mart faced this reality.

On the other hand, I just don't get how or why he maintains his interest in the club. He looks at the website every day, he scans the local papers for news, he thinks about us. But he doesn't go. To stretch the ex-smoker analogy, it's like he's successfully kicked the habit but still enjoys passive smoking.

Saturday, 4 February 2006, Blackburn at home

This morning Mart leaves me a voicemail saying he has a cold and can't come. I'm not sure I believe him but it's not my place to disrespect his decision.

The Blackburn match isn't the only one involving West Brom today. The under-eighteens and under-sixteens are playing

Wolves, kicking off at eleven o'clock at our training ground. Absurdly, I am quite excited, probably because it's Wolves they're playing. I park up near the training ground, right behind a couple hurriedly getting out of their car. We're late. They've already kicked off.

I walk down with the couple. They're trying to walk quicker than me as their boy is playing for our under-eighteens. He's a striker from Northern Ireland called Garth McDonald. His mum and dad are breathless and hassled because a delay to their flight has made them late. His mum says exactly what my mum would have said if she'd been in the same situation: 'I really miss my little boy,' she wails, 'but he's happy. He's fine.' They both say what a big fish he was in the game in Northern Ireland, where he was a bit of a star. 'It's different here,' says his mum and his dad nods.

I have never been to see the youth team play before. It's a bit like a high-octane school match. The vast majority of the spectators are parents. There are cheers when goals are scored, and praise and encouragement shouted, but essentially nobody's here to support a team. For the parents, to all intents and purposes, it's a rather one-sided game of their boy versus at least twenty-one others, plus the referees, coaches and substitutes.

Ian and Karen Nicholson are here, down for the day from Newcastle. They have two boys on our books. One of them, Dean, is playing for the under-eighteens. The other, Stuart, would have been playing, too, but is watching instead because he's expected to be named on the bench for the first team today. This is why Ian and Karen have made the long journey down. They talk to me and each other in the thickest Geordie accents you'll ever hear on a playing field in Walsall. I arrange to meet them in the pub next to the Hawthorns before the game.

I walk round for a look at the under-sixteens match. Again, instead of watching the ball as most football crowds do, the spectators are all looking in slightly different directions at their babies. I talk to some: 'Who are you watching?'

'Wolves. Four.' Four is the number on his kid's back.

'How's he doing?'

'Not too bad.'

They're happy enough to talk, but never take their eyes off their boys.

By the time I get back to the under-eighteens, Garth has scored his first goal for the club. His parents do a poor job of concealing their absolute delight. As I walk away I wonder how many of the forty-four boys and men playing out there now will make it in the game. I ask one of the staff this question. 'About six,' he says. I make that thirty-eight shattered dreams.

On the way to the Hawthorns I call Vic. I know he is on strict doctor's orders to miss his seventh game since the Second World War. I told Jane that I couldn't bear the thought of him missing out again and suggested I might go and sit with him at home and listen to it. 'Nice idea,' said Jane, 'but you won't do it in the end, will you?'

But I needn't have worried about having to make that decision because to my relief – and horror – he tells me he is going to the match anyway, even though the doctor has specifically told him to lie down and keep still. 'Are you sure you should?' I ask.

'Just got to go,' he says simply. 'I've got to have thirteen drops in my eyes,' he says.'

'Thirteen? Unlucky,' I say. He laughs.

In the pub I ask around for Roy Hayden, father of Steve who's having his bone marrow transplant today. He is not here yet, but I'm reliably informed that he will be.

I find Ian and Karen, who are sitting at a big round table. It looks like the kind of temporary structure you might get under a clean tablecloth in a marquee at a posh wedding. Karen has a pile of six programmes in front of her. Stuart and another couple of youngsters are pictured on the front. Ian smiles grimly: 'Stuart's just called. He's not playing. Campbell's fit. He's gutted.' Ian shrugs: 'It happens.'

Also on the table is a bloke rolling his own from a tobacco tin with the club crest on it. I congratulate him on the tin. 'Self-made,' he says proudly. This is Alex Elliott, founder of the Inverness branch of the fan club. Alex was raised in Coleraine in Northern Ireland, where he started supporting the Albion. 'It was all British football in Northern Ireland and this was the days of Jeff Astle and so on, and I just started following them.'

When he moved to Scotland he met a couple of West Brom fans, one a cook from Smethwick and the other from London. They decided to get together and organise a supporters' club. 'We've got twenty, maybe twenty-five, members now, just from the Inverness area,' he says. 'My two sons and my daughter, too, they're Albion fans. They wear the shirts to school. Get a bit of stick, but there you go.

'You know,' he says, 'I used to watch Rangers a bit and saw them win loads of trophies, but for me Survival Sunday was the biggest day ever. To be honest, until then I never knew how passionate I was about the team.'

On the way out of the pub I see Roy Hayden. Steve is at this moment having the operation. His sister's here as well as his father, but his mum has stayed with him. Roy tells me how much this annoyed Steve. 'What a waste of money for the ticket,' he said.

I give the Nicholsons my seats for the game and ask Craig Shakespeare, who's in charge of the academy, if I can talk to some of his players and perhaps sit and watch the game with them. They're all milling around by the entrance to the tunnel, waiting for the teams to come out. 'You, you and you,' he says pointing at three players, 'come and talk to Adrian.'

Obediently, they answer my questions and ask plenty, too. Garth McDonald is one of them and is just as charming as his mum and dad. I'm incredibly impressed by all of them, so it tortures me all the more that most of them won't be in the game in eighteen months' time.

I end up sitting between Jared Hodgkiss, whom Graeme Le Saux and I saw making his debut at Reading, and another full-back, Lee Baker, a Villa fan from Redditch. They both talk intelligently about the game and realistically about their own prospects. Jared tells me to watch our full-back Paul Robinson. 'Look at that, look at that,' he says admiringly as Robinson puts in a tackle in the penalty area right in front of us and clears the ball. 'Class,' says Jared.

Lee says, 'I know I'm on a steep learning curve; got to improve.' I am pretty sure he's just parroting what the coaches have been drumming into him but I'm impressed anyway. He tells me about the game this morning, stuff I barely understand about how he let the bloke in on the outside and got sucked in, or something. I give thanks that this morning when I asked a regular watcher of the youth team who he rated of the lads playing, Lee's name was first on his lips.

I ask Jared if he's a fan now. 'Yes,' he says. 'Sometimes I think, Well, if they went down I'd have more chance of a game, but when I'm here you can't help it, you just want them to win.'

Then we score. I leap up and they do, too, but a fraction after me. They're clapping – not as jubilantly as me, but they're clapping. A little ginger lad is sitting the other side of Jared. He's tiny and his wisps of ginger bum fluff make him look younger than he would if he had no facial hair at all. This is James McQuilkin. 'He was playing this morning,' says Jared. I talk with James awhile and become so intoxicated with the immensity of what they're all trying to achieve that I nearly lose interest in the game because I start caring more about these boys, who probably won't make it, than the ones on the pitch, who already have.

We score again and again we all stand and applaud politely. At half-time we're 2-0 up. It's all going terribly well. Baggie Bird even appears high up on the roof of the East Stand. Everyone cheers and he waves back before abseiling down. I shake hands with the boys and thank them for their company. On the way up to my usual seat, I bump into Craig Shakespeare again. I tell him I don't know if they're going to play for England, or even the

Albion or anybody else, but he's certainly making them great human beings. Craig just smiles and nods.

Vic then appears in front of me, all but blind, wearing a bright red Ferrari anorak. I ask if he could see the goals.

'I saw the goals, yes,' he says unconvincingly.

'How is it?'

'Got no better, got no worse. The doctor said I shouldn't go out. He said, if you have any pain, come straight back. Well, it is aching, but I'll leave it 'til Monday.'

I am not optimistic for the chances of Vic's eyesight returning. I try to imagine what his doctor would make of it if he was here now. I'm troubled by an image of the inside of Vic's eyeball collapsing, caving in, giving up the ghost. And all for the sake of the Albion. I fetch us some tea and as he sips it he describes his vision: 'All I can see is kind of bubbles,' he says, his hand describing them in the air. 'They're wobbling all the while like a river.'

As Ian and Karen Nicholson are still in my seats, I park myself next to Roy Hayden. I'm in his wife Barbara's seat. A few rows in front of us sits Amanda, Steve's sister. It's a bizarre feeling this: sitting next to Roy while his son is having a transplant of bone marrow donated by his sister sitting just in front of us. I ask Roy how it's going at the hospital. A pained look flashes across his face, but then he shrugs, smiles and says, 'All going to plan, I think.'

Here on the back row of the stand, for some reason it feels as if the seats are packed more tightly together. There's a bit of a kerfuffle on the pitch and one or two people in front of us get to their feet to have a better look and register their discontent. 'Don't stand up here or you'll lose your space,' says the man to my right.

It strikes me how each seat in the ground has its own politics and geography, which you acclimatise to very quickly. Here, for example, on the row in front of us, three to my left, a bloke suddenly takes exception to the general discontent all around us. His temper snaps: 'Will everybody stop moaning and be more positive,' he hollers. You just know that this is what he shouts most weeks.

212

It is his theme. It's the same with another man about ten to the right who has either not heard, or chosen to ignore, the command for us all to be more positive. *'Ellington,'* he screams, almost in falsetto, 'You. Are. A. Fucking. Disgrace.'

But we win and it's great. The youth team lads were great; Vic was here, unwisely, but he was here; Baggie Bird abseiled down safely; and, above all, we won. Later Roy calls me to say that Steve is doing fine. Happy days or, as Sandra puts it by text, 'Fanfuckingtastic.'

None of us know it at this stage, obviously, but we will not win another match this season. The fourth of February: dreadfully early to be tasting happiness for the very last time.

Saturday, 11 February 2006, Fulham away

On the Monday before this one I go out for a quick drink with Iain Dowie, manager of Crystal Palace. He is one of the more intelligent people I know in the game. He talks and drinks and thinks very quickly. In about ninety minutes in the pub, we drink two pints of lager apiece, share a bottle of white wine and toast his late father with a large Jameson's. We discuss football mainly, and to illustrate the many interesting points he makes he scribbles wildly on a scrap of paper. I understand some of what he says, but only in flashes. And the more I drink, the less I can fathom out.

It's an enjoyable hour and a half in the pub but, as we walk away to find ourselves cabs, he asks who Albion are playing on Saturday. 'Fulham,' I reply.

'You'll lose,' he says matter-of-factly. This rather spoils everything for me as I take it as an insult. It wouldn't have been so bad if he'd said 'I'm afraid I think you'll struggle there' or 'I can't see you getting much from that.' No, just 'You'll lose', as if I wouldn't be hurt by such a bald statement of fact. It would have felt exactly the same if he'd said, 'You're ugly' or 'You'll never get Gary

Lineker's job.' Both statements are factually correct, but you don't want them spelled out so bluntly, without compassion.

Come Saturday, since Fulham's ground is walking distance from my house, a few of us get together for a meal in a pub just around the corner. Sandra, Kate, Nathan and a bloke I have not met before called Pod came down last night and stayed in a dodgy-sounding hotel in the West End. They bring to our table this lunchtime a story about staying up most of the night and Nathan getting together with some old woman. 'Old slapper,' says Sandra.

'She wasn't old,' says Nathan more with indignation than irony.

Also with us in the pub are Gurdial, her younger daughter Jeevan and her son Joshan. And there's Younos, my Spanish-Moroccan Barcelona-supporting friend, Simmo and Olly from the club's press department, Mehrdad, an Iranian football fanatic I've been working with, and a tubby Jewish lawyer (his description of himself not mine) called David Roody and his girlfriend, a statuesque religious studies teacher.

'So anyway,' Nathan is saying to whoever's listening, 'this bloke wants a fight because he reckons I've been touching this woman's pussy.' Gurdial's smiling but has her hands cupped over the ears of poor, bewildered Joshan, who may or, more likely, may not, have heard such stuff in the playground yet.

Rab Rogers looks on, smiling. Well into his seventies, he's a walking oxymoron: shambolically dapper, brilliantly daft, quite unforgettable company. His hair is as grey as it should be but has a youthfully raffish wave in it. He is legendary for setting up and running the London branch of the supporters' club in the seventies. I say to him now, referring to Nathan, that I've never associated erotica with the Albion. 'Pah,' says Rab, spluttering out broken plumes of cigarette smoke, 'I've been doing it for fifty years now.' There is a contemplative pause while we take this in before, somewhat disconcertingly, he adds, 'I'm going through my oriental phase at the moment.'

David Roody looks round at Sandra, Gurdial, Nathan, Rab et al. and says, 'You know, it's incredible the amount of time you spend with your fellow fans. You see them every other week and yet, usually, you never know anything about them.' As we all shamble uncertainly off to Craven Cottage, I hazily reflect on what a privilege it is to know all these people. I become quite drunkenly sentimental and nearly put my arm around Rab but at the last moment think better of it.

An absent friend comes to mind. I text Steve Hayden, who's been learning to live with his new bone marrow for all of a week now. He is in a bad way: 'Got terrible pain in the mouth. Can't eat, can't talk very well. But they told me it'd be like this.'

A man called Paul Leddington walks down to the ground with me. I've been trying to meet him since his daughter Amy wrote to me: 'I never remember having a choice about being a West Brom fan, I was born one. My father actually wrote a poem to that effect on the day I was born':

> Amy Jane was her name
> Into the world she slowly came,
> When she came she cried a lot,
> A Villa supporter I am not,
> West Brom's the team for me,
> Just like my dad, he loves them see!

'There are more verses and another added on my eighteenth birthday, but you get the idea. And for years when I was tucked into bed we always said the same rhyme, which went as follows: Night night, Sleep tight, Pleasant dreams, Up the Baggies, There's only one Cyrille Regis and One Derek Statham.

'I know this doesn't rhyme, but I truly thought that was the bedtime rhyme, and when I heard about "minding the bed bugs don't bite" in latter years, I thought the other kids had got it wrong.'

Word reaches me that Vic Stirrup is here but, as a very small concession to his doctors' orders not to come, he is not sitting in the away end with us as he's got a ticket for the directors' box. That way Dr Rimmer, the former club doctor, will be able to put his eye drops in for him.

For nearly four minutes it looks as if we're going to play well and maybe even win the match, but then Fulham score and do so again shortly before half-time. My misery is compounded by the embarrassment I feel at having dragged my Iranian friend Mehrdad here. It feels rather like I've taken an acquaintance to see my daughter perform in a school concert and she's turned out to be hopeless.

Bad as we are playing, it's not generally the done thing to abuse your own team away from home, so our fans focus on berating the Fulham fans or, more vocally, the referee, Graham Poll. I can't see how in any way, shape or form he is to blame for our poor performance but a song about Graham Poll being a 'fucking arsehole' is still sung loudly, if a bit mournfully.

Just before half-time the flow of play brings the referee right next to us in our corner of the ground. In a lull in the noise someone shouts, 'Poll, you are a fat cunt.' Unaccountably this cheers me up. It's barbarically rude; Poll's done nothing wrong and, knowing him a little bit, I quite like the bloke. But I still feel better for it. Absurd.

At half-time Kevin Reynolds comes up to me. He is Mark's brother, our man in New Zealand. Kevin tells me Mark said he wasn't going to follow this game live because he's between long shifts but he must be because he has been sending anguished texts. We agree that it's strangely comforting to know that someone in a far-off place and time-zone is suffering with us.

At 2-0 there is hope but soon it is 3-0 and all hope is gone. Released from any residual tension, the singing and chanting get louder and louder. It makes me proud to be part of this lusty demonstration of unconditional love. It's great to see the bewilderment and ill-disguised admiration in the eyes of the home supporters. However, it is also a bit daft. If we weren't being tonked, we wouldn't be singing like this. Also, I'm just sick of walking away from grounds proud of another fantastic performance by the supporters, as if the club ought to be awarded points for our full-blooded singing. Accordingly, I don't sing a thing. I just slump and sulk.

I soon get a sharp tap on the back. The man sitting behind me is displeased. His eyes are blazing with anger: 'What's the matter with you?' he demands. 'Sing up! Aren't you proud to be Albion?' Loyalty and blind, unconditional love: the last refuge of the fan of the dismally hopeless team. But I can't carry it off. I'm furious, because I was just about to leave in disgust but I dare not do so now. Soon, though, with the score at 5-0, I do leave. By this point, even the spirit of Mr Angry behind is broken. He looks at me with as much envy as scorn when I stand up to leave, smiling apologetically at him.

As I walk away there's a cheer from inside the ground. Somebody says, without interest or pleasure, 'That's us.' Five-one. A few minutes later there is a much bigger cheer. Six-one. Gurdial tells me how Joshan kept singing even though he was so upset at the result. To my alarm she sheds a tear. And, as a parent, I'm not sure how I'd behave in her position. So far my efforts to get my daughters involved have failed dismally but if they did one day start taking an interest I'm not sure I could cope with seeing them upset. It would make me angry with the team, and even more angry with myself for putting them through it. Gurdial wipes her eyes, smiles, and we walk on.

I look around as we trudge back along the Thames towards Hammersmith whence we came. 'All religions are represented here,' I say, looking at Gurdial, a Sikh, and Mehrdad, a Muslim. Then there are a couple of Catholics, an Anglican and one or two heathens. 'No Jews,' someone says as if this was our problem all along, and we all nod sadly, thinking of David Roody who was supporting Fulham.

Steve Hayden texts me from his hospital bed: his mouth is still extremely painful; he can hardly talk and is finding it very difficult to eat. 'I thought I felt bad before that shower,' he says. Later that evening Iain Dowie texts me, too: 'That a drubbing. Sympathies.' And the following day he obviously senses that I'm still stewing on it. 'Don't stop believing,' he texts. I text back: 'If I could stop believing, there wouldn't be a problem.'

The following Tuesday our Polish cleaner, Sylvia, comes into the house with a worried look on her face. 'Adrian,' she says, concern etched across her brow, 'what happened to your chim?' It's quite a windy day and I wonder if my chimney has blown off. 'My chim?' I say. 'My chimney?'

'No,' she says, 'your cheem.'

We look blankly at one another.

'6-1!' she says.

'Oh, my team. I see,' I smile. But she's not smiling. She knows this is serious. I never knew that she cared, that she feels my pain.

Sunday, 26 February 2006, Middlesbrough at home

A win is called for. A win we don't get. By half-time, we're 2-0 down. Gavin Peacock, who I'm watching the match with at the *Match of the Day* studio, asks how long it will take me to get over this.

'All week,' I say. He laughs, but I don't. Footballers just don't get it. They never do.

It gets worse. Soon after half-time our new signing Nigel Quashie gets sent off for, well, stamping on a Boro player's throat. He's as certain to get a long ban as we are to lose this game. Afterwards Frank Skinner texts: 'I'm never going to another football match in my whole life . . . still, if we beat Chelsea next week we'd be back on course.'

Quite where Frank gets his optimism from I know not. Usually I envy him, but sometimes I think he's just delusional.

Saturday, 4 March 2006, Chelsea at home

The day before the match I ring the Rev Ken Hipkiss and ask his thoughts. Even Ken, someone with as much faith in his little finger as the rest of us have got in our whole bodies, cannot summon much hope ahead of this one. He can't bring himself to admit we're going to lose but he says, 'It's going to be tough', which is what the Rev says when he is sure we're going to come second.

At the ground I bump into John Homer, head of the supporters' club. As we cross the road our star defender Curtis Davies is waiting at the traffic lights in a huge Porsche four-wheel-drive thing. I'm told it costs about fifty grand. He is not yet twenty-one. Everyone says he's a nice lad but at this moment it feels like he's a visitor from another world. The music inside his dream machine is unbelievably loud – you can almost feel the air vibrating around the car. Curtis sings along, moving his head vigorously from side to side as he does so. His gaze is fixed straight ahead while all around wide, fascinated eyes stare at him in wonder. 'He knows all the words to this one, apparently,' says John Homer.

In the supporters' club I come across Stuart Nicholson's parents. Once again Ian and Karen have driven down from Newcastle in the hope and expectation of seeing their boy start on the bench. Their niece is on her way down, too. Karen tells me that all the old people she looks after at work are rooting for the Albion now. But will he be playing or won't he? Stuart is supposed to ring at 11.15 but doesn't. Finally, at 11.30, he rings and rings off; a signal for them to ring him. They do so and are told that he's not playing. Again. Karen is really annoyed and upset. In jest – I think – she tells me it's my fault as I was in attendance the last time this happened.

Then Karen phones an elderly relative to break the news, knowing that as this match is a lunchtime kick-off and is televised she'll be glued to the screen. 'He's not on the bench,' Karen says. 'No,' she confirms, 'he's not.' Again: 'He's not on the bench, no.' The relative is either hard of hearing or so disappointed that she's refusing to believe what she's hearing. 'No,' poor Karen says again, more firmly, 'he's not playing.'

Today I'm sitting with a woman called Emily Woffinden. She's eighteen and in love with our defender Neil Clement. And when I say in love, I mean in love. I met her at a supporters' meeting I was speaking at in Sutton Coldfield. She showed me her mobile phone. On it was a picture of Neil Clement. 'There must be 120 girls in my sixth form,' she says, 'and none of them like football. But they all know who Neil Clement is.'

Emily first saw the Albion when she was eight. 'I loved it because everyone was so sort of, well, happy.'

'Happy? Are you sure this is the Albion you are talking about?'

'Yes, well, I had just never been anywhere where all these thousands of people were shouting and singing together and I used to love all the funny things they used to say. And then I got to recognise certain players like Paul Peschisolido and Andy Hunt and I really got into it. Sean Flynn used to annoy me.

'My love for Clem started about six years ago, not because of his good looks, more because at that time he was one of our best players and because I thought he was such a nice man. I remember saying to Dad how nice he was. He didn't argue with the referee and I saw him as a dependable, calm but committed player, and I still do really. Even when out of the team, managers always comment on how accepting Clem is. He's able to acknowledge his faults and work hard to put them right and this is something I really admire. However, don't get me wrong, I also noticed his gorgeous head, face, legs, thighs . . .

'I have photos of him on my school folder, my homework diary and on the official Albion calendar where I pin a photo of him each month. I've got a framed picture by my bed (which boyfriends have turned over, for some reason they find Clem's face a bit disconcerting), a framed and signed club photo (including three kisses – I only asked him to put one), a large A4 print on my desk, all the photos out of the club catalogue when he's modelled, a folder of photos on the computer from the official website, photos of his Chelsea days, and he's the background photo on my phone, my computer and my MSN. He has even followed me abroad as Dad gave me photos of Clem to take with me when I went to Russia for a week. And Mum made me a cake for my eighteenth with Clem and me made out of marzipan sitting on top of it.'

Her mum and dad's acceptance and even encouragement of Emily's infatuation I find a little odd. I ask her dad about this and he just smiles, shrugs and says, 'What can I do?'

Emily is in every other way a perfect young woman: jaw-droppingly beautiful, highly intelligent, very funny and incredibly nice with it. Yet she has this obsession. She is one of these people who I suspect can have anything she wants if she puts her mind to it. Perhaps Neil Clement is the one thing she can't have – but it won't be for want of dreaming about him.

I take Emily into the press room where many football hacks stop talking or tapping on their laptops to stare adoringly at her. A bloke from the *Birmingham Post* says, 'Bloody hell, where did you get her from?'

'She only has eyes for one man,' I say, 'and it's not me.'

The Woffindens' seats are the other side of the ground from the press entrance so one of the press assistants walks us around the pitch. As luck would have it, Neil Clement is warming up right by the touchline when we emerge. Emily's face freezes and she manages not to take her eyes off him for a moment. I ask if she'd like to walk backwards with me minding the way for her, but she doesn't seem to hear, so engrossed is she in the sight of her man. 'He has to have trousers made especially for him, you know,' she says dreamily, 'because his thighs are so big.'

'How do you know that?'

'Read it somewhere,' she says.

When we get to our seats the teams are being announced. Emily does a little jig when it comes to his name. Some friends of mine have a son who used to play rugby for England and the British Lions, Dan Luger. I once watched him play against South Africa at

Twickenham. I was sitting next to his parents and sitting next to Emily now is a very similar sensation. She's protective and proud of Clem, and defensive, too.

'I don't like to see him heading it,' she says. And when he collides with Didier Drogba, a battering ram of a player, she oohs and aahs and groans all at once.

Soon everyone else is groaning when Clement is guilty of a poor clearance. She glowers at a few people and shouts, rather shrilly, 'C'mon, Clem!'

She tells me she hates girls who wear a number-six shirt, Clement's number, but don't know anything about him. She pauses to laugh at herself a little but, just as I start to suspect the whole thing's a bit of a pretence, she says something which makes me worry for her, not to say the player and his family. 'You know,' she says, her smile vanishing, 'I really do believe we are meant to be together.'

I stare at her.

'No, really I do.'

Both a bit shocked, we turn our attention back to the match. We get a corner and when Clement nearly gets his head to the ball Emily makes exactly the kind of squeak she might one day make on seeing her child do something good in a school play or football match.

At half-time it's goalless, which, against Chelsea, is no mean achievement. It is generally agreed that we're doing well. But, as usual, we start the second half rather poorly and quickly concede a sloppy goal. Chelsea then have a player sent off and there is a massive ding-dong between our bench and theirs. Lots of grown men shout and swear at each other angrily.

This gets all our pulses racing but before very long Chelsea score again. For both of our goals our defence is sloppy but, in Emily's head, Neil Clement has not been at fault at all. We score very near the end but we know the game's up. We lose. Emily takes a last long lingering look at her man as he shakes hands with Chelsea's players. What a gentleman.

I am very annoyed and upset at the result. 'Lost, then?' says Julian on the till at Warwick Services. I nod miserably. Luckily the indefatigable Frank Skinner has a positive spin to run by me. Later in the afternoon, after the three o'clock kick-offs have finished, he texts: 'I thought we played quite well, esp first half. At least we lost to a good team, unlike our rivals. I also noticed that Blues run-in is very nearly as horrible as ours. If we score first next week, home crowd could turn on their players.'

Saturday, 11 March 2006, Birmingham away

It is ahead of this match I realise I'm in the grip of a madness that will now be with me until our relegation or survival is confirmed. I really don't stop thinking about this game for a minute, all week. It is in my mind when I wake up, when I go to bed and when I'm asleep. I am thinking about it constantly even as I'm having quite challenging conversations, sometimes live on air. It's no longer a question of thinking about it every few seconds. I am never not thinking about it.

I spend Friday night at my mum and dad's as the kick-off is at midday. Saturday dawns quite frosty. I'm talking to my parents when I notice that outside a mouse has managed to kill itself in the bird feeder. In an attempt to get at the nuts the poor little thing has jammed its head in the too-small gap and either broken its neck or frozen to death. I hate mice but I feel quite emotional about this one.

'Do you think that's an omen about the Albion?' my dad says.

'It'd be a great help if that stupid Albion wins,' says my mum. Her heart's always in the right place with the Albion but she never quite gets the grammar or spelling right. A flatmate of mine at university, a Newcastle fan, used to be enchanted by her spelling of Baggies as 'Bagiz' in her letters to me.

I look again at the mouse's frozen bum and I am quite sure that its passing is a portent of doom.

I meet Nathan at Stourbridge Junction Station. He has to be in a pub in Birmingham called the Square Peg at 10 a.m. That seems early enough to me, even for a lunchtime kick-off, but there's talk of a pub somewhere in Dudley that has been open since a quarter to seven. I like that: not seven, but a quarter to, allowing the drinkers that all important extra fifteen minutes supping not long after sunrise.

There are as many police outside the Square Peg as there are football fans inside. It's 10.15 a.m. and the beer is flowing. I make the acquaintance of one of our most renowned hooligans. He's also been in a fair bit of trouble following England around. His claim to fame is that he was once deported from Poland, which is some achievement in my book. I won't give his name or describe him because he's obviously very hard and would kill me quite easily. Suffice to say that through my blue and white spectacles he seems a smashing chap, so I decide not to turn him in on this occasion. He tells me he can't get World Cup tickets. Preposterously I take his number and tell him I'll ring if I hear of any going.

I get a cab to St Andrews and see our supporters' coaches arriving. For some reason I love watching them roll up – perhaps it makes me feel like I'm in the advanced party of an invading army and they represent the arrival of massive reinforcements. A bloke walking past grabs me and says urgently that we're going to win 4-0. 'How do you know?' I ask.

'I've had a premonition: it's my wife's birthday, her fortieth. She had a card. I knocked it on the floor and it was upside down so it said 0-4. We're going to win 4-0,' he says again in triumph.

I tell him this could also be interpreted as a sign of a 4-0 defeat.

'No,' he says firmly, 'it'll be 4-0.'

Incredibly, a wave of optimism surges through my body.

Vic Stirrup's here, obviously. 'How's your eyes, Vic?' I ask him.

'No better. There's this black circle I don't like,' he says, waving his hand in front of his face. 'It's sort of wobbling all the while.'

'How we going to do today?'

'Win,' he says with a shrug. He doesn't seem to care either way but his default position is that we will win.

Standing next to Vic is Les. He is holding the hand of a small, pale boy. Les tells me this is the son of the woman who cares for Les's wife at their home in Smethwick while he's at the football. This is the little boy's treat. 'He's Albion mad,' smiles Les. The little lad's got a scarf on. He looks up at me balefully but says nothing. Les updates me on the progress of the rug he's making for me. He has started it but it's going to take some time because he's busy caring for his wife 'twenty-four-seven', which seems a very modern turn of phrase for him to use.

Roy Hayden's here but Steve is not. It's only a month since he had the transplant to tackle his leukaemia. I ask Roy how he is doing.

'So so,' says Roy, 'he's getting there.'

In the ground, as the guest of our directors, I'm afforded hospitality in the shape of light refreshments and a very, very poor comedian acting as compère. Thankfully I've missed most of what he would probably describe as his 'act' or 'routine'. As I come in he is going around the tables asking people who they're here to support. If they say 'Blues', he yells, 'Come on!' into his microphone so loudly that the sound distorts. If they say something else, like 'Albion' for example, he just grunts.

He pauses to tell an old, old joke about the only recently deceased George Best launching a ship and it being five miles out to sea before they got the champagne off him. Nobody laughs at all. Phil Rimmer, son of our retired club doctor, is here. He raises his eyes to the heavens and says, 'You should have heard the one he told a minute ago about a Villa fan being run over by a steam engine. He was chuffed to bits, apparently. Even with this audience it didn't go down well.'

I speak to a few people, Birmingham and West Brom fans, and we're all as convinced as each other that our teams are going to lose. This is why Blues and Albion fans get on rather well – we are united in pessimism.

In the directors' box Phil and I sit behind John Evans, our club secretary for many a year. On the pitch we start brightly. I say to Phil that we look lively and Phil agrees. Then I pull myself up: 'Famous last words,' I say, at precisely the same moment that John turns round and says, 'Spare us the commentary, will you?'

A little later Phil declares that we look a more balanced side. Again, John turns round to glower at him: 'Stop tempting fate.' And fate, duly tempted, does seem to have taken the bait: we miss two sitters. When the second of these chances goes begging, Phil, a gentle chap like his dad, moans, 'No no no no no', in a kind of reverse of Meg Ryan faking an orgasm in *When Harry Met Sally*.

At half-time it's nil-nil. My all-time hero Cyrille Regis is here. 'How did we miss those?' he wails. Everyone shrugs. A few Blues fans say to me that we're going to stuff them. I say, 'I think we all know what's going to happen here, don't we?' A few Albion fans nod. I'm almost pleased to be right when Birmingham soon get a penalty and score. Jeff Farmer turns to me from a few seats away and mouths one word: 'Unbelievable.'

We go on to miss loads of half-chances. An old friend, Lee, texts me: 'How many bloody chamber do we want?' I think he means 'chances' not 'chamber', so I take my mind off the game by punching 'chances' into my predictive text and, sure enough, up pops 'chamber'. This reminds me of a story Graeme Le Saux told me. When a friend of his asked him out for a drink after he'd lost a match, he replied, 'No thanks, I'm still roasting after yesterday's defeat.' He meant to write 'smarting'.

Our manager makes a double substitution, one of whom, Nathan Ellington, scores. And from then on it really looks like we're going to win. Especially when, with just a minute left, Ellington finds himself clean through. He shoots powerfully against the underside of the bar and it bounces away. Phil does his Meg Ryan impression again. All our directors spring up and then sag back down.

It finishes 1-1. If that chance of Ellington's hadn't presented itself in the first place, we would now be happy but, having spurned it, it feels like we've lost. The following day I argue with Alan Hansen about this. He says: 'You played well, you should be pleased.'

I say: 'No, but that's bad: to play well and lose. You're better off playing badly and losing than playing well and losing because playing well and losing is so heartbreaking.'

'So,' says Alan, 'you're saying it's better to play badly than play well?'

'Yes,' I say.

He shakes his head. He just doesn't get it, poor chap.

Ten

I've had enough of this

Saturday, 18 March 2006, Manchester United at home

The day before we play Manchester United I receive an email from a woman at BBC Radio Berkshire: 'Hi there, Adrian, apologies for troubling you AGAIN, I know you're a busy man . . . just wondering if you would have 2 mins to pre-rec a (begrudging) message for Reading FC, for that day when they follow West Brom into the Premiership? It would literally be something along the lines of "This is Adrian Chiles from *Match of the Day* and *Working Lunch* and I would/wouldn't like to say well done to Reading as they might be taking West Brom's place in the Premiership"! Best wishes, Laura Lyon.'

Laura doesn't seem to understand. This isn't fun. This isn't some kind of jape. It's serious. I spend a good five minutes staring at the email, open-mouthed. It seems she thinks all football emotion is acted out, like some kind of grotesque pantomime. It isn't, Laura, it isn't. She might as well ask me to come on and record something saying, 'Hi, my dad's dead, listen to our weekly medical programme to find out how to keep your old man alive and kicking, unlike mine.'

I can feel myself losing it. I think homicidal thoughts all day on Friday.

Just as well, then, that I have organised a consultant psychiatrist to come with me to the match today. Jo Emmanuel is the twin sister of a friend's brother's wife – and if you can follow that you probably need to consult her.

All season – all my life in fact – I've been trying to work out why, psychologically, I and others like me feel the way we do about our teams. As usual at the sharp end of the season I start getting cold sores on my lips. On the packaging for the cream I use it says to consult a doctor if symptoms persist. Well, my symptoms of football mania are not only persisting, but getting worse, so a talk with a psychiatrist is probably long overdue. I want her to examine me and some of the more serious cases I've diagnosed at the Hawthorns.

Jo is married to an enormously tall, enormously clever, enormously charismatic Sri Lankan doctor called Anton. They have four children, ranging in age from early teens to not long born. All of them have higher IQs than me. Her two boys, Jeyam and Mano, are coming today. I pick them up from their home in Harrow. Jo's sitting at the window looking, it seems to me, a little concerned.

But her boys are right up for it, waiting eagerly at the front door. They are incredibly well behaved and well spoken.

Just to complicate matters – adding to the existing team of me the maniac family friend, the football-mad boys and their psychiatrist mother – I've arranged to pick up Rab Rogers. He told me he'll be waiting for us outside South Harrow Tube station 'in a big car coat, the kind of thing that was fashionable in the seventies'.

Rab is the founder of West Brom's London supporters' club and a genuine one-off. Everything about him is unique, down to the oddest answerphone announcement I've ever heard. It's absolutely specific to what he's doing at that moment: 'Hello, yes, hello. Just going to B&Q in Kingsbury to look for something, OK, thanks, bye.'

Rab first saw the Albion sixty years ago. 'I went to Solihull school. My grandfather was from Wednesbury. He was a very famous cyclist, a renowned Midlands sportsman. He came second in the road racing world championships in 1922. My grandfather took me to my first game. I think it was Birmingham–Albion in 1946; that's when the bug started.

'Everybody wore flat caps,' he says. 'And people seemed tinier then. Most men wore jackets and sort of collars and ties even at football matches. People didn't travel away from home in those days because, don't forget, everyone worked a six-day, or five-and-a-half day, working week. There was no away support except local derbies.

'I tell you when it started to matter to me: it was the season that we got promotion, forty-eight/forty-nine, with Dave Walsh, the great Dave Walsh. We had a bloody good team. Billy Elliot, who was the centre half; the captain of Northern Ireland, Jack Vernon. This is the age you do get into it. If you're into it at sixteen, seventeen, it sticks with you for ever.

Rab did his national service in the RAF and went to Cardiff University but by 1954, when the Albion won the cup, he was back in Solihull. 'It was the greatest day of my life up to that point, really it was. I tell you one little story. We were playing Port Vale in the semi-final. I got up at six o'clock in the morning to queue for hours to get a bloody ticket for the match, which was at Villa Park.

'Anyway, there were three of us, all mates, and on the day of the match we went to the Albion and stuck the counterfoils of our tickets through the box with open postal orders for them to fill in as they wanted, you got me? Because we were so certain of beating Port Vale we wanted to be sure of getting tickets for the final. We had to blag our way into Villa Park 'cos don't forget the stubs were missing. You can imagine how we felt at half-time when Port Vale were leading 1-0. Anyway I got a ticket and we won the final, but these were really great years.'

Rab moved to Peterborough, and then on to London. He pauses and says, for all the world as if he's sucking a particularly nice toffee, 'Ah, the sixties – the greatest decade ever known, and the Albion won the cup as well.

'My first wage when I came to London was £800 a year. I was a rep for a company which had off licences and pubs all over London. They had thirty-odd shops – I had to go round to see they were doing their jobs. I was living with a Greek lady called Daphne in Palmers Green and she was a football fan. She didn't have a team or anything like that but she did like football. I was with Daphne for six years.

'Daphne used to love going to the games with me. We'd go by train. We met in a club in London. She was divorced. Her husband was a psychiatrist who turned out to be the number-two man at Broadmoor. Daphne had a little girl of five who was absolutely besotted with football. She used to have all the things in her bedroom, the scarves and all the little dolls and teddy bears.

'I waited 'til she was eleven before I actually took her. It was a floodlit match. She'd not been before and we come up through the gates. Night air. January.' He's talking slowly now, transported back. 'Snow on the ground and everything. It's beautiful, she said to me.' He pauses awhile and then says, 'An eleven-year-old girl's first sight of the Hawthorns', as if it could be the title of a poem he's just written.

'Anyway, the problem was,' Rab says, snapping out of his reverie, 'I do a little bit of bullshitting where ladies are concerned.' He hesitates, then says, 'Daphne thought I came from Kenya.'

I laugh.

'Don't laugh,' says Rab, laughing himself.

'But why did you tell her that? Why would that make you any more attractive to her?'

'Ah. Er.' He thinks. 'It was a different era. Don't forget, I lived in Earls Court. Earls Court was full of Australians, South Africans, Kiwis.'

'So, if you said you came from Solihull, it wouldn't have the same impact?'

'Well, yes.'

'What was your cover story?'

'I was a journalist, wasn't I?'

'You were a white Kenyan who was a journalist in London?'

'Yes.'

'But you were working for a chain of off licences. When exactly did she think your journalism was happening?'

'She thought I was freelance,' says Rab sheepishly.

'And you sustained this untruth for six years?'

'Well,' he says, 'one match was a close shave. At half-time there was an announcement: would Mr Rogers please report to the secretary's office after the match. Daphne said to me, did you hear that, did you hear that? And I said, what's all this about? and she said, we'd better go, we'd better go.

'And what she'd done, she'd written to the Albion and told them about this Kenyan who was an Albion supporter and how much he supported the Albion and everything else. So she takes me and we go round to the secretary's office. One or two of them knew me round there and they knew full well I wasn't a Kenyan journalist but I got away with it. And we got two ten shilling tickets behind the goal for the cup final.'

In 1976 Rab started the club – the London branch of West Brom's supporters' club. 'I put an advert in the QPR programme saying, if you're interested in joining the London branch of the West Bromwich Albion supporters' club please get in touch with R A B Rogers, and I gave my address. My real name's Richard Anthony Burkuill Rogers. Burkuill was my grandfather's name. But in the programme they put a capital 'R' and a small 'A' and 'B' and, to Albion fans, I've been Rab ever since.

'I had fifty-five letters. It was a great feeling, the first meeting, all these Albion fans walking in. That Saturday we were playing Tottenham at home. We took twenty-two, including three blokes from work who were Spurs fans. We won 4-2. Peter Taylor scored both Tottenham's goals. That's how it started.

'We used to meet at the bottom of Fleet Street at a pub called the Albion in Ludgate Circus. The owner was Mick somebody who was an Arsenal fan. And I was so pleased that we had a pub with our name on it. I ran the club for ten years. By eighty-one/eighty-two we had 140 members.'

All of which is less interesting than how Rab came to be running a sex shop. 'Well, that came about because my mate got the sack, he was an Albion fan, Phil. He had this bookshop. He always gave the impression it was his.'

'Did you know what kind of books he was selling?'

'Oh yes yes yes yes, I used to go in there, yes. And Phil asked me if I wanted a part-time job when I took redundancy from the government. On the ground floor it was a normal, nice little shop in Charing Cross Road but downstairs it was all the adult stuff and video booths. That's where the money was. Then it got raided. Phil got a year. He did six months and he wouldn't come back to the shop. And I ended up managing it for three years.

'Could you concentrate on porn and the Albion at the same time?' I ask.

'I can compartmentalise,' says Rab. 'I never mix the two up. Don't worry.'

'But I suppose,' I suggest to him, 'that when we've lost it must be a great comfort to go home to the best porn collection in London.' He doesn't answer this directly but the question conjures up mental images that neither of us, I suspect, are particularly comfortable with.

At South Harrow Tube station Rab is there in a dodgy-looking coat, as promised. I ask him if this is the coat that was fashionable in the seventies but he says, 'No, this is a different one. It was fashionable in the eighties.' He is also wearing a very old, possibly home-knitted, hat and scarf combination.

On the way up the M40 Jo asks about our addiction. Rab, a keen smoker, smells like my Auntie Doris's house: smoky, for sure, but in a way only decades of smoking can cause. He keeps awkwardly corkscrewing round to face Jo in the back and emphasise a point he's making. He always prefaces what he is saying with 'What you've got to understand is this . . . ', and so on.

Jo explains that she's seen research suggesting male testosterone rises during football matches. Even at seventy-five, it seems to me that Rab's testosterone is quite high enough without football's help. Jo also says some research suggests fans really do believe they are contributing to a team's success. This makes me think: Do we? I suppose we're better off being there than not being there but I'm not even sure about that. Our travelling fans are always right behind the team, yet at home it's a different story. If we're behind after half an hour everyone's moaning; if we're ahead, everyone's panicking that we won't be for much longer.

The research Jo has seen was done, coincidentally, by the psychologist I also happen to know, Sandy Wolfson from Northumbria University. 'With football,' Sandy told me, 'everything about it reinforces a sense of *us*: the home ground, the seating, the strip, the colours.' This all creates a very strong bond. 'And when you're there with others as committed as you it's hard to believe others are more committed. When we polled fans, asking them how they felt about fellow fans, in every case they portrayed fans of their team more positively than those of other teams. They thought them more knowledgeable, more loyal, more supportive.'

To which I said: 'Well, they would, wouldn't they?' But to a psychologist like Sandy this was merely 'irrational, some kind of distortion'. And, of course, she's right. Every fan can't be better than all the other fans any more than every male driver can be right when he considers himself to be an above average driver. Irrational. Then again, nobody said football fans are rational. But this illusory superiority, as Sandy calls it, is important because we fans need it to help justify our crazed attitude.

Incidentally, supporters consider fans of their own clubs superior in every way apart from one: physical attractiveness. I think this is hilarious. Are you the most loyal fans? Yes. The most vociferous? Yes. The cleverest? Yes. The best-looking? I look at Rab next to me, and then at my own face in the rear-view mirror. No.

At the Hawthorns Rab wraps his chunky-knit scarf several times around his neck and slopes off to catch the tram to the Black Eagle in Hockley, long a meeting point for London Baggies. Meanwhile Jo, her kids and I are going to meet five of those who, in my estimation, represent the most interesting psychiatric cases. For this informal consultation I have booked a table in one of the club's executive lounges. Nathan is there waiting for us, dressed terribly smartly. I've warned Jo that, as she is in her forties, she's well within his usual target age range. I have warned him not to do anything daft but not to pretend to be anything but daft either. The poor bloke's not quite sure what to say or do but he seems up for some analysis anyway.

Before Jo gets the chance to speak to him he takes me to one side and says he was rather hurt by something I wrote in the programme about the drubbing at Fulham and the meal we all had beforehand: 'Around that table,' I had written, 'we had Muslims, Sikhs, Christians of all dominations. And, let's be honest, the odd heathen. And he knows who he is.'

'I was quite hurt by that,' says Nathan simply.

'It wasn't you I was talking about,' I say.

'Oh, right, no problem,' he says, 'it's just that I am actually quite moral.'

'I know, I know, mate,' I explain, 'but it was Rab I was referring to.'

Gurdial Singh appears, dressed as immaculately as ever. And Vic Stirrup, too. He looks well, all things considered, but one eye's very red. He says he banged it on something. In his own rather grumpy yet friendly way he doesn't seem quite sure what this occasion is all about, but when I tell Nathan how impressed I am with his attire Vic butts in and demands, 'What about me? My wife dressed me up specially!'

Gurdial leans towards Vic and asks if he's excited about the game. She nods her head encouragingly as she says this, rather as if she might be speaking to a child.

'No,' says Vic.

'Oh,' replies Gurdial. Anxious to establish that Vic isn't being rude here I explain that he's just being literal: he genuinely is never excited. 'You're not, are you, Vic?'

'No,' he says.

Perhaps Vic is the polar opposite of those fans who get so tense and miserable that they have to stop coming. Maybe the only way you can have an attendance record like Vic's is not actually to care that much. Roy Hayden and Steve join us. Steve has lost all his hair but, as ever, he's smiling away. He is pleased, and rather perplexed, that I find his loyalty to the Albion under such ghastly circumstances quite so remarkable. I hear Roy say to Jo, 'You've got to draw the line somewhere: I don't go to the reserves' away games.' Jo listens, astonished.

Vic asks for his salad starter to be served without dressing. At a loss, the waitress opens and closes her mouth and makes shrugging movements. 'It comes with the dressing already on,' she pleads. Vic shrugs and when it comes he wolfs it all down regardless. At the other end of the table Jo's boys, aged eleven and ten, are politely quizzing Nathan; interviewing him. Even seated, Nathan towers over them, but they're very much in charge of the conversation. They nod with interest as he answers their questions, one of which is: 'Have you ever been to a football match that West Brom weren't playing in?'

'That's a good question,' replies Nathan thoughtfully, smiling.

Vic taps me shyly on the arm and hands me an envelope. It's an invitation to his fiftieth wedding anniversary. I'm flattered to be invited. As always, my first reaction is to panic that the event will clash with an Albion match. Instantly, though, I realise that Vic would never arrange anything to clash with a game.

While Jo talks to a worried-looking Nathan at the other end of the table, Gurdial, the Haydens and I discuss the poor form of the team. Vic listens for a while, then harrumphs firmly: 'If we go down this season, that's it for me.'

'You're joking,' I say.

'No,' he reiterates grumpily.

'What would you do with yourself on a Saturday?'

A rather cruel smile spreads across his face as he says, 'Watch the ice hockey! Edinburgh, Belfast . . .' He reels off the places he could visit with Coventry Blaze once he's left the Albion behind. His tone is derisive, even patronising, as if none of us knows that there is life outside the Albion. This is a fair point but, it has to be said, a bit rich coming from someone who's hardly missed a game in eighty-one years.

'You'll have to come, Vic,' I tell him. 'It just wouldn't be right here without you.'

The sneer vanishes from his face and he seems genuinely flattered. 'Is that right?' he says.

For once, the Albion start well and even nearly score. I hate it when we start well, it almost always means we'll go on to lose. When I was a kid, here with my granddad, it made me uneasy if we scored early on. Even as we celebrated I'd be looking anxiously at the clock. If ten minutes hadn't passed I knew we'd scored too early. I've always been a worrier.

'You're playing well,' says Jo.

'Won't last,' I say. 'Always a bad sign.'

She rolls her eyes in a baffled kind of way.

Reassuringly Man Utd score after sixteen minutes – a free header from a corner. I try to avoid looking at Jo, Jeyam and Mano. When I do I see three pairs of eyes looking anxiously, compassionately up at me. Soon, though, as our play deteriorates, they're avoiding eye contact with me completely. At half-time Jo points out that there is only one goal in it. I tell her we are doomed. Compounding our misery, it's announced that our relegation rivals Portsmouth are winning away at West Ham, who, with a cup tie to play imminently, are said to be resting an indecent number of players. Malcolm Boyden, the broadcaster who does the public address announcements, reads the score out as follows: 'West Ham reserves nil, Portsmouth three.' Everybody groans miserably. I say to David Jones, who sits behind us, that Birmingham will win, too. He says they won't. Jo laughs and says to David, 'We're very much of the opinion here that things can only get worse.' I try to smile but it really hurts.

I hear one of the boys say that he thinks United'll win 2-0. Jo urgently shushes him and I feel a bit ashamed that she feels the need to do this, as though her son has shown some disrespect to a member of my family. But in fact it feels to me that this is exactly what he has done.

United score again. No one says anything. One of the boys asks me what the Man U fans are chanting. I can't work it out. All I can pick out are the words 'fuck' and 'off'. So I tell him I can't hear.

Next to me, Jo is making all the right noises. I can feel her tense up and relax with the flow of the game. This season, having sat next to a variety of people whose emotional responses I've tried to gauge, I have become aware of what a physical thing it is to watch football. My heart rate rises terrifyingly during a game. I've also learnt that my companions' physical response to what's happening on the pitch gives their game away. The most passionate fans tense up and relax half a dozen times a minute. And some newcomers, like Jo today, do so, too. Others, like my work colleagues

Adam and Rob at Fulham, are deadweights, emotionally unmoved by the spectacle and so physically unmoving, too.

Jo groans, 'Oh no', with the rest of us when a pass goes pointlessly astray. 'Oh come, come on,' she pleads. 'Oh no, not there,' she says when we hoof the ball out of defence straight back to United for them to mount another attack. 'Why are they doing that?' she asks. We haven't got an answer for her.

We score from a corner, but Jo isn't looking. 'You said you never score from corners,' she explains. Now, really, at 2-1, we should have hope. I have none and neither does anyone else as far as I can ascertain. It finishes 2-1. As we're leaving Jeyam says, 'The referee was bad; he was for Man Utd! If it hadn't been for him, we would have won.' For saying 'we' and for caring enough about my feelings to allege bias on the referee's part, I could kiss him.

We drive back to London. Jo and her boys stagger out of the car, exhausted, in Harrow. They seem grateful for the experience but the look in Jo's eyes says it all: 'How on earth can you put yourself through this week in, week out?' She promises to be in touch with her thoughts, which I expect is what she says after coming across a particularly difficult case at the hospital where she works.

Then it's just Rab and me in the car. He says, with the air of a man who has decided after a lot of thought to get something off his chest, 'By the way, I've been meaning to ask you something. You know that thing you wrote about there being a heathen with you against Fulham?'

'Yes.'

'Well, I must say I was quite hurt about that.'

'But it wasn't you I was thinking about Rab – it was Nathan.'

Rab laughs.

'But, funnily enough,' I continue, 'I told him it was you I was referring to.'

'That's hilarious,' says Rab. He laughs and suddenly doesn't care that I might have been referring to him. It's as though he doesn't mind being described as a heathen as long as he's not the only one in the room. He is still chuckling and shaking his head happily when I drop him off at his flat.

Wherever I am, I'm always thinking of the Albion. On Tuesday, I fly to the US, to Wyoming. I am with a cameraman, sound recordist and producer to make some films about British people who have made a new life out here. We're interviewing about two dozen people. So, in all, around thirty people are involved in this project. Why this week? Well, it's the only week I could be away and not miss a West Brom match, since we're not playing until Monday. So the whole trip has essentially revolved around me or, more specifically, the Albion.

On Friday we drive several hundred miles north to interview one of the original Marlboro Men on his ranch. When we get there he refuses to speak to us. This is something of a calamity. I have other worries, though: Portsmouth are playing Arsenal tomorrow and Birmingham are at Man Utd. Unfortunately we have no mobile phone reception, so on Saturday morning, driving through wild, desolate mountain ranges, I only have eyes for the screen of my mobile, willing it to come to life.

Halfway through a six-hour drive back, we stop at a Taco Bell in some godforsaken, half-deserted railway town. I ask if I can make a reverse charge call but the obese woman behind the counter can't understand what I want. I persist. She starts to look a bit frightened. It must be the wild, desperate look in my eyes. I give up.

It's five o'clock in the afternoon in Cheyenne, eleven at night in the UK, when I finally get a signal as we pass the city limits. Heart thumping, I phone a friend back home. After six hours of agony I can barely breathe. 'What were the scores?' I gasp.

'Portsmouth–Arsenal called off. Waterlogged.'

My heart nearly breaks with relief. 'What about Blues?'

'Playing tomorrow.'

'Thanks, mate.' I don't feel as foolish as I should.

The following day Birmingham lose at Old Trafford, opening the way for us to pull further ahead of them on Monday night in London. It's time to go home.

Monday, 27 March 2006, Spurs away

I arrive back at Heathrow on Monday lunchtime. I'm absolutely shattered. The butterflies are raging away in my stomach, mainly because we're playing Spurs, but also because I am not quite sure what attitude Jane's going to have about me going to the game. I know she knows that we're playing tonight. And she knows that I know that she knows. Yet, in our telephone conversations across the Atlantic I have neither sought nor received permission to go. It would be entirely reasonable for her to suggest that, having been abroad for a week, I should stay at home, dote on my wife and children and watch it on the box.

I get home. We embrace. Our older daughter is at school, our younger one is heartbreakingly happy to see me. I give them all presents. Then Jane asks, 'What are you doing now, then?'

'Have to get a bit of sleep,' I say tremulously.

'Then what?'

'Er . . .'

'You're not seriously going to go to Tottenham, are you?'

'Well . . .' I flannel, looking anxiously at my feet. Then I look up into her eyes. There's no way of telling what kind of eyes they'll be. There are two options: angry, bitter eyes shining with contempt or – and these are the eyes I married her for – eyes raised to the heavens communicating a mixture of resignation, pity and even, sometimes, amusement. I get the latter. I am going to Spurs. Relief wells up inside me. I kiss her again, and Sian, and go to bed. The relief gives way to anxiety about the game. I can't sleep.

Four hours later, having paced around the house and the neighbourhood, I'm in a car on the way to White Hart Lane. It is being driven by Phil Bernie, a cherished colleague and Spurs fan who's quite important in BBC Sport. We won't be sitting together, but I ask him what kind of spectator he is. He tells me he goes berserk during games and never really thinks much about it the rest of the time. I envy him because I am exactly the opposite: quiet during matches but in bits the rest of the week. I'm in bits now. Somewhere in north London we pass a road called St Regis Close. An omen! I think of Cyrille Regis and suddenly I'm full of hope.

Everything starts off so well. After twenty-one minutes we're ahead and our Polish goalkeeper Tomasz Kuszczak is having a blinder. A tall man sitting just behind me taps me on the shoulder. 'We haven't met,' he says, 'but we have exchanged emails.' This is Matthew Taylor, once head of a leftie think tank but now, he tells me, the Prime Minister's chief advisor on Strategy at Number Ten. Normally I'd be breathlessly impressed and bombard him with questions. At the moment, though, I have no more questions than he has answers – all we want is for the Albion to hold on to the lead.

'You're powerful. Can't you do something?'

'I could always pass emergency legislation to get the game ended now,' he replies grimly, as though if he could he really might.

The home fans start getting on their team's back. I make some over-clever comment about the Spurs supporters being like the Labour Party's rank and file. Matthew fires back with something about George Orwell being described as, politically, having the attitude of a home fan. The clock at Spurs has no seconds, just minutes. Time seems to pass even slower. But we get to half-time. And it's still 1-0. A tall Scandinavian comes over to say hello. He tells me he's been a fan since 1978 and this is his thirty-second game. 'Unbeaten away in eleven years,' he says, which worries me even more.

'My surname's Stian Böe,' he says, 'the "o" has a thing on it.' I'm not sure what the 'thing' is, all I want to know is why, why Albion?

'I'm not sure – I think it was in the seventy-eight/seventy-nine season. They had a strange name and I was learning to read and looking through papers, and they were pretty high up in the table. We used to see a Saturday match every week.'

I ask him where he's from and he says, 'Norway. From as far down south as you can get.' He tells me he sells hardwood flooring 'like everyone else in Norway'.

Stian first saw West Brom in the flesh in 1989. 'We won 3-2 at West Ham. Had three away wins in a week.' I ask him what it was like to see us for the first time.

'Pretty special,' he says. He's a man of few words.

'Are there any other Norwegian Albion fans living near you?'

'No.'

'Do you get nervous listening or watching at home?'

'Yes, of course.'

'So, wherever, whenever we're playing you're usually worrying about it?'

'Yes.'

He's a little more expansive on the games he has seen. 'In the play-off final against Port Vale I was there and the first promotion was on internet radio.'

But now, with a family – two children – it's hard and he says he only gets to one game every two seasons but 'my kid, who is seven years old, has already been to thirteen pre-season matches in Denmark'.

I ask him when he might next see us after tonight. 'I don't know yet.'

A bloke with two young children says hello. 'Haven't they got school tomorrow?' I ask.

'Yes,' he says, with more pride than shame in his voice.

'Good parenting,' I say, without irony. I hope I one day get the chance to drag my children to an evening game on a school night.

While I'm talking to them I see a middle-aged man with a serious expression on his face lurking just over the dad's shoulder. As our conversation comes to an end this man approaches, speaking urgently in a low voice, with his finger pointing at me: 'I want a word with you,' he says. 'I understand you've been having dealings with Garry Mottram. Well, he owes me and a lot of others round here, a lot of money. He's never paid it back and never said sorry or anything. Just so you know.'

As it happens, I have had dealings with Garry Mottram. He is an Albion fan in HMP Birmingham. I wrote to him asking what it was like to be incarcerated in a cell so close to the ground that if it was in the right place you could probably see the floodlights. He wrote back with an answer to my question: 'It is torture, but you have to be a bit of a masochist to follow Albion anyway, so that helps.'

Early in the second half Spurs score. But instead of capitulating we go on to improve. Then, very near the end, our Pole in goal makes a complete hash of a clearance and, in trying to retrieve the situation, concedes a penalty. As Robbie Keane steps up to take it someone says dolefully, 'He don't miss these.' Keane scores. Still, I feel no pain at this stage. It's like when I stub my toe on something – I'm in that awful hiatus between the stubbing of the toe and the pain setting in.

The final whistle goes and then the pain does kick in. I shake hands with Matthew. He slopes off to try, and fail, to worry about the future of the Blair administration rather than the Albion. On my way out a kid stops me to ask for a photo. I try to smile but just can't. Yet this little kid, in his Albion shirt, is all smiles. I feel ashamed. I get all morose thinking about Stian on the journey back to Norway, brooding over his eleven-year undefeated away record lying in tatters.

Getting away from White Hart Lane is an awful business, especially if you've just lost. I can't bear to travel back with Phil who rings to apologise for what I've just been forced to witness. It's a long walk to the Tube. On the train I just stare at my feet, angrily determined not to speak to anyone. At first I have to stand, but by the time we get to the West End there's a seat. I slump into it and ignore the Spurs fans sitting opposite who don't seem to have noticed me anyway.

At South Kensington a rather plump but very attractive blonde woman gets on and stands by the door. She looks like she has been out at a ball or some such. She clocks me and comes to sit beside me. She tells me she recognises me off the telly and that she's been to some awards ceremony. Her breath smells strongly of wine, which is strangely repellent to me at this time of year as I never drink during Lent.

She seems a nice woman, though. As we slow down into Barons Court Station, she says, 'This is my stop.' She pauses and then says that she's dying to go home for a big glass of wine. Now I'm no philanderer, but even if I was, I doubt if I'd do much philandering on the same evening the Albion had lost in the last minute. In any case, I'm not sure if this is some kind of proposition or not. My mouth opens and closes a couple of times before I stammer that it's Lent and I'm not drinking.

'Oh,' she says, in such a way that I feel sure she wanted me to go back with her. She gets up and leaves alone.

I catch the eyes of the Spurs fans opposite: 'Did that woman just ask me back to her place?' They all nod. I stare at the floor again, still determined not to discuss the match with them.

At that moment the supporters' club coaches are on their way back to the West Midlands, a journey that Dave Holloway will later tell me is the most miserable of the season. He puts a Peter Kay video on to try to cheer everyone up and it almost works. On board, Michelle Wilkes is going back to a very early shift at Sainsbury's in Oldbury. She gets back to the home she shares with her mum in Halesowen at quarter past two, washes and changes and goes straight to work.

'I walked in,' she tells me later, 'and they said, you lost, and I said, no, did we? And they turned round and asked me a silly question like, did you go? No, I sat at home and watched it on telly, what do you think?' spits Michelle.

In the morning, at work at the BBC, I get a series of emails from

Matthew Taylor, lamenting our performance. This is a quite normal part of the grieving process, but by lunchtime it's struck me that while I am wasting time emailing him about the Albion instead of concentrating on the show I'm supposed to be presenting, Matthew must, to some extent, have actually taken his eye off affairs of state. I feel very pleased with him for getting his priorities right.

Football is a great social and political leveller. There aren't many places where a high court judge and a street cleaner can engage on a subject with the same level of expertise and respect for each other. This is true for political views, too. I can say with some degree of certainty that there is only one thing in common between me, Matthew Taylor and the deputy leader of the British National Party.

I first met Simon Darby when I interviewed him in Handsworth for a programme about racial integration. I was gearing up for a full-on verbal assault on him but he threw me completely by getting out of the car, shaking my hand and saying, 'Up the Baggies, mate.'

He can't be an Albion fan, I thought. How could he be? We were the team that brought all the black players through in the seventies. I soon put this to him. I'll never forget his reply: 'Adrian,' he said, 'I loved Cyrille Regis, and I still do. But that doesn't mean I want my grandchildren to be black.'

Now I ring him and he throws me again: 'Hello, Adrian, how are you, mate? I was talking to a vicar yesterday who knew you.' But before I get to the bottom of which vicar he's on about I'm distracted by the sound of birdsong. 'I'm birdwatching,' says the deputy leader of the British National Party. 'I give myself an hour every day so I don't turn into a fat slob sitting at my computer, and I go for a walk over Cannock Chase. What you're hearing is a whitethroat and a blackbird, and you'll hear a yellowhammer in a minute as well.'

'They're birds of all cultures and colours, I suppose?'

'They're all British birds,' he counters, equal to the jibe.

'I never had a choice about being an Albion fan,' he says. If my father found out I supported anybody else I'd have been in trouble. I suffered. I suffered a lot. You have to ride the course, but then it's even more sweet when good things happen, when you've battled against adversity. I remember losing 5-0 to Stockport but I remember beating Man Utd, too.'

And then Simon starts, without irony, eulogising our black players: 'I remember Cyrille Regis when he first played. We all loved Cyrille Regis. Cracking player. And Laurie Cunningham.'

'Simon,' I say, 'when you talk about loving Cyrille Regis there's an obvious irony there, isn't there?'

'I suppose there is, but we didn't look at it like that. He was just a young happy go lucky lad, and he put on an Albion shirt. I'm not totalitarian; it hasn't got to be an all-white Albion team. You didn't mind one or two in the side – then you could still say it was a fairly reflective thing.

'Anyway, once they pulled on that shirt that was it. I mean, obviously he can't help his colour, the lad can't help his colour. He was just enthusiastic. He'd run his heart out for the Albion.'

'But what do you think about him now with your BNP hat on? Do you think you were naive to love him or do you still love him in retrospect?'

'I do actually. The memories that he gave us as Albion fans you'll never be able to erase those. The problem is, you take things to extremes and you end up with an England side that is all black, which is not good; everything in moderation. We can put up with a little bit but not too much.'

I change tack: 'On the old Throstle Club, near where my grand-dad used to park, someone had written on the wall, in big white letters, "Laurie Cunningham . . ."'

'" . . . is a black cunt",' says Simon, finishing off my sentence.

'Well,' I ask, 'what do you think of that?'

'Wolves supporters,' he says. 'Wolves supporters. That's who put that there. I don't approve of it now and I didn't then. There's no need to be personal like that.'

Simon says the game is not the same any more now there are so many foreigners playing. 'When I say foreign players, I mean people who simply cannot be construed as English or British at all. It's just making the game nonsensical.'

I point out that if being English is the test then surely Simon must feel more kinship with our huge black defender Darren Moore, who's from Aston, than Cosmin Contra, the Romanian we've had on loan.

'In a bizarre way I actually agree with you. I'd much rather if it wasn't players from Africa. For instance I mean, I've got nothing against Kanu, but I'd feel much more comfortable with somebody like Darren Moore than Kanu. I think that to me makes sense.'

I realise with a start that the bond between Simon and me, the Albion, is dangerously close to being stronger than anything, such as politics, that could divide us. To open up the gap between us again, I tell him he could hardly come with me on an away coach as I have friends like Gurdial and her wonderful Asian family. 'What would you say to them?' I demand.

'They probably vote for us,' he says.

I checked: they don't.

'Pressure on Prescott as Blair's Troubles Show No Sign of Abating' is the headline in the *Independent*, which I'm reading on the way to see Matthew Taylor at his place of work, 10 Downing Street. The Friday we've arranged the visit has come at the end of a very bad week for the government. Apart from anything else, John Prescott, the Deputy Prime Minister, has been caught having an affair with one of his secretaries.

Matthew has also invited Frank Skinner. In a flurry of emails I've been told to make sure we bring our passports and that, no, there is no dress code. I've suggested that I come dressed as Baggie Bird but Matthew responded as follows: 'I think, given the general perception of the Government at present, that may not be a great idea and then there is the issue of the full body search.'

There is airport-style security when we get past the huge iron gates. Every single guard has something to say about the Albion being certainties for relegation. Frank and I smile politely. Soon we're walking through the big black door with Matthew, up the stairs past the paintings and photographs of former Prime Ministers, into the cabinet room for a quick peek and, finally, into a giant drawing room overlooking Horse Guards Parade. A pot of tea materialises and Matthew settles down to tell us how a left-wing intellectual born in London, raised in Leeds, and university-educated in Southampton, ended up an Albion fan.

'I didn't support the Baggies until my mid-twenties. I was working in Birmingham, for a trade union. I went to Villa Park, and they were, I think, third in the old first division, and there was no atmosphere – you know what it's like there. This was about 1988 or 1989.

'Then I went to the Hawthorns. Brian Talbot was the manager and we'd had quite a good season, so the fans were in a good mood. It was just full of these big fat blokes with impenetrable accents, arguing. They were unhappy about Sandwell Council being the shirt sponsors because they said this was the thin end of the wedge and we'd end up being called Sandwell Albion. And they were saying what is Sandwell anyway? It doesn't exist. And I thought, I love this, I love these sorts of arguments.'

Just above us there's a mark in the cornicing – damage from an IRA mortar bomb that John Major, then the Prime Minister, decided to leave unfixed as a reminder.

'I was sort of, sort of . . .' continues Matthew, falteringly trying to explain how he felt about the Albion. 'It really was a bit like romantic love, it was just love at first sight. And within about three weeks – and some people say, you know, you're not allowed to do this – but within about three weeks I had the devotion of someone who'd been there all the time, who'd seen Jeff Astle score the goal at Wembley and all that sort of thing. It just fitted, and, I think, that is the thing about love really: it's as much about whether you're ready for it and I was completely ready. I wanted a football team, and I wanted a football team that was like that.'

249

Frank and I are quite moved by this speech about how Matthew came to it so late and so passionately, but later Frank says, 'I don't know how he let it happen to him. It's like smoking: if you start when you're a kid, fair enough. But if you start when you're older, well, you know the dangers . . . '

The conversation turns to a couple of players from that dismal era in which Matthew fell in love with our club. There was a little Staffordshire Bull Terrier of a player called Stuart Bowen and a blond, sort of bow-legged wing-back we bought from Kidderminster Harriers called Steve Lilwall. 'He ran in a really peculiar way,' says Matthew. 'There was a huge gap between his knees.'

Frank says, 'There was a feeling he was going to be Derek Statham, and then he suddenly disappeared.'

This is standard stuff between football fans mulling over their shared history but when Matthew leaves the room to make a call, Frank and I fall silent as it occurs to us both how incongruous it is to be talking about these people here, with everything around us just groaning under the weight of its history. 'I wonder what Steve Lilwall's doing this morning,' I say.

Frank laughs and says, 'He probably thinks he's been completely forgotten and here we are discussing him in some depth in one of the great seats of power in the western world.'

For a moment we are silent again as we wonder where Steve is and how we've come to be where we are.

Frank and I have both been fans for as long as we can remember and suffer accordingly, but Matthew's late start doesn't seem to have spared him any of the pain. 'When I was younger I used to think about sex all the time to get a bad result out of my mind, but as you get older you can't do that so much.

'My boys have made a difference. Joseph is an Albion fan and I can't afford to get too down for them. So that has made me slightly more grown up about it. But then it does grab you, and it's hopeless. This morning at quarter past six I should have been worrying about the future of the government but instead I was wide awake worrying about the Albion and whether we can survive this season. The minute I think I've got it under control I realise I haven't.

'But for my kids' sakes, I suppose I don't want them to think I'm immature really. Joseph has a tendency to gloominess and he gets very, very angry when we lose. Last year he was absolutely convinced we were going to stay up and he told everyone we would. I sat him down and I said to him, don't do this to yourself, son. But he said, no, no, it's going to be fine. And he was right. Mind you, he's not saying that this year.

'I always seem to be thinking about it. You know, I ran a think tank. I mean, I'm supposed to be an intellectual and I'd be worrying about the Albion, and I'd think, No, you shouldn't be thinking about the Albion, you should be thinking about the strength in the future of the progressive left.

'I used to get impatient with myself for the amount of time I thought about it and the missus would get impatient with me because, the other thing is, you know, I'm a bit dishonest in the sense that if the Albion lose and I'm miserable I have to find another reason, I can't admit that it's the Albion. So I have to come up with some existential crisis and the missus does say sometimes, I wish you'd just admit it was the Albion.

'My father catches me out as well. A couple of weeks ago I was in a grump and he said, he's in a terrible mood, because he found out the Albion have lost. So I do get caught out. You see, the thing is, I'm slightly ashamed of caring too much. So paradoxically, in this job, because I do think about the job all the time, the Albion feels more like a benign form of escapism. I don't feel like I've got to purge myself of it. But there have been times when it has taken up all my emotional energy.'

We talk about how miserable we all were after the Spurs game and Matthew, as you would expect from a smart bloke, intellectualises his feelings on the winning, drawing and losing of football matches. 'I suppose there are times when they've played badly,' he says thoughtfully, 'and you just think, you know, part of it is a moral thing. You play out in your head – do we deserve

251

this? Is there some way you can construct this story which means that we deserve something. It's an interesting insight into people's psychological make-up. I remember reading a book by Margaret Atwood years ago – she was talking about Calvinism. She said when she grew up there was this strong sense that everything evened out, that if you had a bit of good luck it was really bad luck. And I'm a bit like that with the Albion in that I think, Well, in a way, if something really awful happens and we don't deserve it, then we are owed a bit.'

I know what he means, and to a certain extent I feel the same, but it only works one way for me: if something good happens I think something bad will surely follow. But if something terrible happens, it never occurs to me that something good will soon happen to even things out.

I tell Matthew that his Calvinist approach is flawed as it is no better than waiting on a roulette table for it to come up red five times, then betting on black. Matthew considers this response: 'Yeah,' he says, 'but you're not lecturing me on rationality, are you?' Fair point.

Frank comes to my rescue: 'I think the reason that one can take football so seriously is because deep down you know it's not important. So whereas in life when you're faced with tragedy and disappointment you have to fight it to deal with it, with football you know that it doesn't really matter because no one is going to die, so that gives you a kind of freedom to be down and miserable, to express all that stuff.'

We ponder this for a few moments before Matthew says, rather as if he's rounding off a seminar on the subject, 'I think this is really the big challenge for football fans – to manage your emotions so football provides valuable escapism from the humdrum or the stressful but not to let it invade your whole life.' ·

Am I, or is any football fan, capable of managing their emotions? Later, Jo the psychiatrist calls me with her verdict on what she saw at the Manchester United match. I'm intrigued to know: does she think we are all mad? 'With my psychiatrist's hat on, I'd say none of you are suffering from a mental illness although some of you seem to have psychological problems which might predispose you to becoming formally ill later.

'For the moment you'd be asking whether it's affecting you in a positive or negative way rather than whether you're anywhere on the spectrum of mental illness. With most of them I took it as being an overall positive influence in their lives that gives them pleasure mostly.'

'Pleasure?' I gasp.

'Well, I certainly felt that with some, who you'd consider more vulnerable, like Nathan, it's served as some sort of protective influence. I suppose you wonder, with him and others, that if he didn't have football what would he have. And I don't know how to put this without sounding horrible, but maybe with Vic, who had a very routine job, it gave him some sort of notoriety and status and so on, something that made him stand out as not being Mr Average.

'And I felt a little bit the same with Gurdial – she said as much, how she thrived in the sense of being a bit of a non-conformist and it was a source of great pride to her that she, as an Asian woman, was there.

'I must admit that even I, not really into sport, did get into it, and that was being there beforehand and seeing how much it means to everyone. And a sense of really wanting it to be good, and that awful tiny sense of what it must be like to go through gut-wrenching disappointment regularly. But there was such a wonderful welcoming feeling. Everyone was critical and yet also completely behind the team: just like you talk to a child actually. Unconditional love.

'I found myself watching the match again on the telly and saying, oh God, this is where this happened, and why did they do that, and where was the marking. And, trust me, this is most unlike me. It came about because of the community I was welcomed into and therefore I adopted the community's extremes. I can feel it happening to me. I am going to kill you!'

Now she falters and says, 'I really thought this. I know it

sounds horrible, but there was a very different feel for them than you.'

It dawns on me what she's trying to get across, without hurting my feelings: 'So, what you're saying is that I took you along to see all the mad people and ultimately you think I'm madder than all of them.'

'Well, your attitude is the most interesting,' she insists. 'For everyone else it's just there and, though it's emotional, there's not that lingering pain you seem to suffer. For them, the feeling is that it's always there and thank God we've got the club because it's this wonderfully continuing support in our lives.'

Jo's right: I love it but at the same time I do let it blight my life. Still, I feel strangely proud that a consultant psychiatrist has suggested I'm showing signs of madness. In fact it's oddly reassuring. But am I formally addicted? For a diagnosis I go back to Sandy Wolfson. She tells me there's no standard definition of addiction although it's generally agreed that addictions meet most of the following criteria: salience, conflict, unawareness, tolerance, withdrawal and relapse.

Salience. Does it dominate my life? Yes. One-nil.

Conflict. Do I continue to engage with the activity even though it causes problems? Yes. Two-nil.

Unawareness. Do I lack awareness of the extent and magnitude of my behaviour and its effects? No (but, as my wife will confirm, I'm selfish enough to proceed regardless). Two-one.

Tolerance. Do I need increasing amounts of the activity in order to feel satisfied? Yes, the more I go, the more I want to go. And the older I get, the more I want to go. Three-one.

Withdrawal. Do I experience, as Sandy puts it, 'strong negative responses' if I can't go to a game? Well, once the game's over I can cope but in the build-up to and the duration of it, I'm in hell. So, yes. Four-one.

Relapse? Are my attempts to cut down unsuccessful? Since I've never really tried I have to answer yes to that one, too. Five-one.

Conclusion: I'm addicted.

Eleven

Blimey, we really do pull faces like that

It is a beautiful spring morning when I visit Garry Mottram at Her Majesty's Prison Birmingham in Winson Green. I won't be the first person who's read Oscar Wilde and visited a prison on a sunny day to be troubled by his famous words:

> I never saw a man who looked
> With such a wistful eye
> Upon that little tent of blue
> Which prisoners call the sky,
> And at every drifting cloud that went
> With sails of silver by.

I have never been to a prison before and in the visitors' reception I'm all at sea. There are two other people here: a very fat woman

255

with the top of her bottom showing above her jeans, and a very thin girl who has hardly any bottom at all. They look as if they know the ropes so I just mimic their every move and follow them over the road to the entrance.

I see a sign saying no paper money is allowed. I feel in my pocket and there's a fiver in there. 'Can't take that in,' says the man.

'I'll leave it here,' I say.

'Can't.'

'Have you got a charity box?'

'No.' Stalemate. We stare at each other. Finally he rolls his eyes and says, 'Might be able to help you out here', and fishes some pound coins out of his pocket.

'Pleasure doing business with you,' I say, handing over the money. And he smiles for the first time.

I go through an airport-security-type thing and two heavy sliding doors, and up some stairs into a bleak under-lit waiting area. There is no reading material apart from countless posters warning about drugs. I sit next to a young Asian couple talking loudly, half in English, half in a language I can't understand.

Sandra told me about Garry. She described him as a quiet bloke who often used to come with them on away trips. 'Then,' she said, 'he just stopped coming. And it turned out he'd been sent down for robbing building societies. None of us could believe it.'

This is how the *Birmingham Post* reported his crime and punishment:

Nutcracker Robber Gets Eight Years

A businessman who owed more than £100,000 and carried out a series of bank raids armed with a nutcracker hidden in a brown paper bag has been jailed for eight years.

Garry Mottram (43) forced cashiers at Barclays Bank branches in Birmingham, Stourbridge and Penkridge, near Stafford, to hand over nearly £6,000.

He also tried to rob three other branches in Brownhills, Stourbridge and Northampton, said Saleena Mahmood, prosecuting, at Stafford Crown Court.

Eventually I'm called: 'Visitor for Mottram.' I go through into a small area in which I'm sniffed by a dog and then into a huge room, as big as a couple of tennis courts. Prisoners face one or more family members. I take a seat and, trying not to catch anybody's eye, keep a watch on the door through which the prisoners are emerging. Garry soon appears. He is pale, slightly built, with short thinning hair and his jeans are too big for him. He's smiling shyly. His shirt is blue and white striped. 'At least you're in our colours,' I say.

'This is the bit they put on for the public face,' he says, looking around the room. He's not being ironic. 'This is horrible,' I say, 'what on earth is it like back there?'

He just smiles.

He tells me he was forty-three when he did the robberies, 'and I'm still forty-three,' he says, as if it's just dawning on him that he is not even a year into this nightmare yet. 'My wife divorced me, that's what cut me up the most. I don't blame her, though. I get to see my daughter twice a month. I'm seeing her this weekend. And next weekend. Then it'll be three weeks. My mum brings her in. Last time she said, Daddy, will you come out this summer? And I said to my mum, no, nor next summer, nor the one after, nor the one after that.

'I did it, though,' he says, more than once. 'I'm not complaining. I've got to serve my time. I did it. It was wrong.'

He tells me his story. He had a courier business which ran into trouble and he had a bit of a gambling problem, which didn't help. 'I ended up borrowing money from loan sharks and it wasn't too bad at first. I had to pay so much a month, £22,500 on £15,000 loaned. I could manage but then another couple of clients let me down and I couldn't make the payments and they threatened to kill my babby.'

'So,' I say uncertainly, 'you decided to rob a bank.'

He smiles. 'I know, incredible, isn't it?'

'You don't look like a bank robber.'

'I know,' he says. 'A friend of mine worked in a bank and once told me that if anyone came in with a gun they had to hand over the money to get them out of the building. This stuck in my mind.

'So I went and did it. I lost my bottle a couple of times but I carried a picture of my daughter. For the last one, it was an afternoon and I had to get the money in; I was desperate. I did one last job. But I took my own van and they got my number on the CCTV and arrested me a couple of weeks later.'

It was in that two-week period that he went to our Survival Sunday game. I asked if at the time he could put to the back of his mind that he was the subject of a manhunt. 'I suppose it was the only time that I could put it to the back of my mind.

'In here,' he says, 'I feel detached from the Albion. I suppose I have to be. Just miss the away games more than anything – the crack, the drinking. I watch *Grandstand* on the telly for the scores. I borrowed a radio off my mate for the Blues game and the Villa game so I could listen to the commentary.' He pauses, looks up, and asks plaintively: 'How did we not score?'

'If I miss *Grandstand*, then that's because we're locked in our cells on a Saturday. If we ring the bell it's got to be for an emergency.' He mimics a screw coming to the door, sliding open the hatch, and him asking, 'How did the Albion get on?'

Garry says he gets lots of stick from Wolves, Villa and Blues fans. 'It's good, though,' he says, believing there's something healthy about the banter. He tells me how crap the food is and how he only gets four teabags a day. I buy him coffee, Minstrels, crisps and a caramel. He wolfs it all down and says it's a real treat. He's pathetically grateful. We talk for ages of matches we were both at. He tells me he remembers seeing me at Gillingham once. And he, like me, was at Twerton Park for the calamity of the relegation to Division Three. We have this connection, but he's in here and I'm out there.

I ask him who his friends are and he tells me his best mate is in for conspiracy to murder his wife. I raise my eyebrows and he laughs and explains that 'the way he tells it, he says he was having an affair with another woman and didn't want to upset his wife so he decided he'd arrange to have her killed. Mad, isn't it? But the thing is that he's still with his wife! She comes in to visit him.'

And he tells me about a bloke in here who murdered two people and put their bodies through a woodchipper. 'He's in for twenty-five years at least.'

'Do you know him?'

'Yeah, he's the bloke who lends me his radio.'

Before I leave I make the mistake of telling him about the angry bloke at Spurs who said Garry owed him money. This upsets Garry. He swears blind he'll pay him back and he thought he'd contacted him to tell him as much. We shake hands and I tell him I'll come again. I watch him lope back to the cells in his too-big jeans. He looks back and waves sheepishly. I feel terribly, terribly sorry for him.

Saturday, 1 April 2006, Liverpool at home

I never go to a West Brom match feeling we're going to do anything but lose, but today I feel even more sure than usual. In our five Premiership encounters with Liverpool we have won none, drawn none and lost five. Goals for: zero. Goals against: seventeen. Andy Thompson, the Albion fan from Kent, picks me up. As we head up the M40, Birmingham City and Chelsea have already kicked off. We've not been worried for a moment that Birmingham will get anything from this game. It's only now we remember, to our alarm, that all matches begin with no goals on the score sheet. They're into the second half and there is still no score. We listen for five minutes before Andy turns it off: 'I just can't stand it,' he announces, putting some music on. We proceed wordlessly

259

north for ten minutes before Andy switches the commentary back on. It's still nil-nil.

'Fuckers!' he shouts, bashing the steering wheel.

It's approaching 2.30 p.m. and the final whistle isn't far off. There is no thought of switching the commentary off now. In the dying moments Chelsea mount an attack and the commentator's tone suggests they cannot but score. They don't.

'Fuckers!' blasts Andy. The final whistle goes.

It occurs to me that with us kicking off at 5.15 p.m., and Portsmouth playing Fulham at 3 p.m., the anxiety we are feeling will stay with us, assuming we're not stuffed out of sight by Liverpool before half-time, until gone 7 p.m. 'So,' I say, 'the pain started at 12.45 p.m. when Birmingham kicked off, and will last, in total, for well over six hours.' Andy doesn't reply.

At the ground I walk into the press room and am horrified to see that Portsmouth are 3-1 up and Fulham have had a player sent off. This is awful: one relegation rival has got a massive draw, another's heading for victory. I grab a Balti pie, devour it, then eat at least ten pieces of pork pie. Next I stuff about six sandwiches into my mouth. Then I have another Balti pie. Madness. I feel better for about five seconds before feeling just awful.

A friend of mine calls from outside the ground and I pop out to see him. He, like me, is from Hagley just down the road. He was always a Liverpool fan but recently he confided in me that he quite likes the Albion, too. To test him out, I have given him a ticket for today's match. He's been driven up here today by my mate Martin, whose season ticket is next to mine. Steve doesn't know Martin particularly well but, upon getting in the car, before any niceties could be exchanged, Martin simply said to him, unbidden, 'We're definitely down.'

Having hung around outside the ground for a short while, chatting to a few people, Steve has reached the conclusion that never in his life has he encountered such a negative body of men and women. 'Everyone is moaning,' he says. 'It's like I'm at a national convention of pessimists.'

Sometimes a stranger in your midst can tell you so much more about you than you can work out for yourself.

I'm watching today's match with a player. I will do so with some trepidation. Most of my encounters with players have been a reality check. I think of Mart, the fan who has not seen the inside of the Hawthorns for the fourteen years that have elapsed since he saw our relegated team filing off the coach laughing and smiling. I can only really love the Albion if I feel the players love the Albion as much as I do. Of course I know they don't, and they can't, but I try to avoid putting myself in any situation – like Mart did – where the fact will be staring me in the face.

Here, now, Nigel Quashie is staring me in the face. We signed him from Southampton in January but he's since managed to get himself banned for five games by the simple expedient of kicking George Boateng of Middlesbrough while he lay on the ground. This is the last match he'll sit out and he has agreed to do so with me.

Even aged nearly forty, with a relatively successful television career which gives me access to all sorts of famous, clever and influential people, my legs still go a bit wibbly-wobbly when I meet a West Brom player. 'Hi, Nigel,' I say, 'how are you?'

'Fine, how are you?'

'Everything in my life is fine,' I say, 'apart from the Albion.' I've blurted this out before I realise that he might well take it personally.

'Oh, we'll be all right,' he says with a passion and confidence that I find pleasing even though I know he's been relegated with three of his previous clubs and probably said the same kind of thing before each of those calamities came to pass. And now confidence visibly drains out of him as he sees the Fulham–Portsmouth score flash up on the television: 'Three-one,' he exclaims. 'Fuck, we've got to win this.'

We stand in silence. My phone rings. It's Jane. 'Excuse me,' I say, and he says he'll see me in our seats in the press box. My wife has locked herself out of our house in London. She has our two girls with her and it is raining torrentially. It seems to me that, somewhat unreasonably, she's focusing all her anger on me. It's not my fault she has locked herself out. Nor can I be blamed for the rain. But it is, I have to admit, plainly my fault that I'm not there.

A man I met recently outside the ground comes to mind. 'Adrian,' he said, unprompted, 'the Albion ruined my first marriage.' I'll call him Tony. Before I knew it he was telling me about when his sister came over from Australia. 'She'd never met my first wife and my sister was in a right state: she'd been having a really bad time. But I just left her with my wife and went to see the Albion. My wife wasn't terribly impressed.

'I think football and the Albion really came first, second and third but,' he said with not a little regret his voice, 'as you get older I suppose you have to put other things first. Your family have got to come first. We didn't have kids then but we've got kids now; they're big Albion fans. My wife now says to me, why do you go if it makes you so upset?'

This is a pretty tricky one to answer – I've tried to do so many times myself. Tony just shrugged and said, 'Well, it's even harder when you're not there. And I always say I've been married to the Albion much longer than I've been married to you. But if you treated me the way they do, I'd divorce you.'

This is an excellent point. Blokes like Tony, and me for that matter, not only tolerate our team but actually celebrate the loyalty we have for the Albion despite everything they put us through. The fact that we have been with them so long is to be cherished and boasted about. If only all football fans, me included, could have the same attitude to their spouses, their marriages would be so much better for it.

As Frank once said to me, if I went off with some foxy young thing he'd think I was a bit of a plonker but he'd probably harbour some measure of grudging admiration. However, if I told him I'd decided to support Chelsea instead of the Albion he would probably never speak to me again.

Back in our seats, I tell Nigel about Jane being locked out in the rain. To my surprise, he suddenly looks really very interested, hanging on my every word. When I finish the story he carries on staring at me, agog. I feel sure he's about to say something profound about marriage but, after a short pause he says, 'Is it raining in London, then?'

'Er, yes,' I say.

I am just reaching the conclusion that this is going to be really hard work when Nigel launches, more or less unprompted, into the most extraordinary monologue I think I've ever heard. 'The thing is,' he begins, 'I've had a lot of tragedy in my life. My son, he died in my arms when he was five and a half hours old.'

He tells me the whole ghastly story about how the tragedy affected him and how good his club at the time, Nottingham Forest, were to him. He concludes by saying how he could only have coped with the help of football: 'Football helps you forget. Only football can help you forget. When you're on that pitch you forget everything.'

In this, it strikes me, footballers and fans have at least one thing in common: the game acts as a drug, as an opiate for some people. For me, it's an escape from the success in my life. Elsewhere I'm more or less in control and most things go very well for me. Here, though, I'm not in control and emotionally I'm out of control. Bad things happen and make me miserable. Perhaps, it's good for me. It drags me back down to the middle. But for many others it has the opposite effect. For those with real unhappiness, or at least dissatisfaction, in their lives, it alleviates the pain. It might only last a while, and it might well only alleviate pain by causing more pain, but it seems to work. It has for Nigel.

'I was seeing a shrink for a year,' he volunteers suddenly.

'Oh yes,' I say, feeling a little faint by now, breathless under the weight of all this intimate information.

'Tony Pulis organised it when I was at Portsmouth,' he continues. 'He said he knew someone I could see. I went in and the shrink asked what I had to say. I said, what do you mean, what have I got to say?'

'"Well, what have you got to say?" he said. And I just started talking and I didn't stop for three and a half hours. It really helped me. To relate to people. To my partner.'

The match is about to start but, desperate as I am for a result, I don't feel it would be appropriate to show much passion for the game. In the light of everything I've just heard from Nigel, football feels less important than it did half an hour ago. But now Nigel wrong-foots me again. He's saying something profound about his childhood when the ref blows up to start the match. He stops talking mid-sentence and a transformation takes place. His whole body becomes taut and the urgent lucidity he has been displaying for the last quarter of an hour deserts him. 'Good start,' he says, in a way which suggests he's not interested in a response.

A cliché comes to mind about the non-playing player, or manager, 'kicking every ball'. But there is no better way of describing Nigel's movements now. Each leg jerks involuntarily as the ball comes near any of our players. And he blurts out instructions, admonitions and encouragements: 'One more', 'Not there' and 'Go on, brilliant.'

Liverpool score. We convulse simultaneously and gently collide. Albion are struggling now. A cross-field pass is pumped firmly over the intended recipient's head straight into the stand. I look at Nigel and open my mouth to say something but, warningly, he says, 'It's easy to do it up here.' Point taken.

I am not a critical fan. Unlike many of those who sit around me, I don't normally spend much time slagging off our players. But sitting next to Nigel, where observations about his team-mates' inadequacies are unwelcome, I realise just how critical I habitually am. Time and again I turn to say something to him but have to stop myself for fear of annoying him.

Not long before half-time, Liverpool's Xabi Alonso picks up the ball on the edge of his own penalty area. 'Ping it,' mutters Nigel, 'he's going to ping it.' Alonso duly pings it – kicks it a long way – straight to one of his own players, who scores. 'I said, didn't I?' Nigel keeps saying. 'I said he'd ping it.'

In the second half Zoltan Gera, our gifted but under-performing Hungarian, comes on and we have a couple of half chances but nothing much materialises. There are no more goals. Nigel is very quiet. With about a quarter of an hour to go he nudges me and asks, 'Is that everything?' And he mutters something about his hamstring. Then we shake hands and he leaves.

I don't really know what to make of him. He's kind of intimate and distant all at the same time. Does he care? Yes. Does he care as much as me? No. The one player who does care as much as me doesn't play for us any more. Apart from his prison team, he doesn't play for anyone.

Lee Hughes was beloved of Albion supporters because he's a proper fan, just like us. His career flourished at the Albion as a raw but lethal striker. It then stalled at Coventry City before he came back to us. Now it could be over completely. On the evening of 22 November 2003 he crashed his £100,000 Mercedes into another car: the passenger in the other car died. But, disgracefully, Lee didn't stop, didn't report the accident and didn't give himself in to the police for thirty-six hours. He was jailed for six years for causing death by dangerous driving, and he had his contract terminated by the club.

Dave Holloway gave me Lee's dad's number. Bill Hughes answered the phone and listened doubtfully as I explained who I was and that I'd like to go to see his boy in prison. He said without enthusiasm that he'd pass on the message, but put the phone down quite abruptly, saying his other phone was ringing.

I gave up on the idea of getting to see Lee in prison. But five minutes later my phone rang. It was Bill. 'It's Lee's dad,' he said cheerfully, sounding like a changed man. 'That was Lee on the phone. He said you'm a good bloke and he'd be happy to speak to you.'

'Oh great,' I said. 'How was he?'

'OK,' said Bill, sounding really sad again, 'It's his thirtieth birthday today. That's why he rang.'

Having visited Garry Mottram in Winson Green I'm quite blasé about setting foot in another prison, but I'm disorientated by HMP Featherstone, just north of Wolverhampton. Most prisons you see are the ones you happen to drive past, in big cities; they look like Winson Green, which looks like the one in the opening titles of *Porridge*, sort of Victorian. But the only time I've seen a prison which looks like Featherstone is in American films. I suppose you'd never come across it unless you lived nearby or visited somebody there. It looks like a penitentiary, squatting in the suitably featureless flatness of this part of Staffordshire. The buildings are low and flat. The fences are high and white and strewn with barbed wire. There are floodlights everywhere.

There is a big sign at the entrance which reads, 'Featherstone: Creating New Futures'. I think of Lee's quite glorious footballing past and what might remain of its future. There's another sign saying, 'Prisoner's Visitors Car Park'. The apostrophe situation is catastrophic but I park there anyway.

Visiting time begins at 2 p.m. but I'm in there fifteen minutes early. I look around at the other visitors waiting on the plastic seats. They're arranged in fixed formations of one versus four. The single one is red, the four are blue. I sit in the red one at position thirteen to where I have been instructed to proceed. Then I realise the single seat is obviously for the inmate. I move to one of the blue ones. No one's noticed. Everyone else is waiting, just waiting, staring into space.

There are a couple of women with babies whose squawks are swallowed up by the awesome emptiness of the room. In front of me a man in his sixties has the sallow face of someone who

266

smokes too much. He is wearing black slip-ons with ferociously white socks. To my left there is a plump Asian woman, to my right a heavy but attractive woman in her early thirties with dark hair. I catch her eye and smile but she looks away.

Just before two o'clock the shutter slides open at the café. Everyone but me jumps up and walks that way. I get up to follow suit. Then I realise I don't know what Lee will want so I sit down again. Everyone else soon returns to their tables with crisps, tea, chocolate, Coca-Cola. The raven-haired woman to my right has four teas and a bag of crisps.

Bang on time the villains file out donning orange vests as they emerge. The things are just like the training bibs Lee would have worn countless times. One of the first cons out is a middle-aged guy with a purposeful stride. He makes for the raven-haired woman with the four teas and a bag of crisps. He looks too old to be her partner but too young to be her father. They kiss passionately and talk as they do so.

An Asian man comes out, slipping his bib over his head. He smiles sheepishly at the Asian woman to my left as if to say, Oh God, this is ridiculous, I can't believe it's like this. They kiss, too. The sallow-faced man opposite is approached by a younger version of himself who says, 'Are you on your own? Have you come on your own?' The older version nods and they sit down. 'How the fuck has that happened?' demands the younger version, crumpling. They fall into quiet conversation. The younger man's head is bowed in despair.

A kid I mistake for Lee is next out but he's much younger, in his early twenties. He sits down on a red seat but there is no one waiting for him there. Finally, smiling, Lee emerges. We shake hands and I point at the bib. 'I know,' he says delightedly, nodding his head and grinning, 'just like a training bib!'

I ask what he wants from the café. 'Pop,' he says. The former Premiership footballer and convicted criminal on a six-year stretch wants 'pop'. I nearly laugh. Pop? He's like a kid in a sweet shop. 'Do you want some chocolate or anything?'

'Yes, bar of chocolate, thanks,' he says, nodding eagerly.

I ask how he's keeping. 'Good,' he says, 'put on a bit of weight but not in bad shape.'

I'm not planning on asking about the car accident just yet but Lee deflects all my initial questions about how he is by saying that he deserves this and that he's written to the family of Douglas Graham, who was killed in the accident. 'But you never read about that in the papers,' he says, matter-of-factly, apparently without rancour. 'And I spoke to a victim support group and they asked if I'd see the victims and I said I would, but I never heard anything from them. Can't blame them, I suppose.

'But it was an accident,' he continues, unbidden. 'I just made a mistake. I had the accident and my head just went. I'd had three drinks, I swear. We'd kicked off late and I got home at 9.30 and then I had three drinks. They said I'd been drinking all night but I couldn't have been because the accident was only an hour and half after that. I remember shouting, is anybody hurt? and I heard someone say no, but I don't know whether it was someone in my car or the other one. My head just went. I ran away. I know it sounds mad but my head just went and I ran.

'I didn't know anyone had been hurt 'til I saw the news the following day and I just couldn't believe it. I called my agent, who called the solicitor, and we called the police and they told us to come in in the morning. I was just at my mate's house.

'The first three weeks at Winson Green, that was an experience,' he says with feeling. 'I'd just got sent down and I really didn't know what was happening. Everyone knew I was in there. Blues fans, Wolves fans, they were all screaming and shouting at me until three in the morning and I was in a cell with a heroin addict and he was shouting and screaming all the time because he couldn't get enough gear or whatever. But right from the beginning I wouldn't feel sorry for myself. I'm quite strong minded like that. I knew I just had to get through it for my family. It's a sentence for them, too, for my wife especially. Luckily the kids are too young to really understand what's happening. Sometimes we have family days here when they clear all these seats away and we can play around on the floor with our kids. They love that.

'It has been terrible at times, though, terrible. When you get down in prison, you get very down. There's no one to pick you up. No one. It's difficult to explain, but it's hell.' Later, I speak to the Rev Ken, who visits Lee a lot, and we agree that he copes well inside. 'The thing with Lee,' says the Rev astutely, 'is that he's the kind of bloke who could make himself comfortable in a cardboard box.'

Lee says it helps that he grew up in Smethwick, 'on the streets' as he puts it. 'One or two I was at school with are in here,' he says. I make a weak joke about school reunions, which he laughs at. I tell him a story that his dad told me about a holiday at Butlins when Lee was perhaps nine years old. You could get T-shirts printed with newspaper headlines on them. Bill Hughes told me that they've got a picture of Lee in a T-shirt on which the headline shouts, 'Lee Hughes Signs for Albion'. I worry that this memory will make him emotional, but he just smiles and nods delightedly again, in the same way he did about the prison bib.

From an early age all Lee wanted to do was play for the Albion: 'I played for my school and was picked for the district but not the county. I was a full-back. Always wanted to play up front but I was a bit small. I was on the Albion's books from the age of eleven. Nobby Stiles was great with me; great coach. But then, when I was fifteen, they told me I wasn't good enough and wouldn't make it. I was devastated. I thought that was it. All I wanted to be was a footballer.

'I went to Swansea and there were a hundred kids there and I was picked with about six others. I scored a load of goals. But they said the manager wanted to see me play – that was Frank Burrows. And when I went back down and played in a practice match I had a really bad cold. I could hardly breathe. It was all on my chest. But I thought if I told them, they wouldn't play me and that would be my last chance. So I played and played badly and

Frank Burrows told me they didn't want me. I reminded him about that later.

'Then I went to Kidderminster on a trial and banged some goals in, didn't I? They didn't give me a contract but I played for the youth team and did all right. Then I broke my bloody leg against Wolves. My bone was sticking right out. I came back and did all right and got offered a contract: fifty quid a week to play football. I was made up; it was a dream come true. I was playing for Kiddy but still following the Albion.'

I remember Graham Allner, Lee's manager at Harriers, once telling me that he had to give him a bollocking for going to Barnsley to watch the Albion on a Friday evening. He got back at three in the morning and was kicking off for Kidderminster twelve hours later. 'I went everywhere,' says Lee. 'To Blackpool in the back of a transit van. Everywhere.'

Meanwhile, he was scoring freely and getting noticed by big clubs. 'I had a trial at Sheffield Wednesday. Chris Woods, Des Walker, Steve Nicol, Chris Waddle, they were all there, but I did my hamstring on the Monday and couldn't train the rest of the week.

'And West Ham wanted me on a trial but Graham got sick of it and said that if they wanted to have a look then they could come here and have a look at me. I said, fair enough.

'Then Bristol City came in for me with a quarter of a million, but Graham thought someone better would be coming in. I was worried then because this was my big chance of playing league football. And then one day,' he says, speaking more slowly as if still savouring the memory, 'I got a phone call at home saying the Albion wanted to sign me. Charlton did as well. Alan Curbishley wanted me, but Graham knew there was only one team in it.'

So the lad who'd been dreaming of this all his life, who wore Albion shirts most of the time anyway, now had to wear one in his place of work. 'Pre-season was unlike anything I'd ever played in before. Bob Taylor was my hero and here I was playing with him.

We played Chelsea and I was up against Zola and Vialli. Frank Leboeuf marked me. I came on at half-time and got man of the match.

'My first league game was on the subs bench against Tranmere. It was the first game of the season. I could hardly breathe. I had to keep pinching myself. All my life I'd wanted to be a footballer. Now I wondered if I was good enough; could I actually do it? I was a roofer. I'd been on the roofs a few weeks before, now I was playing for my team. I couldn't believe it. I came on with ten minutes left and hit the post.'

If he was pinching himself before that appearance, he must have been pinching himself harder after his next game, away at Crewe. 'We were losing 2-1 but then I came on as sub and scored twice and at the end all the fans came on the pitch. My dad and my mate were there. It was buzzing; it was special. I couldn't believe what was happening.

'Sometimes it worked against me, though, being a fan. Playing against the Wolves, well, I should never have been playing really. I was just so hyped up. I never did any good against them. I only scored once, a penalty.

'I definitely wanted it more than other players, because I was a fan and because I'd had a real job. I remember Jason Roberts winding Gary Megson up by being late, and it's not exactly an early start, is it, ten o'clock? I used to be up on a roof freezing to death at seven in the morning. But I always found it incredible how little some of them cared because for me it was a dream. I'll always be a fan. Even when I stop playing I'll still go and watch them.

'On Survival Sunday I was in my cell here. I called the players in the dressing room, before and after. There were five of us in here listening to the radio. It was agony. And when we stayed up it was mental. There were cell doors being banged and screaming and shouting.'

I ask if he regretted not being out there going nuts with the rest of us in pubs all over the Black Country and beyond. As ever, he

271

just shrugs. He doesn't seem to do regret: 'I just went and bought two chocolate milk drinks. Not one, two. That was my treat.'

Lee plays football for the prison team, 'but only in midfield. I get too frustrated up front because they never pass to me where I want it. And I'm always getting kicked. I got banned after being sent off.'

It's soon time for me to leave. I ask Lee what he is doing for the rest of the day. 'Oh,' he says happily, 'I've organised a table tennis, pool and dominos tournament, during association. It passes the time.'

We shake hands and, awkwardly, almost embrace, but don't. He strides away, still smiling. Like Ken says, he could make himself comfortable in a cardboard box.

Tuesday, 4 April 2006, Birmingham vs Bolton

At this stage of the season it feels like we're playing even when we're not. We might as well be tonight. After losing to Liverpool we stayed fourth from bottom, but if Blues win they go above us. I am working this evening in the Great Room at the Grosvenor House Hotel on Park Lane. I hate to boast but I am master of ceremonies at the annual Building Awards. If I was hoping for my mind to be distracted from the Albion, I hoped in vain, because the organisers have decided on a football theme. Luminaries of yesteryear are in attendance to hand out awards: Pat Jennings, Frank McLintock, Martin Peters, Martin Chivers, George Cohen and Bob Wilson. Most ask me about the Albion when I'm introduced to them.

John Motson, who has been booked to do the voiceover this evening, is sitting next to me. Any attempt to steer the conversation away from football when you're talking to Motty is doomed to failure. I keep checking my watch. It's a 7.45 p.m. kick-off. Mercifully, probably, there's no mobile phone reception down here in the Great Room so I've asked Simmo, the Albion's press officer, to text me the result. The final whistle won't blow until nearly ten o'clock. It seems a long way away.

I'm talking to Motty but my mind's at St Andrews. Bob Wilson makes an appeal for his charity, the Willow Foundation, which gives seriously ill young people special days out. Bob tells the story of how he and his wife founded the charity after the death of their daughter, Anna, from cancer when she was thirty-one. His voice eventually cracks and thickens with emotion. I realise with a start that I've quite forgotten about what's happening between Birmingham and Bolton. But a couple of minutes later I am ashamed to find my mind back at St Andrews and the suffering's all mine again.

At 8.30 p.m. I contemplate excusing myself from dinner to find out what's happening, but I have to resist this because once I know what's going on I have to stay with the source of information. It's like going for your first wee during a night on the beer – once you have been you've got to keep going.

Dinner goes on and on. At 9.50 p.m. I can wait no longer, not least because I'm due on stage any second. I run upstairs and out of the ballroom entrance on to Park Lane. I switch my phone on and with eccentric briskness march along until a signal materialises. Shortly after it does so a text message appears. Before I go in to it I see that the first four words are 'I'm the bearer of . . . ' I pause and speculate for a moment more: bearer of what, for fuck's sake? Good tidings? Bad tidings? What? ' . . . bad tidings m8. Blues win 1-0.' The use of the present tense makes it even worse. We're now in the bottom three, the relegation places, for the first time in ages. I have no time to mourn, though, as the awards ceremony is about to start. I quickly tell Motty my bad news. He's very sympathetic, as if I've told him of a family bereavement.

As well as cold sores and constant fretting, the other sign that the end of the season is approaching is the catalogue of superstitions I assess our chances with. We're playing the Villa away on Sunday which makes me even more tense. I walk my kids to school trying not to tread on any cracks in the pavement and I implore them to do the same. They think it's a bit of fun; they don't know how serious it is.

On Thursday I am flying to Manchester and I start a Sudoku puzzle as we begin our descent. It's the extra hard one in the *Independent*. If I complete it before we touch down, the Albion won't get relegated. At first I struggle, but then I steam ahead. I am going to do it; the Albion are going to do it. My heart is pumping as the ground gets closer to us. But then I find two threes in the same box, and two fives in another one. It's all gone wrong; it's not going to happen. I despair as the wheels touch the runway.

On Friday I'm filming at Chester Zoo. I drive the crew there in a hired people carrier. If the temperature gauge in the car comes out of the cold bit by the time we get to the zoo then the Albion won't get relegated. I will be doing this kind of thing all day. This particular challenge is a nice easy one because it's miles to the zoo so the engine will be good and warm long before we get there. Except the pointer on the gauge doesn't move at all because, it turns out, the bloody gauge is broken. This freakish coincidence leaves me surer than ever that we are going to be relegated.

Having 'failed' this easy test, later in the day I set myself a harder one. If it comes off, then it will cancel out the failure in the earlier, easier temperature gauge test, and we might avoid relegation, after all. I'm waiting in the penguins' feeding shed for the keeper to arrive. Gingerly, I switch my phone on, telling myself that if a message received alert comes up before the penguin keeper arrives, then the Albion will be safe. This is a ludicrously big ask because I know the bloke is only seconds away. The phone finds its signal. My eyes dart nervously between the phone and the door. In walks the penguin keeper, closely followed by a message alert flashing up. Oh no, we're doomed.

The weekend's matches couldn't be more crucial. Before we go to the Villa on Sunday, Portsmouth are at home to Blackburn on

Saturday and Birmingham are at Wigan. I do the boiling water test as I make breakfast on Saturday morning: will the bit of water I've put in the pan boil quicker than the water in the kettle? It does! Everything's going to be all right!

Portsmouth and Blackburn draw. Birmingham will kick off shortly. I go for a run. I'm running without my radio, as it would be just too stressful to run and listen at the same time. I am wearing a heart monitor, though, and every time my mind wanders back to the football my heart rate seems to tick up a bit.

While running my heart rate is normally at about 150 beats per minute, but by the time I've warmed down and staggered back into the house it's dropped to about 100. Then, as I shakily call up the Ceefax page, it shoots up to 141 bpm. Birmingham have got a draw at Wigan. I go to the cinema to see a film called *Inside Man*, but all I can think about is Aston Villa tomorrow.

Sunday, 9 April 2006, Villa away

Sunday. I wake up at 3.23 a.m. for a good worry about the game and it's well past four before I get back to sleep. The match is a noon kick-off, and I'm watching it at work with Frank Skinner. He tells me he put his contact lenses in in a different order than usual this morning. We're both hoping this might be an omen.

It's an awful, awful game. On another monitor *Keeping Up Appearances* is on. 'Keeping, up and appearances are all, like, football words, aren't they?' says Frank. I nod. 'Perhaps it's an omen,' he says doubtfully.

In the second half we're all over Villa and do everything but score. For long periods the ball seems to be rattling around their penalty area. Two huge appeals for penalties go up. Neither is given. Frank wants Stuart Nicholson to come on: 'Young lad, comes on, scores at Villa. Feels good, might happen.'

I say, 'Alternatively, young lad comes on, fluffs open goal, never recovers, career in ruins.'

'That's another possibility,' admits Frank.

Kanu and Nicholson come on, but it finishes nil-nil. I wonder if Alan Hansen will now understand why it is that playing well and not winning feels worse than playing badly and not winning.

On *Match of the Day 2* Alan asks me, on air, if we are going down. I don't know what to say but if I say no he'll scoff and I'll have tempted fate. So I just say, 'Yes.' Then I feel a little ashamed, disloyal.

Wednesday, 12 April 2006, Portsmouth vs Arsenal

Portsmouth, our rivals for relegation, are playing the team we've got to face on Saturday. I try to forget about it but end up glued to the radio. I'm really not feeling very well. Then Arsenal score and I immediately feel a bit better. In the second half Portsmouth equalise and I start to feel all hot and bothered again. It will be fine, though: Arsenal are all over them. Except Arsenal can't put it in the net. I feel dreadful. I try to take my temperature with the kids' ear thermometer but the batteries have gone. I look for some new ones but we haven't got any. The final whistle goes.

Worryingly, even Frank seems to be losing the plot now: 'Fucking cunting bollocks. Horrible fucking Arsenal have missed all the sitters they will fucking bury for fun on Saturday against us.'

Things really are desperate if Frank's giving up the ghost. Feeling desperate I describe my evening, by email, to Jo the psychiatrist. Then I take some Night Nurse and go to bed.

Saturday, 15 April 2006, Arsenal away

On Saturday morning I get a reply from Jo to my email. She's quite chatty and jovial in it but then, almost as an aside, writes 'perhaps sometime we can go for a drink or whatever and talk about any ways to reduce the negative impact it clearly sometimes has on you'. Blimey, she really does think I need help.

Outside Highbury I meet a middle-aged Albion fan dressed all in black. He pulls back his overcoat to reveal a blue jacket. 'Last wore this rig-up away at Sunderland,' he says, 'what a game that was.'

I tell him he'll be wearing it for ever if we win today. He talks to me approvingly about something I wrote in the programme on Man Utd fans and how we almost feel sorry for them. 'I think we're on the same wavelength,' he says, with an air of confidentiality.

An Arsenal fan shouts good luck. I thank him. 'You'll need it,' he says, rather callously. I've never ever got into a fight at a football match and never will. But I'm not quite sure how because at this moment, and at many others like it, a part of me feels inclined to chase him down and beat him savagely.

I meet Paul Friend, a teacher at a school in Zambia. He doesn't get to many games and is thrilled to be at this one. His childish enthusiasm for just being here is a sharp slap on the cheek for the idiotically dull, joyless trepidation I feel. Inside the ground by the refreshment stalls it feels like every Albion fan I have ever met is in attendance. Gurdial and Jadeen are eating sweets. They both say that we're going to win. Dave Holloway, transport manager, tells me that Mary, who finally gave me some fruit cake on the way back from Manchester on the first day of the season, is very sick. Dave Rolfe, his face reddened by drink, but his ponytail looking as magnificent as ever, tells me he resolved not to shave until we won another match, 'but I had to pack it in because I was looking like Robinson Crusoe'.

I talk to Pat Luke and Jean Wilkes, the ladies I met at Manchester City right at the start of the season. As I do so a tall kid, maybe seventeen years old, catches my eye. He's got grubby jeans on, an even filthier Fred Perry polo shirt, and some very battered trainers. He is very pale and his gingery hair is unkempt. He's talking to a friend. They both have a beer in their hands. The shambolic ginger one suddenly leans forward, mid-conversation, and vomits copiously. He and his mate both look faintly surprised but then carry on chatting and drinking as if nothing much has happened.

Dave Watkin says hello. He's the one whose wins and defeats tallied up exactly the day we beat Man City. I suggest to him that his wins must be some way behind his defeats now. He nods solemnly. The away end is packed out. There has been a fair bit of fuss about this being our last chance to visit Highbury but I really couldn't give a toss if I never come here again. At the ages of eleven and fifteen I saw us lose FA Cup semi-finals here and the best I've seen from us against Arsenal has been some plucky draws. No, good riddance to the place.

To my left sits Paul from Zambia. To my right are two empty seats. We're just about to kick off when those sitting at the end of the row stand to let the latecomers through. To my dismay it's the big, pale, scruffy, smelly, ginger puking machine. I hold my breath as he takes his seat next to me looking decidedly unwell. The only positive thought I can muster is that at least I'm not sitting in front of him. The bloke who is is wearing a waterproof garment, I note with relief.

We give Arsenal a game until just before half-time, when they score. I am almost relieved: I just want to get the inevitable defeat over with. I'm no less relieved that the ginger puker has kept whatever's left in his stomach in there, but he still looks terrible. I make my way to the end of the row and chat with Dave Holloway. Soon, though, I see the puker making his way along the row with an urgency that can mean only one thing. He is doing that funny thing you do with your cheeks when you're about to be sick but trying not to. Those fans he's trying to brush past don't seem to notice. I'm gripped by the ghastly drama of it all. He finally gets to the end of the row, past me and up a couple of steps before, with a muted roar, spewing up.

A couple of people look up from their programmes or their pies, note the performance without interest, and go back to whatever they were doing. I say to Dave Holloway it would be just perfect if we lost and he ended up vomiting on me. Dave nods, has a think and then says, 'It'd be worse if he vomited on you and we won because then you'd have to get him to vomit on you every week.' A good point well made.

Nathan's another one who has had too much drink. I go up the back to see him. He tells me that Sandra's already given him a bollocking. Not long into the second half word gets around that Portsmouth are one up against Middlesbrough. The hope I had of anything good coming out of today recedes even further out of sight. Remarkably, though, we equalise. I can't even bring myself to celebrate because I just know it's hopeless. A big guy I don't know hugs me really tightly and I try to hug him back but I can't summon the enthusiasm. He loosens his grip and brushes down his coat and says, 'Sorry about the hug.' I tell him that if we get a winner he'll be on the receiving end of more than a hug.

We don't get a winner. We soon concede another goal, then we're denied a blatant penalty, then they score again. The bloke who hugged me tells me to cheer up but I do feel thoroughly pissed off with the whole business. Paul from Zambia thanks me profusely for the ticket. He has not had the best of luck with the few games he's managed to get to, and this is the first time he's seen us score in seven years. He is even happier now than he was when we kicked off.

Although Lent doesn't end until midnight tonight I'm seriously considering filling myself full of beer at the first opportunity. This presents itself at a pub near Marylebone Station in the company of Sandra and Kate. They left Nathan to it somewhere near the ground. 'He's just too drunk,' says Sandra. 'I can't bear to get on the train with him.'

After six and a half weeks without a drop of alcohol in my body five pints of strong beer have an immediate impact. After a couple of hours, swaying in a manner not dissimilar to the ginger puker, I accompany Sandra and Kate to the station, where we

279

see Nathan, loudly drunk, making his presence felt. Luckily they see him before he sees them and they manage to avoid him.

By the time I've got home I feel miserable again. Miserable about the result and miserable that I've broken my Lenten fast. Just to make myself feel even worse I eat a huge lump of cheese, several digestive biscuits and a great big Smarties Easter egg. Then I drink a large scotch and go straight to bed. Happy Easter.

Monday, 17 April 2006, Bolton at home

Yesterday Villa beat Birmingham City which, cruelly, gives us a flicker of hope again. I know enough by now to realise that it's the hope that kills you. Jane, the kids and I go round to our friends' house. Cath's expecting twins and we talk in hushed tones about what a challenge it's going to be. Lee is an Albion fan, though, so he, like me, has more than half an eye on the television. Portsmouth are at Charlton and Sky Sports, predictably, drearily, inevitably, flashes up that they've scored. Lee and I roll our eyes at each other. Then, eyeing Cath's growing belly, he says, 'Don't s'pose I'll be going much next season anyway.'

As we drive away I turn the radio off. I can't bear to listen any more. But then when we get back to my parents' house, where we're staying tonight, I switch it back on before we get out of the car. Charlton have equalised. I yelp. Jane bollocks me for making the kids jump. I sit alone in the car and nearly scream the roof off when Charlton score again. I'm physically shaking. Beat Bolton tonight and we'll be within a point of Portsmouth who are fourth from bottom. We needed a miraculous end of season run of luck to survive and the miracle, though late arriving, might yet come to pass.

I need a drink. I call Nathan and we agree to meet in a pub in Stourbridge. He's not quite over his hangover from Saturday yet. Pod shows up. He is often on Nathan's drinking team. In reference to Portsmouth's defeat at Charlton he says, without much relish, 'Tonight's the night. Again.'

Pod's got a big tattoo of the club crest on his forearm which he's pleased to see me admiring. 'I had it done four years ago when I was forty. The wife says it was a mid-life crisis. She's probably right. But where I sit there's a woman about four or five rows down and she's got one on the top of her arm. Over the years I've thought, that's nice, I'd like one of them. It gets noticed. Even now I'm working in this manor house and when the woman who owns the place saw it she kept looking at it. I thought she was going to say something because I knew she noticed it, but she didn't. And we're not allowed to speak to her.'

As I mull over the somewhat Victorian nature of this relationship between contractor and client, Pod explains why he's called Pod. I can't make head or tail of what he is on about: 'It was just something at school when we was kids. Do you remember Hannibal Heyes and Kid Curry – two rogues? He's Pountney Pays and Pays went to Pod, and that was it.'

'Oh, right.'

'So what's your real name?'

'Mark.'

This, it later turns out in another pub somewhere, is a black lie. Pod was actually christened 'Tracey' which, to add to the confusion, is also his wife's name. 'But you told me it was Mark,' I say indignantly.

He shrugs. 'At least now you know why I'm glad my nickname stuck. When *Thunderbirds* came out, that was a bloody nightmare,' he says with feeling, while we all wipe tears of laughter from our eyes. 'My brother's called Spencer,' he adds. 'Spencer and Tracey Pountney.

'I've been an Albion fan since 1964. My granddad, he was a Villa fan, but he took me to see the Albion once and we played Liverpool and beat them 1-0. And something just stuck from there, plus we won the cup in 1968, but it was mainly the Liverpool game that done it. I don't know what it was – the lights, the colours, or what. My granddad didn't like it for a few months. I remember his face now when he said, why the Albion? 'cos I told him I didn't want to go to the Villa no more. He'd been a Villa fan all his life and it took him about six months to come round. Then he started buying me Albion shirts and Albion this and Albion that.'

Now that's what I call loyal grandparenting – not something my granddad would have done for me. And certainly not something I'll be doing for my grandchildren should they ever dare to support anyone other than the Albion.

'Apart from a little break when I was between fourteen and sixteen, because basically I had no money,' says Pod, 'I've been going home and away. I think about it all the time when I'm working. I think my worst time for not sleeping was the first time we got promoted. I got the shits. I was sick.' Him and me both.

Pod left the Midlands twenty years ago. 'Maggie Thatcher told us to jump on our bikes so I got in my car and went down to London. And I went off to Spain for six months. I'm married now but we ain't got any kids. My wife's not interested in football. Next season we've got plans to move abroad – we've got a house in Cyprus. Don't know whether it will come off, though.'

I ask Pod how he'll cope without the Albion. He thinks and then says, with feeling, 'That is hard mate, 'cos two years ago I did go over for three months and I took two phones with me so I could text and take calls at the same time and get all the results coming through. I didn't think I'd miss it but when Saturday come I was the first in the town round the bars watching the tellies. And I was having the *Argus* sent to me.'

'So the Albion would play a part in your decision-making as to whether to go or not?'

'Yeah, yeah.' He's lost in thought for a moment before digging up more bad memories about being away from the Albion: 'Saturdays were terrible,' he says. It sounds more and more as if I've talked him into talking himself out of going.

On the car park over the road from the ground there are, as usual, three blokes having something to eat and drink out of the back of their car. I have always admired their pioneering spirit –

the way they're trying to bring the tailgate-party tradition of the American sports fan to West Bromwich. 'We're trying to get something going here, but it's not catching on,' one of them says. Another one reveals excitedly that they have wild boar and apricot sausages today. I smile politely and say, 'Ooh, very nice,' assuming that they're going to offer me one, but their meaning is altogether more profound. 'Look,' he says, pointing at the foil tray they were supplied in. On the lid, in marker pen, it says, 'WB+A'. It's an omen, we all agree.

The match is truly, terribly, awful. The low point is reached when Steve Watson, our hugely experienced defender, takes a throw-in right in front of us and throws it straight out for a goal-kick. You don't see that very often. In the second half I move to sit with Andy Thompson on the other side of the ground. This did the trick on the last day of last season, Survival Sunday, but it won't tonight. There's a rotund bloke who sits behind Andy and annoys the hell out of him. He keeps very quiet in the first half but, apparently having taken ale in the interval, is always voluble in the second.

Amusingly (at first) he only ever screams four things though. And when I say scream, I mean scream. He screams like a girl. If something good happens, it's *'Yes!'*; if something bad happens, it's *'No!'*; if the opposition have the ball, it's *'Close 'em down!'*; and if we ever have the ball ourselves, it's *'Wing it!'*. 'Wing it!' is his favourite. Tonight, this late in the season, he's trying another one on for size: *'Pick. It. Up.'*

I once slagged this bloke off a bit in a national newspaper and, to my horror, he saw the article. However, he seemed quite grateful for the mention and shook hands with me very firmly. Now, at the final whistle, at which point we are all but relegated, he's overcome with love for me. He nudges me and says, 'Ada,' – hardly anyone calls me Ada – 'we'll be back 'cos it's about the heart.' And with this he thumps his chest really hard. We shake hands and I wish him well but he won't let go of my hand and I end up embracing him in an effort to bring about some kind of closure.

On the way home I keep thinking about what Pod said earlier about tonight being 'the night. Again.' Why did we think tonight would be any different from any of the other nights? 'Insanity is doing the same thing over and over and expecting different results.' It's not clear who first said that. It might have been Rudyard Kipling, but whoever it was must have been a football fan.

Saturday, 22 April 2006, Newcastle away

I'm running the London Marathon tomorrow which means I can't be there. Instead, Frank Skinner and I go to the Albion pub in Hackney, where the match is featuring on Saudi Arabian television. The place is already packed full of Arsenal and Spurs fans watching the north London derby.

The trouble with being a famous comedian is that everyone tries to be funny with you. Frank is bombarded with wisecracks. Of course, being a comic, he's got to be funny back. Someone shouts, 'Lend us a few quid!'

'I can't,' he fires back, 'I've got to buy a whole new team this summer.'

The match kicks off and the game quickly finds a groove in which Newcastle attack relentlessly and we defend incompetently. 'This is bad for your health this is,' says a man sitting next to us. It turns out he's an Albion fan from Essex. With him he has a much younger woman who looks foreign. She pays attention to the match but doesn't say anything. It turns out this gentleman is the man who was jailed for running the sex shop, opening the way for Rab Rogers to take over. Small world.

Newcastle score following the customary cock-up in our defence. A few people cheer. All eyes are on Frank and me, waiting for a reaction. I say to Frank that we better show some emotion or they'll think we don't care. How are they to know that we're unemotional simply because we're so used to it? Or, as Frank puts it, 'Even the padres watching executions in the electric chairs got immune to it after the first fifty.'

If humour's an effective coping mechanism, Frank is coping well with the calamitously bad performance unfolding before us. A second goal goes in – a dodgy penalty we can't even be bothered to moan about. More cheers. Again, no reaction from us. Frank says, 'Well, the darkest hour is just before the dawn. And I don't know about you but I can't see my hand in front of my fucking face.'

At half-time it's 2-0. We're lucky to have nil. I'm distracted, though, by a shot of Tony Brown, an Albion great and now a radio pundit, popping up on Saudi television. At that moment a friend of mine calls to say that Tony Brown is on the radio saying it's the worst performance of the season. Odd really: Tony 'Bomber' Brown, scorer of the first West Brom goal I ever witnessed, pictured live on Saudi TV while broadcasting live on radio all over the West Midlands. All seen on a huge pub telly somewhere in east London.

At half-time Nathan Ellington, Kanu and Junichi Inamoto all come on. Frank says, 'It's like the Pilgrim Fathers arriving in North America among the savages.' But the Pilgrim Fathers had an easier time of it than this holy trinity. The match finishes 3-0. And Portsmouth win, so they're fourth from bottom with six points more than us and two to play. So to stay up we need them to lose the last two while we win both of ours.

The following day I run the marathon. The organisers have given me an elite athlete's pass which entitles me to ride on one of the double deckers ferrying the real runners to the start. I look utterly ridiculous next to dozens of uber-fit Africans. I sit down on the seat in front of Haile Gebrselassie's. I don't think he considers me a threat. The top deck is full of the world's finest distance runners. And me. The seat next to me is empty. I have rarely felt as lonely. Then a wiry middle-aged man comes and sits next to me. He looks extremely fit. This is Bud Baldaro, UK Athletics' marathon coach and, it turns out, a West Brom fan. He has a neat grey beard and quick, alert eyes. 'Do you think we're doomed, then?' he asks.

Saturday, 29 April 2006, Wigan vs Portsmouth

We are not playing but if Portsmouth win we're down. I'm at home listening on the radio. Wigan are ahead. Hope starts to infect me again. Angry with myself for being so daft, I go into the back garden to do the most ghastly job I can find: cleaning out the worm farm. The worms are supposed to eat all your perishable waste to save it from going in landfill and damaging the ozone layer, or something. But, like the Albion, it's been slowly failing all winter and now absolutely bloody stinks. I gag on the smell. Jane shouts out that Portsmouth have equalised. I go inside, wash my hands and hear that a penalty's been given.

Jane says, 'Who's got a penalty?'

I say, 'Who do you effing well think?'

Portsmouth score.

I sit in the kitchen and stare into space.

I text Frank and Simmo the club's press officer: 'This season could go on until Christmas and still nothing would go for us.'

My father-in-law's staying this weekend. He comes into the kitchen and asks, without anything like enough emotion or compassion, if Portsmouth are still winning. I grunt a yes. Frank replies: 'Twenty minutes of hope to go.' It's tragic really. The poor man still believes that Wigan will come back and win. I actually start to worry how he'll react when the moment comes that even he will have to stop hoping.

The final whistle goes. We are down. A journey that started in mid-August in Manchester is over. All those miles, all those hours, all those hopes, all the talk and the worry and the odd bit of joy. All for what precisely? I was sitting in exactly the same position the moment we were relegated from the Premiership last time.

Then, as now, relegation had long been inevitable, but the moment was still strangely painful. A bit like one of those relatives' deaths when you know they're going and all agree it will be 'a mercy' when they do. But when they die, it's still shocking. Not that this is as important as life or death, or anything.

I write a text to Frank: 'As soon as you've put a positive spin on this do let me know.' But before I can send it I get one from him: 'Y'know, at the end of the day, we don't go there to watch premiership football, we go there to watch West Bromwich Albion. It's just another chapter in a very long love story.'

Brilliant. Then I get one from Sandra: 'Fanfuckingawful.'

Twelve

Because we need a bit of magic

Monday, 1 May 2006, West Ham at home

There is revolution in the air. The tone of the internet message boards and the media reports feeding off them suggest that tonight could see the first public lynching in West Bromwich this millennium. There's anger about our relegation. Everyone seems to agree it's a complete disgrace, but opinion is divided as to who's to blame. Some point to the manager, others lay it all at the chairman's door.

I call Jeremy Peace, the chairman, to ask if I can sit with him. 'Are you mad or just a true friend in my hour of need?' I tell him it's a bit of both. I got to know him very well when he first took control of the club. I was the first in the directors' box to hug him this time last year, so it seems only fair that I should be here when things are as bleak as they were brilliant in the bright sunshine of Survival Sunday. I tell him to duck if anyone throws anything at him, and I'll take the hit instead.

Before the game I go to the Old Crown in West Bromwich, where I first met Sandra and Kate last September. The Albion are down and out, dead and buried, but the place is still packed full of blue and white shirts, which is how it should be. Sandra's brother is here with his son. My heart sinks when they solemnly tell me that they're not renewing their season tickets. 'Oh yes,' I say, 'pissed off with it all, then?'

'No,' says the younger one, 'we're just skint – can't afford it.'

After beer and scratchings and kind words all around, I drive to the ground. In the car park the tailgate-party pioneers are there as usual. But they're grim-faced and there are no fancies like wild boar and apricot sausages on offer. In fact there's no food at all, only booze. One of them tells me unsmilingly that they've got loads of beer and half a bottle of scotch. I tell them that won't be enough. He doesn't realise I'm joking: 'There's another full bottle in the boot,' he says.

The atmosphere around the ground reminds me of nothing so much as a funeral. There are plenty of people here but it's rather quiet. Friends, acquaintances and strangers make doleful, kindly eye contact and exchange firm, silent, consolatory handshakes. In the Hawthorns pub coping strategies are exchanged. Vicky, Dave Holloway's partner, tries to soothe us all with this: 'Let's face it, as Albion fans the best we can ever hope for is promotion and to get promoted we've got to get relegated first.' I smile benevolently at this nonsense for as long as it takes me to realise that she's probably right.

Alan Cleverley, president of the supporters' club, is smiling away. He tells me we're going to get promoted next year with 107 points. Where he gets that exact figure from I don't bother to ask because, apart from anything else, he has told me earnestly before every match this season that we're going to win. So far he's only been right seven times out of thirty-six.

Barbara and Amanda, Steve Hayden's mother and sister, announce that they are not going to Everton because they're looking after the dog. 'I tell you what,' says Nathan, 'you go to Everton and I'll look after your dog.' Many others volunteer to look after the Haydens' dog instead of going to Everton for the last game of the season.

In the ground I see Vic Stirrup. 'How many relegations is this?' I ask.

'Don't know,' he replies.

'You are coming back next year, aren't you, Vic?'

'Dunno,' he says sharply.

'Vic,' I plead, 'you've got to.'

'Have I?' he says, his face brightening.

'Yes.'

He beams now and goes off to his seat.

Sue Ball, German Val's daughter, whispers to me of her mother that 'her's been crying. I was out shopping and her was on her own all day on Saturday, which wasn't good. Crying, her was. And I was. We were both crying yesterday when her told me about Paul Robinson crying on Sky.'

I'm sitting three rows behind our chairman when the players come out on to the pitch. A few, and only a few, white flags and banners are raised. Most feature demands along the lines of 'Robson Out!' But I also spot one, on our side of the ground, against which the chairman's head is silhouetted. I can't properly read what it says because it's facing the other way but, in reverse, I can make out the words 'Peace' and 'Cheat'. I suppose

290

whoever's holding it has weighed up the comparative benefits of showing it to the television cameras, on the other side of the ground, or turning it round to face us so 'Peace' the 'Cheat' can have a good look at it. With admirable savvy the demonstrator's gone for the mass media, rather than the personal option.

As usual, we do OK, nearly score, nearly concede, then actually do concede. At half-time it's 1-0. In the boardroom it's quiet. A couple of the directors have noted that Paul Robinson's managing to get himself applauded every time he touches the ball by the simple expedient of having cried on television. They suggest to me that they might try it themselves.

Denise Robson's in here, too. I worry that I've not spoken to her. This time last year, on Survival Sunday, I kissed her. I don't want her to think that I'm ignoring her now, though I sense this would be the wrong time for a kiss. I go to the toilet and ponder what I should say, but by the time I return she's gone back to her seat in the directors' box. As I walk out there myself, I catch her eye, smile and open my mouth to say something but at that very moment I trip up a step and go flying. For what seems an eternity I am a whirl of arms and legs flailing everywhere as I try in vain to avoid landing flat on my face. I pick myself up and turn round to smile sheepishly at Denise but she's staring straight ahead at the pitch. Directly opposite us, her husband is standing by his dug-out, arms folded, staring back with a similarly unhappy expression on his face.

In the second half we should score but don't. And we should get a couple of penalties but don't. A Mexican wave starts and sweeps around the ground. The West Ham fans refuse to participate, many of them make wanker signs at us. This seems rather heartless to me – all we're trying to do is squeeze a tiny last bit of fun and enjoyment out of a miserable season. The final whistle goes. The boos are as half-hearted as the cheers.

It's warm. Summer has come. I feel fine. I've dreaded these moments all season, really feared them, but now relegation has come to pass I'm astonished to realise that I truly do feel fine. I wonder if I'll feel like this on my deathbed. All my life I have been terrified of dying. Perhaps, just like now, when the worst has happened and you have reached that moment, it's actually OK, rather nice even. Perhaps, after a lifetime of worrying about death, you just smile and reflect on all the happy times and gently sort of drop off.

I'm still smiling when I pull into Warwick Services. 'Did you win?' says Julian on the till, puzzled. 'No,' I say happily.

Sunday, 7 May 2006, Everton away

For our last match in the Premiership for who knows how long, I've organised a bus trip for the fans I've come across this season. How Dave Holloway and Sauce keep their tempers, I know not. For weeks now I have had a spreadsheet on my computer. There are fifty-four seats on the coach Dave's hired for me. In the last week the number of passengers has fluctuated between a worryingly low thirty-nine and an impossible fifty-five. But this morning Rab rings me to say he is sick as a dog and can't come. So, we'll be Rab less but at least no one will be seat-less.

Jo the psychiatrist, remarkably, wants to come on another field trip, so I pick her up from Harrow. And we collect Garth Pearce, the gentlemen journalist, at High Wycombe. Jo tells us of a study in which people with psychological problems, living in dread of something, were asked to throw themselves forward and visualise how they'd feel if whatever they were dreading came to pass; how would they cope; what would they actually do. It turned out that getting them to imagine the worse-case scenario and how they'd deal with it was a real help.

She says that seeing me now we are relegated, relieved of all tension, makes her wish she'd read about this study earlier in the season because it seems to her that I invested so much in the dread of relegation that the dread became my focus rather than how I'd cope when it happened. She's absolutely right; this is exactly what my problem's been.

292

It's all starting to fall into place. Sandy the psychologist has told me that I suffer from what she calls anticipatory regret. If we're leading 1-0 with five minutes left, Frank Skinner will be anticipating how happy he'll feel when the final whistle goes. I meanwhile will be anticipating the misery I'll feel if the opposition score. It seems to me that I need to get a grip on myself and suck a bit of Skinner's optimism out of him. Or I should anticipate my regret more fully and think about how I will cope with it when the worst comes to pass; because, as I've found out now, I will cope in the end since it's the hope that's been killing me all along.

Garth tells us of a time he once bent down to switch on his television to find out from Sky Sports how the Albion were doing. We were winning 1-0 with twenty minutes left. He was kneeling as Sky communicated this to him. Garth was delighted but worried that if he moved from this position and went to sit down he'd break the spell and the opposition would equalise. So there he remained, on one knee, for more than twenty minutes. And I thank him for that, because if he had moved we surely wouldn't have won that game.

Jo and I conjure up an image of this tall, distinguished, accomplished, middle-aged man on one knee, effectively in prayer, in front of the television. 'I ask you,' Jo will say later, 'is that any way for a grown man to behave?' When I relay this to Garth he says, 'Well, she's got a point, hasn't she?'

It's a spring morning but, being rather misty, it feels more like autumn. On the car park at the Hawthorns a gaggle of my party are already gathering next to our coach.

Sandra's here with Kate and Rob, her kids. 'How are you?' I ask. 'Rough,' she says. Last night was Sue Ball's fiftieth birthday. They've had a late night. Rob's got a big long beard for some reason. He looks like Great Barr's answer to Cat Stevens. I tell him this and he nods and smiles wearily but doesn't say much. He never really says much.

Vic Stirrup is neatly attired in his blazer. David Garrett, a businessman from Stourbridge who watches DVDs of matches in his own proper home cinema, goes straight over to him. David used to do a paper round for Vic when he was a kid. He is the second person, after Frank Skinner, to tell me that Vic was well known for paying his paper boys the least and for sending them on the longest rounds. They fall into conversation. Eventually Dave Garrett comes over and says Vic admitted that he didn't pay his paper boys as much as he should have done. Poor Vic, he must be going soft in his old age.

The Singhs are here: Gurdial, Jeevan and Jo. When Frank Skinner arrives Gurdial immediately gives him a fierce bollocking. Apparently she once sat next to him at a supporters' club dinner and he ignored her. Frank looks half ashamed, half nonplussed. Jo the psychiatrist looks on, a little embarrassed.

Nathan looks very much like a man who really should have gone to bed several hours earlier than he did. His cheeks are slightly flushed from whatever he was drinking last night. His T-shirt, though, is spectacularly white. I congratulate him on this. 'Two pounds ninety-nine,' he says, belching.

Roy and Steve Hayden appear. Steve has an odd kind of colour about him, sort of brown but not as though as he's been in the sun. Roy whispers to me that 'he's not been so good this morning'. But Steve, as usual, is smiling.

One-legged Kev Candon shows up. He is dressed as an undertaker with a big black hat on. He smiles, but only briefly and grimly. He's not letting go of his disappointment with the season just yet. Dave Watkin taps me on the shoulder. He is clutching a new bundle of facts and figures for me to look at.

The Woffindens are here, John and his daughter Emily, whose love for Neil Clement remains undimmed. I tell those around us all about this. She blushes prettily and proudly and shows Frank the picture of her Clem on her phone. In reference to Clement's incompetence with his right foot, Frank says it's the only phone in existence on which it's just the buttons on the left hand side that work.

The chairman, Jeremy Peace, appears. A few people eye him

warily. He smiles and asks if there's a spare seat for him. As it happens, there is, but the prospect of him being on the bus makes my nerves jangle. Of the other fifty-three on board precisely none of them have not slagged him off to me at some stage this season. Bob Taylor, one of our greatest ever players, is coming with us and Dave Holloway mutters something about Bob and the chairman not getting on. But Bob is a study in civility: 'Mr Chairman,' he says firmly in his authentic north-eastern accent, shaking Jeremy's hand, vice-like.

And Tim Higgs, a keen watcher of training sessions, is another massive critic of Jeremy's – the last time Tim was talking at me about the chairman he turned so red that I thought he might explode. But Tim looks like a sheepish schoolboy as Jeremy walks past him to find a seat on board. Earlier in the season, as he stood in the cold watching training, Tim told me how most fans didn't understand the good that Bryan Robson was doing. Now, five months on, I ask him if his view of the manager has changed. 'He's got to go,' says Tim sadly. 'Got to go.'

Les James shakes my hand warmly and softly, as he always does. I rang Les a few weeks ago to ask if he'd like to come today.

'I don't think so, no.'

'Oh, why's that?' I enquired brightly.

'Adrian, I'm sorry, I lost my wife on Saturday night.' And with that he burst into tears.

By the time I'd said how sorry I was he seemed to have recovered. 'I'm not on my own. I've got grandchildren and my son comes up to see me. And if I get bored I just go out into the greenhouse.'

I sent some blue and white flowers to the funeral, and went to see him when I was next in Birmingham. His house in Smethwick is a tiny little council place, almost like a holiday bungalow. A huge disused tower block looms overhead.

'Welcome to my humble abode,' Les greeted me, leading me through to his front room. It's small but looks smaller because it's crammed with furniture and lots of dolls. 'My wife collected them,' he explained. Les has a little dog called Rusty, who barks squeakily in a way which suggests he has a very sore throat. 'He's seventeen' said Les, as he went off to make some tea. 'He barks funny because of this operation he had.'

I asked how the cremation went. 'Great,' Les said, 'apart from one thing: Dave Gutteridge said the curtains shut before the coffin went down. Not for us it didn't.' He smiled grimly.

He told me that he first saw the Albion in 1948 paying 'two bob' for the privilege. I asked where he was born and he hesitated before telling me he was brought up by local authorities. 'I lost me mum, she died in labour – not with me – and me dad took to the drink and I ended up with a different auntie ever night.' The tentative way with which Les builds up to what he says next tells me he still feels the stigma of it more than seventy-five years on. 'I'm not proud to say it, Adrian, but me and my brothers, three lads, and me sister, all ended up in the workhouse in West Bromwich. This was thirty/thirty-one. I was five.

'From there I went into another home. Then I went into the Royal Navy as a boy seaman but I came out. I didn't like it. I went to live with my dad in Bilston but I was conscripted down the mines as a Bevin Boy. I did my two years there and then joined the Fleet Air Arm. I was an air mechanic, went all over the world: Korea, Hong Kong, Japan, Thailand, Philippines, Australia.

'I came out in fifty-four and followed the Albion ever since. I got married, lived in Tipton. I used to come from Tipton on me bike. There used to be a mobile caff on the Birmingham New Road called the Boundary Caff. I chained my bike to the back of that. I stood under the old scoreboard at Woodman Corner. I stood there for years. I took me son but he ended up supporting Wolves. Don't know why. And his son, my grandson, he's a Villa fan.'

He tells me his lowest moment as a fan was when we lost at Twerton Park to get relegated. I tell him that's mine, too, and I ask if he was there as well. 'No,' he says, 'I was having trouble with my wife then. She was in hospital. I lost my first wife with breast cancer. She was forty-six; we were married fourteen years. This time it was thirty years.'

As his late second wife was immobile, Les was her full-time carer, 'but she was never on her own when I went to the football', he's at pains to point out. 'She'd sometimes get a bit annoyed, though. She'd say, Newcastle? What time are you leaving? I'd say, Eight-thirty.

'What time? she'd say. She'd be angry, but then she'd just stagger off on her Zimmer frame asking what I wanted on my sandwiches. And I can honestly say we never had harsh words, we never had an argument.

'In the early days I used to come home and my wife would ask how we got on. I'd say we bloody lost. And she'd say, so I suppose you're going to take it out on me then. No, I'd say, I'll take it out on the bloody garden instead. It was then that I started gardening 'cos I had to let my frustrations go somewhere. And it was in the garden I let the Albion go. The garden doesn't make you frustrated. I can get over anything in the garden. I can make anything right. I can dig it up and replace it. But if anything goes wrong on the football pitch, I can't do anything about it.'

This had to be some garden, with years of Albion-induced frustration dug into it. He led me outside and I swear that I gasped out loud. It was like the scene when Judy Garland arrives in Munchkinland for the first time in *The Wizard of Oz*. It's tiny, maybe the size of two snooker tables, but it is absolutely immaculate. Everything is planted, having been nurtured from seed in his greenhouse, in precise rows. It's simply beautiful. 'I've done this for you,' said Les, handing me an enormous hanging basket. 'I grew them all from seed.'

Before I left he suddenly remembered something and grabbed my arm. 'I must apologise, Adrian,' he said very seriously, 'I'm afraid that rug I've been making you has had to take a back seat. I'll show you what I've done so far.'

And with that he pulled out a huge rug. 'WEST BROMWICH ALBION FC' it read. '2004/5 ESCAPED' and below that '2005/6 RELEGATED'.

I almost forgot to ask if he felt able to come to Everton with us.

'Yes,' he said firmly. 'After the service we had a get-together, you know, all the family. And I asked them all if they had any objections if I went. And they all, every single one of them, said, no, Dad, Granddad, that's the best thing you could do, if there's anywhere you can get your frustrations out it's watching that team.'

Vic and Les sit together on the coach. Seeing them there I get the same feeling as when I see my little daughters snuggling up together in the back of the car. Frank sits with the Singhs. Jo the psychiatrist asks him if this is his punishment. 'I'm doing my penance,' he says. He's sitting next to Jeevan, who looks terrified.

On the motorway Frank and David again discuss the length of Vic's paper rounds. Frank says, 'I've just seen one of his paper boys on the hard shoulder coming back from a round. He set off in 1986.'

Bob Taylor ('Superbob' to Albion fans), Frank and I serve refreshments. I pour the teas and coffees, Superbob sugars them and Frank does the serving. Danny Grainger, the lad who emailed me about his dad crying at Jeff Astle's funeral, is just as overwhelmed by Superbob and Frank Skinner serving him his tea. Danny's sister Jackie has come along, too. She seems less overawed by the celebrities and is busy reading a novel by Ian McEwan. I tell her I'm impressed. She shrugs and says, 'I've got to read it for college.' In turn, her dad shrugs, too, and says, 'I'm a bricklayer. I don't know how I produced these two.'

Paul Perry, alcohol counsellor, and his partially-sighted son Liam, sit just in front of the Graingers. Liam's reading a newspaper. He holds it very close to his face. The Jacksons are here: Dean and his daughters Tea, who's fourteen, and Albion, who's twelve. Yes, Albion. Dean Jackson christened one of his four daughters Albion; it is not, repeat not, a nickname.

As a writer some stories are so good that you don't want to check them out just in case they're not true. For this reason there was a very long gap between my hearing about Albion Jackson and actually calling her dad. When I finally did so a little girl answered the phone. I couldn't quite bring myself to ask if this was Albion I was talking to. 'Hello, is Dean there, please?' She went off to get Dean. It sounded like there were a lot of kids in the house. 'You've got your hands full there,' I said to him.

'It's all right,' he replied, 'I've got a big family. Five children.'

'Six more you've got a football team.'

'They're all girls, though, that's the only problem. Me son's seventeen and I've got five daughters.'

I'm all mixed up: 'So you've got six altogether?'

'No, sorry, five altogether. I'm getting confused – it's been a long day.'

I asked Dean, somewhat unnecessarily, if he was a big Albion fan. He told me he was a season ticket holder but couldn't afford to go to many away games.

'So how do you get to go at all with five kids?'

'I've got a very understanding wife.'

'You must have. Is it true one of your kids is called Albion?'

'Yes,' he said, matter-of-factly.

Why? is the obvious question, but instead I asked how on earth he got that past his wife. 'She wasn't too sure at first when I come up with it, but she warmed to the idea. She decided it was quite a nice name 'cos it's so unusual.'

Albion was born in 1993 when, apart from anything else, her namesakes were rubbish. 'Yes, we were awful at the time,' admitted Dean. 'I think it was the year after we came up through the play-offs and we were struggling in Division One. It could really have wounded her for life, couldn't it?' he said cheerily. 'When people ask me why I did it I say I'm proud of the name, proud of the club and proud of my daughter.' And, put like that, I must say it sounds an eminently reasonable move to me. 'It's such a proud thing to call your daughter after your football team. I mean Adele's golden, really, to allow me to do it. To be able to do something like that was just such a thrill to me.'

Adele came to the phone. I told her that if she wasn't already married I'd propose because she sounds the perfect wife to me.

'I'm insane,' she said. 'I must have had a brain cell missing, but I've come round to it, I quite like the name. And she does. Occasionally she'll say, oh why did you call me that?, but on the whole I think she doesn't mind the name. We used to call her Ally for short but when she got to about six she said her name wasn't Ally, it's Albion, so we had to call her Albion.'

'So what do you call her when you have to tell her off? Do you shout, Albion, come here!'

'Yeah. And when I shout it in town, when I'm in Sainsbury's and I'm going, Albion! Albion!, honestly, sometimes people stop us in the street when they've heard me and ask her name. I tell them and they say, "Good on you".'

It's a fantastic story but the one bit missing is the football itself: Albion doesn't like football, so it's my sad duty to report that Albion doesn't like the Albion. If you ask me, that is a crying shame. 'I know,' said Dean with feeling. 'Her brother's a season ticket holder and Tea – that's the one we nicknamed Baggie – she loves football and she'd go every week if she could, but Albion, unfortunately, she just won't get into the game, which is a bit disappointing really 'cos I'd be proud to take her down. I think the problem is that the first time she went, she was only about five and of course they were all shouting, Albion Albion Albion. And she said, why are they are all shouting my name? It frightened her. I'm hoping when she gets older she gets a bit more keen and involved in it really. I keep emphasising to her the importance of her name. It's such a shame,' concluded Dean sadly.

Kids, eh?

Inviting them on this trip was my contribution to Dean's informal 'Get Albion into the Albion' campaign. But I've stopped introducing Albion to people as their delighted consternation is clearly embarrassing her. Vic has obviously been threatening to give up the Albion again, to go to watch Coventry Blaze instead. Frank comes up to me while I'm pouring the tea and says, 'Quick, give me another sugar –

looks like we might lose Vic Stirrup to ice hockey next season. I'll stick another lump in to see if that cheers him up a bit.'

At the back of the bus, like the naughty boys they are, Pod, Nathan and Pete the ex-fireman are discussing life and football, but mainly football. Bernie the prison officer is with them. 'We've been thrown so many lifelines this season,' he says sadly, 'and we've just kept throwing them back.' Everyone nods in agreement. But then he tells of a discussion he had in the prison gym about choosing between Albion to survive relegation or England to win the World Cup. He chose England. Derision rains down on him.

Ken the Rev is sitting near the back, too. He's not one for small talk, Ken, but he never looks anything other than benignly happy. He is sitting next to a friend of Bernie's, a rough and ready look-ing bloke. I ask if Ken's putting him right, spiritually. 'No, I'm putting him right,' he replies. Ken beams. Dale and Rich, the ter-race choirboys who I first saw in action at Fulham, are sitting at the back as well. They don't say much. They're saving their voices.

We're at the ground ninety minutes before the game is due to start. I tell Nathan I've never seen him so close to kick-off without a drink inside him. 'I know,' he says, 'I'm feeling a bit shaky.' He sets off at a brisk pace in search of a pub with most of the bad lads from the back of the bus in hot pursuit. Presently only Les and Vic are left on the bus, remaining aboard for a little snooze.

Normally, on the occasion of our last away game, everyone comes in fancy dress. The last time we were relegated everyone dressed in black in ironic tribute to the referees who we judged to have been so unfair to us all that season. This year there is no apparent theme. There's Kev in his undertaker's outfit, one or two people in beachwear, the odd comedy wig and three teenage girls dressed as fairies, or angels possibly. As we're queuing up to get into the ground, Frank shouts to the fairies, 'Why?'

'We need a bit of magic!' one of them shouts straight back. And for a moment we all just smile at them adoringly, entranced.

I sit between Jo the psychiatrist and Albion Jackson. As we take our seats our fans are all singing, 'Albion Albion Albion', over and over again. She mouths the words shyly, trying to join in. I ask what it's like to have a thousand people chanting your name. She blushes. Her dad is singing his head off. Then the chant changes to 'Baggies Baggies Baggies.' Dean joins in with this one, too. As Baggie is what his other daughter is known as, he couldn't be happier.

Frank is sitting just beyond the Jackson family behind a huge shaven-headed bloke who is giving the Everton fans near us fearful abuse. Frank looks astonished. Jo nods furtively in the big bloke's direction and says, 'He's someone who you're rather glad is on your side, not the opposition's.'

The match starts and within a quarter of an hour, remarkably, we are in the lead. Our fans are making the most extraordinary noise. The big guy in front of Frank keeps up a steady stream of invective against the Evertonians. After one particularly vociferous exchange with an Everton fan, or all the Everton fans, or whatever, the big man slumps back into his seat. The shouting, the language, the frantic succession of obscene hand signals have apparently exhausted him. Frank leans forward and massages his neck, as if to say, 'Calm yourself, calm yourself, there there.'

Bob Taylor stands up to go to the toilet and two thousand people start singing his name. No wonder he likes coming along. At half-time we're still winning 1-0. The three fairies are sitting just behind us. One of them tells me she is going out with Dean Nicholson, who's in the youth team. I think how thrilled she must be to have bagged an Albion youth player. And then I wonder what I wouldn't have given as a teenager to spend just one evening with an Albion-mad girl dressed up as a fairy.

Frank professes himself gobsmacked by the conduct of the large man in front of him. 'I don't think he has watched a second of the game,' he says. 'He just doesn't take his eye off the Everton fans.'

In the second half, astonishingly, we make it 2-0. Jo, who is feeling more of our pain and our joy all the time, jumps to her feet, startled, when we score.

The big skinhead is beside himself. With him is his son, a young lad, who has the same haircut as his dad and is conducting himself in a similar manner. At one stage he rips his Albion shirt off revealing a pale, skinny little boy's body. He whirls it above his head and chants and shouts with an unbroken voice.

Frank, Jo and I look on in appalled, amused astonishment. Then the boy's father abruptly stops in the middle of some loud, arm-waving chant, turns to his son and speaks sharply to him. The boy sits down. It turns out that this is because he has uttered a swear word – something his father doesn't tolerate.

Dave Rolfe, my friend with the pony tail, is sitting near the big bloke and seems familiar with him. 'Who is that?' I ask. 'He's scary.'

'He ain't scary,' says Dave, 'that's just Cotter.'

I speak to Neil Cotter later, on the phone. Shy and softly spoken, he tells me he's been an Albion fan for thirty-four years. I tell him how scary he looks and what Jo said about being glad that he was on our side. He laughs quietly and says, 'I'm completely the opposite, honestly. I'm just going bald so I got the hair cut.'

'But it wasn't just that,' I say. 'You never seemed to watch the game, you seemed a hundred per cent focused on the Everton fans more than anything else.' I ask him if he was concentrating on one particular fan or all of them.

'I don't know,' he says, 'it was just banter, nothing serious. We decided on the coach on the way up that we were going to let them know that we know we're going down and we're not too bothered about it.'

'So,' I ask, 'this was just a special occasion – normally, you're more focused on the game then?'

'Completely,' he says. 'It was just a bit of banter.'

I feel rather namby-pamby middle class now. Here's Jo, Frank and I thinking of him as seriously unstable, even evil, and all he's doing is engaging in a 'bit of banter'.

I ask about his son, who is eleven. 'Is he as passionate as you?'

'Yes, he's absolutely fantastic,' purrs Cotter softly and proudly.

'We were thinking of not having a season ticket next season and I asked him what he thought and he said, no we've got to have one Dad, I enjoy the days out.'

Gingerly, I broach the subject of bad language. 'Cotter,' I say, 'I couldn't help but notice that while you were using so much bad language in your, er, banter, with the Everton fans, you gave your boy a bollocking when he swore.'

'Yes. It was the way I was brought up, to be honest. You hear it but you don't want to repeat it.'

'But you were using bad language with the other fans?'

'Only in the songs,' he says defensively.

'So when will he be allowed to use that sort of language with you?'

Cotter thinks. 'In front of me, when he's thirty.'

I laugh, but he's serious. 'That's the same rule I had with my dad,' he says firmly.

Back at the match Everton attack relentlessly and Kuszczak, our goalkeeper, performs heroically. Each time he does so Cotter leaps to his feet, roars with derision and makes obscene gestures with both hands at the Everton fans. But disappointingly, with six minutes left, Everton pull a goal back through Duncan Ferguson. Cotter, apparently relaxed about this setback, stands with his arms outstretched, inviting the derision of the Everton fans he's been bantering with. But they are too busy celebrating the goal to take much notice of him.

Then, well into injury time, Everton are awarded a penalty. Jo can't see what's happened and when I break it to her I feel bad. Kuszczak saves it but the rebound is scored. I can feel Jo looking worriedly at me. I smile at her and shrug. Her pity embarrasses me but the truth is that if there was anything resting on this game I'd be asking her for medication now.

With more or less the last kick of the game we have the ball in the net. Cotter leaps to his feet, his arms and fingers flailing about in a whirl of derisive obscenity in the direction of Everton fans to our left. Jo leaps up, too. But I have an ironclad rule not to celebrate until I've checked the linesman's not flagging and the ref's given it. The linesman's flagging. I tell Jo and the disappointment and shame on her face quite upsets me.

For the journey home Dave Holloway, who's a caterer by day, is laying on some food. This is solemnly handed out and even more solemnly chewed over. Pete and Pod eat blearily. They left the ground for the pub with ten minutes to go when we were 2-0 up. 'Nothing to be proud of Peter Talbot,' says Nathan mocksternly, aware that he's been known to leave a match for the pub well before half-time. 'It was only when we got to the pub we realised it was 2-2,' says Pete through a mouthful of pork pie.

Tom Harding has joined us for the return trip. He's Danny Grainger's mate, but couldn't come up with us because he was playing in goal for the Albion's under-fourteens this morning. It fell to his poor mother to drive him up here. I ask how he did. 'Lost 4-1,' he says.

'So, you've seen the Albion concede six today?' I say.

'Well, I only let two in,' he says defensively. 'I only played a half.'

Dave Watkin gives me some good news: 'The consolation is that, despite the ninetieth minute equaliser by Ferguson, we've still actually scored one more, 2063, than we've conceded since your first game against Luton in 1974.' Rejoice.

Elena Sergi, who has never seen us concede a goal, apart from one scored by Bradford in September, told me on the way up that she was going to try to watch if Everton scored today, but when I check with her now she shakes her head: 'No, I tried but I couldn't. Once we were 2-0 up I just couldn't look again.'

Alex Butler just stares out of the window watching the M6 slip slowly, very slowly, by. For two years he has been masseur at Wolverhampton Wanderers. As big an Albion fan as you can be, yet an employee of Wolves. Everyone I introduce him to shakes their head sadly, disbelievingly. They're sad for him because he had to do the job, not because he's just lost the job, having been

305

made redundant. Alex, Albion fan or not, is totally pissed off to be out of work.

'When I got the job it felt bizarre, going in the first day, putting the kit on. I caught myself in the mirror and thought, God, what do you think you doing? What do you look like? My sister, bless her, when she found out I'd got the job, didn't talk to me for three months. When I first brought my tracksuit back and all the kit I'd been given for the year, I caught her trying to line the cat litter with it.'

The nightmare job turned into his dream job and now it's been taken away from him. We'll be playing the Wolves next season. I ask if he is looking forward to it. He shrugs. He doesn't seem to be looking forward to much at all. I'm gutted for him. The jibes he suffered working for Wolves must have started to wear a bit thin when he was still there; they must be really hard to take now.

The expression on Vic Stirrup's face is as neutral as ever. I tell him how smartly dressed he is and he opens his jacket proudly to show me the label inside. It might be thirty years old. It says: 'Burton's. Personally tailored for Vic Stirrup.' I ask how his eyes are. 'Still can't read,' he replies, as if he's really not that bothered. 'Only the headlines.'

Pete Talbot is well oiled. He causes consternation when he's overheard on the phone telling somebody about how Bob Taylor served him tea earlier: 'I was served tea by an aspiring former player,' he says.

Albion Jackson and her sister are asleep, leaning against each other with their hoods over their heads. Their dad whispers to me that he'd love to take them every week but he can't afford it: 'I only got a couple of cleaning rounds,' he says, 'factories and stuff.'

Pod is soon asleep, too, bolt upright with his big arms folded and the club tattoo magnificently displayed. Finally we arrive back at the Hawthorns. We all shake hands like, I imagine, over-worked teachers in a tough comprehensive school as they break up for the summer holidays. Interestingly, nobody says much.

We just make eye contact, shrug and don't even bother saying that we will or won't be back next year because we all know we will.

Steve Hayden looks as unwell as he looks happy. He and his dad shake hands with me and walk away contemplating a few months without the Albion. I doubt Steve is planning on missing many games at all next season. I'm left with Yvonne, who told me on this very spot back in August that she'd only missed four home games in forty years. Now she has only missed four home games in forty-one years. I tell her she's wearing the same, flat sensible shoes she was wearing the day I met her. 'They're my Albion shoes,' she says, smiling. And she walks away up Halfords Lane.

Epilogue

Steve and Roy Hayden

Friday, 4 August 2006

It is the day before the start of the new season. I'm working, doing some filming on a grassy airfield in Gloucestershire. Roy Hayden leaves me a message to call him, which I do. 'Oh hello, Adrian,' he says, brightly enough, 'thanks for calling back.' Then he pauses before saying, 'I'm afraid I've got some bad news. We lost Steve last night.' Roy's voice cracks and he falls silent. My legs threaten to give way so I sit down on the grass.

I was in touch with Steve all summer so I knew he wasn't well but it never occurred to me that he would die. He developed something called GVHD, Graft-Versus-Host-Disease. As I understand it, this is common in those who have had bone marrow transplants. There is some kind of reaction to the new material in the body and essentially the immune system breaks down, giving rise to all manner of ghastly symptoms.

Steve spent the summer feeling very unwell. He was tired and water retention was a big problem. He had difficulty walking. I spoke to him while I was in Germany at the World Cup. 'I'm better now, in the sense that they've got the cancer out,' he told me, 'but, to be honest, this is the worst I've felt during the whole time.'

'So,' I said, 'basically you've got a good excuse to sit at home, watch the football and have your poor mother wait on you hand and foot.'

'Yes,' he laughed, but for the first time since I had known him there was a bit – just a little bit – of despondency in his voice.

At about that time I mentioned Steve in an interview I did with the *Observer* newspaper. I cited him as an example of a truly committed fan who lay in hospital worrying not about his health, but the Albion. I slightly exaggerated the story – or so I thought – in saying that he 'could be dying'. To my embarrassment the journalist, not unreasonably, wrote down exactly what I said. So I had to call Steve and tell him I was quoted in the *Observer* as saying that he might be dying. 'Though you're not dying, obviously,' I stammered.

'No,' he said, and laughed. 'No problem. Don't worry about it.'

'He was ever so peaceful in the end,' says Roy. 'It's incredible, but he was diagnosed two days before the start of last season and now he's died two days before the start of this season.'

I ask if he can still bear to go and see us play Hull tomorrow. 'I don't know,' he says. But we both know that he'll be there.

Roy and Barbara normally sit right behind me in the Halfords Lane Stand. Sure enough, they're both there. Next to them is Steve's empty seat; on it, some flowers. I reach up and hug Roy awkwardly and I kiss Barbara.

We win the match 2-0. I steal a glance at them when each goal goes in. They both applaud and even smile, but their eyes are glistening. Afterwards Steve's sister Amanda joins them from her seat a few rows in front. Jane and I go and stand with them while the ground slowly empties, the life draining out of it. Yvonne, my friend from the coaches, comes up, too, tears streaming down her face.

There is a card on the flowers which reads: 'To our dear son and brother Stephen. Saturdays will never be the same without you here in your seat. We will continue to be here to carry on your support for the football club you love. Good night. God bless. Mom, Dad and Amanda.'

With the ground almost empty now some stewards in high visibility jackets shout up for us to be on our way. We leave the Haydens to be alone. I stop to use the toilet and when I come out I see them walking slowly away past the refreshment stalls, all shuttered up.

Steve is cremated ten days later. As I pull up at the church I don't expect to see so many familiar faces, but Graham Williams is here, our captain when we won the cup in 1968, and Tony Brown, and other members of that team. Laraine Astle, Jeff's widow, is here. So are many players of recent years, some retired, some playing elsewhere now: Cyrille Regis, Darren Moore, Bob Taylor, one of the Chambers twins – I could never tell them apart. The chairman is here, too, as are Gurdial, Dave Holloway and many people from the supporters' club.

I ask a couple of Steve's mates who I've not met before what he was like before he got ill. One of them shrugs and says, 'The same. He was always smiling.' The coffin bearers, all Steve's friends, are wearing West Brom shirts with 'STE 1' on the back. As the service begins they stand in the front row with their arms on each others' shoulders like international players do when they sing their national anthems.

I make a speech in which I say that while servicemen and women get sent on their way with full military honours this, for Steve, is full Albion honours. I tell them how Steve would call or text me while I was in Germany at the World Cup and, even though he was going through such a bad time, he only ever sounded thrilled that I was having such a great time.

I try to make the point that whenever I met Steve I left him feeling rather uplifted. The Rev Ken, his face reddened and shining with passion, expresses this much better during his speech when he says, 'You went to see Steve to give him strength but you came away feeling stronger yourself.' Everyone nods.

After the service we mill about outside. I can't go to the cremation as I have to be back at work. I hug Amanda, Barbara and Roy and tell Roy I doubt I'll be able to get to the wake. 'See you on Saturday, then,' he says.